The Ukraine War & the Eurasian World Order

"Diesen has written a terrific book about the emerging world order. The multipolar system that is now forming, he argues, has the potential to be much more peaceful than the U.S.-dominated unipolar moment that recently ended. But the Ukraine war, a legacy of American policy during unipolarity, has poisoned international politics and made it difficult to transition to a more harmonious Westphalian order. A must read for anyone who wants to understand the great shift in the global distribution of power that is taking place before our eyes."

JOHN J. MEARSHEIMER, R. Wendell Harrison Distinguished Service Professor of Political Science at the University of Chicago

"A most thoughtful and realistic account of the evolution of the world order, the perils that transitions in it create, and the relationship of these to the tragic conflict in Ukraine. Diesen dispels and replaces the fog of war with the much-needed clarity of historically informed reason."

CHAS FREEMAN, Ambassador and former U.S. Assistant Secretary of Defense for International Security Affairs

"Brilliant, in-depth analysis of the roots of the Ukraine war and the emerging changes in the world order."

JACK F. MATLOCK, JR., U.S. Ambassador to the USSR, 1987–1991

"Excellent book! Glenn Diesen offers a highly informative analysis of the change and continuity of world order over the centuries. Must read to understand the complexity of the Ukraine War as a historical inflection point."

SERGEY KARAGANOV, Council on Foreign and Defense Policy, Russia Honorary Chairman of the Presidium

"A wide-ranging and stimulating examination of contesting models of world order and the roots of the Russo-Ukrainian war. A corrective to mainstream Western narratives, providing a powerful conceptual framework for critique. A brilliant foundational work."

RICHARD SAKWA, University of Kent

More Praise

"A superb book! Diesen dismantles the war propaganda and outlines why the Ukraine War is a symptom of a collapsing world order."

CLARE DALY, Member of the European Parliament

"Professor Diesen has addressed the geopolitical issue of our era—and likely beyond. What is the future geo-politics: How will states interact between themselves in the future? Does the shift to multipolarity championed by Russia and China hold the promise of more harmony or simply the move to a different mode of contention? He traces the irruption of the powerful nation-state notion of Westphalia, through the Pax American 'forever wars'—to the waning of the Rules Order presented as the mandatory 'vision for all.'

"Diesen shows how Ukraine became the rock that holed the Western myth below the waterline—and discusses the likely tribulations a new world order will certainly encounter.

"An important read. Important insights—as we need to face up to the unwelcome task of challenging our own preconceptions and having to navigate in an unfamiliar (non-western) landscape where old, steady handholds simply are no longer present. No longer there."

ALASTAIR CROOKE, former British diplomat

"What luck! Professor Diesen takes the role of Christopher, patron saint of travelers, as we stumble across the threshold into 2024—a truly liminal year. With laudable candor, Diesen presents little-known facts—on Ukraine, for example—showing how we arrived at this dangerous juncture. If facts lead to action, we may yet survive the demise of the tottering hegemon of the West."

RAY McGOVERN, former CIA Presidential Briefer

THE UKRAINE WAR
& the
EURASIAN WORLD ORDER

GLENN DIESEN

Clarity Press, Inc.

ISBN: 9781949762952
EBOOK ISBN: 9781949762969

In-house editor: Diana G. Collier
Text designer: Becky Luening

Cover photo (bottom): Shanghai Cooperation Organisation summit, 13 September 2013. Attribution: Kremlin.ru.

Library of Congress Control Number: 2023951310

Clarity Press, Inc.
2625 Piedmont Rd. NE, Ste. 56
Atlanta, GA 30324, USA
https://www.claritypress.com

To my wife Elena, and our children—
Konstantin, Andre and Maria

Contents

1.

Introduction

EVERY WORLD ORDER aspires and appears to be permanent. Preserving the status quo is conflated with stability, even though the world is constantly changing in terms of the international distribution of power, technologies, economic development, societal challenges, values, and ideals. It is the ability to manage change and reform that determines its stability, as the failure to adapt results in stagnation, decay, and collapse.

Wars, revolutions, and the collapse of states can cause huge disruptions, which may overwhelm the ability of the world order to adapt. The collapse of the Holy Roman Empire gave birth to the modern world order manifested in the Peace of Westphalia in 1648, which was based on a balance of power among sovereign states. This order lasted for 150 years but was then reformed after failing to preserve order following the disruption of the French Revolution and the Napoleonic Wars. The 1815 Congress of Vienna became the successor world order and lasted for 100 years until it failed to resolve the rivalry between rising industrial empires that challenged British leadership. Following two world wars, the Cold War produced a new world order based on bipolarity and ideological rivalry that ended with the collapse of communism after 45 years. The ensuing unipolar world order of liberal hegemony lasted even shorter, for approximately 30 years, until it became clear that the hegemonic system had failed to adjust to new realities and the excesses of liberalism had failed to deliver order. New centres of power have emerged that strive to restore multipolarity and reject liberal universalism.

The transition from a unipolar to a multipolar world order is spearheaded by the Eurasian giants of Russia and China, while it is seemingly supported by states representing a majority of the world's population. The objective is to return to a balance of power in which the competing national interests of the great powers are addressed, and common rules cannot be imposed unilaterally with claims of universalism. Perceiving that a world order based on hegemony and liberalism is imperative for its national security, the U.S. has resisted multipolar realities that manifest themselves economically, politically, and militarily.

A world order outlines the system and rules for how to live peacefully on the same planet, and a conflict over defining that world order suggests that the present order is suspended and chaos governs. Failing to reform the world order through diplomacy and peaceful mechanisms puts the new world on the path to being born through war. In the late 1920s, Antonio Gramsci wrote about the troubling times as a period of interregnum. The term *interregnum* was originally intended to denote the period of transition between the death of one royal and the inauguration of the successor. This period was characterised by an absence of authority creating a political and legal vacuum. Explaining the conflicts then in store, Gramsci wrote: "The crisis consists precisely in the fact that the old is dying and the new cannot be born; in this interregnum a great variety of morbid symptoms appear."[1]

Defining World Order

World order refers to the international distribution of both power and legitimacy that is to mark the system of how states and non-state actors should conduct themselves for order to prevail over chaos. Therefore, the topic of world order must address sociological theories of human nature, economic systems, and political systems.

Since the collapse of the hegemonic Roman Empire and the subsequent diffusion of power in Europe, the Peace of Westphalia in 1648 established state sovereignty and a balance of power as the main pillars of order. Order is based on a mutual commitment to collectively balance any expansionist and hegemonic impulses with a view

1 Z. Bauman, "Times of Interregnum," *Ethics & Global Politics* 5, no.1 (2012): 49.

to preserving equilibrium. Universalist ideals must be rejected to the extent they become instrumental in advancing sovereign inequality and justifying expansionism.

The Westphalian international system is defined by international anarchy as the state is the highest sovereign. Every state is subsequently in a perpetual competition for power and survival insofar as enhancing the security of one state can cause insecurity for other states. Over the centuries, there have been idealist temptations to transcend the international anarchy with universal values and a hegemonic distribution of power that aims to undo the entire Westphalian order. In such instances, the objective would be to restore the equivalent of Pax Romana, a reference to the two-hundred-year-long period of Roman hegemony and universalism that delivered relative peace, prosperity, and progress.

After the Cold War, the U.S. emerged as a global hegemon in terms of military, economic, cultural, and political power. The modern Westphalian world order based on a balance of power among sovereign equals was thus challenged by its claim for hegemony and for universal liberal democratic values. Liberal hegemony thus required and sought to legitimise sovereign inequality, recasting the earlier international order of sovereignty for civilised states and reduced sovereignty for "uncivilised" states. Full sovereignty for the liberal West, and limited sovereignty for the rest.

Initially, there was great reason for optimism that the belief in the universal values of free markets, democracy and global civil society would create an entirely new and benign world order. The Berlin Wall collapsed, communism across Eastern Europe was abandoned, the former rivals of Russia and China prioritised friendship with the U.S. and the wider West in their foreign policy, the EU took on a socialising role by conditioning membership to that body on liberal democratic reforms, the Arab Spring appeared to reform authoritarian government in the Middle East, NATO expansion brought a sense of security to states that had lived under Moscow's rule for decades, the economic rise of China pulled hundreds of millions out of poverty and pushed the world economy forward, while the processes of globalisation appeared to bring the world closer together.

Globalisation under Pax Americana was thus commonly expected to usher in a new era of stability and prosperity. At that point, a strong case could be made for a world order based on liberal hegemony, in which liberal democratic values spread under the seemingly benign leadership of the U.S. What created the post-Cold War peace and why did liberal hegemonic order eventually begin to crumble?

This assumption of benign global hegemony, that economic and political liberalism was a silver bullet for transcending power politics, proved to be a liberal delusion fuelled by hubris. The failure to reform the zero-sum security architecture revived the Cold War rivalry with Russia and China. NATO expansion predictably inflamed tensions with Russia as Moscow reasonably perceived it as an existential threat, while the mere economic rise of China became a challenge to U.S. global primacy. Globalisation as a neo-liberal and Western-centric process became unsustainable as the global financial crisis of 2008 exposed an unsustainable development model. The excesses of liberalism are now repudiated from within the West and beyond, causing polarisation within societies and in the international system. While an empire can afford to make mistakes as the costs can be absorbed, the accruing costs of the empire measured in terms of both wealth and legitimacy eventually became unsustainable as the West's military adventurism against Yugoslavia, Afghanistan, Libya, and Syria failed.

The world order based on a unipolar distribution of power, and legitimised by universal liberal democratic values, has already collapsed. On an even wider time frame, the 500 years of Western-led world order has come to an end. French President Emmanuel Macron has voiced the recognition that "Western hegemony is nearing its end." New centres of power have emerged that are laying the foundation for a multipolar system along the principles of the Westphalian system. The world order taking shape is repudiating Western-centric globalisation in terms of the dominance of maritime powers, economic and political liberalism, and a liberal global civil society. The West can also no longer impose the conditions for states' acceptance as a full member of the community of sovereign states. The international distribution of power, ideals, rules, and the nature of diplomacy is accordingly being reorganised.

The Proxy War in Ukraine

The proxy war in Ukraine revealed the fatal dysfunction of the hegemonic world order that has accelerated the transition to a multipolar world order. While the Westphalian world order seeks a balance of power to avoid conflicts, the unipolar order necessitates perpetual conflicts to ensure allies are dependent and rivals are weakened.

The Ukraine War could easily have been prevented if the Westphalian principles had been followed. However, the West rejected non-interference and the balance of power principle by supporting a coup in 2014 to expand NATO. A minority of Ukrainians supported the constitutional coup and only a small minority desired NATO expansion. As ample evidence reveals, the West knew that converting Ukraine from a bridge to a bastion against Russia would likely spark a civil war and a Russian invasion. Diplomacy failed spectacularly as Western states admitted using the Minsk peace agreement of 2015 as the "only path to peaceful resolution" to merely buy time to build a powerful Ukrainian army. The peace platform that won Zelensky the presidency in 2019 was reversed by Western support for far-right groups in Ukraine that even the West itself recognise to be influenced by fascist elements.

After Russia invaded, the pending settlement between Russia and Ukraine was sabotaged primarily by the U.S. and UK. Diplomacy was again rejected as the West viewed defeating Russia on the battlefield and the destruction of its economy as required to restore its hegemony as the foundation for peace and the so-called rules-based international order. The NATO Secretary General argued that weapons are the way to peace; paraphrasing George Orwell, war is peace, ignorance is strength. Censorship of Russian media and of dissent within the West left the public with very little understanding of the Russian position. Not a single major Western leader advocated for diplomacy as negotiations became a naughty word used by fifth columnists. Instead, "peace summits" were organised in Copenhagen and Jedda; Russia was not invited and Russian security concerns about NATO expansionism were not addressed. The Ukrainian government openly acknowledged that the purpose of these peace summits was to weaken Russia by organising the world around Ukraine.

The West intended to defeat Russia on the battlefield, destroy its economy and leave it isolated on the international stage. Instead, the West displayed the weakness of liberal hegemony when it provoked a military conflict and rejected all efforts at pursuing a peaceful solution. It became apparent to the world that the international economic architecture could be weaponised against anyone, whether through primary or secondary sanctions. However, the rest of the world refused to align with the West and isolate Russia, but instead intensified the transition to multipolar economic and political structures. The liberal hegemonic world order was intended to elevate principled liberal values to transcend power politics. The war lifted the liberal veil and exposed that democracy and human rights had devolved to crude instruments of power politics.

Liberal hegemony glorifies the dominance of one centre of power, but this narrative has collapsed. It has been suggested that NATO is merely a third party seeking to defend the Westphalian principle of national sovereignty against unprovoked Russian aggression, yet the Ukraine War was in actuality the direct consequence of the West's effort to undermine the Westphalian world order and advance a hegemonic world order. The Ukraine War began in 2014 when the U.S. and its European allies supported a coup in Ukraine to advance a pan-European security architecture based on collective hegemony. Over the next eight years, NATO countries converted Ukraine from a neutral state to a frontline against Russia by marginalising the domestic opposition in Ukraine, demonising Russia, curtailing the democratic rights of its own Russian-speaking population, building a large army, and preventing any peace settlement and reproachment with Russia.

The proxy war in Ukraine represents a conflict between two competing world orders—the West's liberal hegemony and what can be conceptualised as a multipolar Eurasian-Westphalian world order. The high stakes in what is now an all-or-nothing game reveal the reason why both NATO and Russia have been prepared to take such unprecedented risks, including the possibility of nuclear war.

Overview

The book answers the research question: To what extent does the Ukraine War influence the world order? The book focuses primarily on the West's actions as it has been the collective hegemon and main custodian of the world order over the past centuries. Subsequently, it focuses on the West's failure to offer common rules to prevent and resolve conflict. Instead, the unipolar world order contributed to, instigated and prolonged the Ukraine War. Exploring the war as a consequence of a collapsing world order should not be interpreted as supporting or legitimising the war.

To answer this research question, the book first outlines the theoretical assumptions about world order and explores the rise of the Western-centric world order, providing an overview of the foundations of world order. Thereafter, it explores the rise and decline of the world order defined as liberal hegemony after the Cold War, and the significance of NATO expansion on the unravelling of the pan-European security architecture and a common world order. In the second part of the book, the Ukrainian crisis is explored as a key battleground for determining the preservation or abandonment of liberal hegemony. These chapters explore the rivalry for influence between 1991 and 2014, the civil war between 2014 and 2022 following the coup, and the Russian invasion from 2022. The final chapter outlines how the emergence of a Eurasian world order has intensified because of the Ukraine War. It is concluded that the world is entering a turbulent time as the Ukraine War has ended liberal hegemony, yet a multipolar Westphalian system has not yet asserted itself.

Chapter two theorises the concept of world order. The modern world order originating with the Peace of Westphalia is contrasted with the incentives of restoring a Pax Romana system to transcend the international anarchy with hegemony and universal values. The balance of power is also translated into a geoeconomic "balance of dependence" to explore how the disruption of the Industrial Revolution altered the mercantilist system. The struggle for world order is theorised to represent a series of dilemmas such as a balance of power versus hegemony, cultural distinctiveness versus universalism, and order versus justice.

Chapter three explores the rise of the Western-centric world order. Military superiority and control over the maritime transportation corridors enabled the rise of a Western-centric world from the early 16th century, which advanced further as the Industrial Revolution endowed the West with economic statecraft from the late 18th century. The world order was reformed by liberal principles due to the American and French Revolutions, the transformation of industrial capitalism, and the subsequent rise of ideologies following the First World War. The influence of economic and political liberalism on world order became a reflection of the international distribution of power.

Chapter four addresses Pax Americana, the new world order of liberal hegemony. After the Cold War, there were debates about the case for and against constructing a world order based on unipolarity and liberalism vis-à-vis restoring a balance of power. The hegemonic system lacked sustainability as the U.S. became reliant on military interventionism, exhausted its resources, failed to address domestic problems, suffered from declining legitimacy in the world, and inadvertently incentivised foreign powers to rival the U.S. in terms of military power, geoeconomics and political institutions.

Chapter five analyses the decline of liberalism as the organising principle of the world order. Liberal hegemony replaced international law with the rules-based international order and reinvented diplomacy as a subject-object civilising mission. The excesses of political and economic liberalism undermined the foundation for social cohesion, and a new authoritarian liberalism made it increasingly difficult for the West to present itself as a teacher of democracy. Cultural decline weakened soft power, the military-industrial complex corrupted democracy and governance, domestic political squabbles increasingly influenced foreign policy, and the concept of global civil society became a tool of state power.

Chapter six explores NATO expansion and the collapse of pan-European security and a common world order. After the Cold War, two rival models for world order emerged that influenced the European security architecture. A Westphalian balance of power system represented by an inclusive pan-European security architecture was institutionalised with the establishment of the Organisation for Security and Cooperation in Europe (OSCE), which was based on indivisible security, sovereign equality, and a Europe without dividing lines. Concurrently, liberal hegemony in Europe manifested itself by expanding NATO, which implied abandoning the pan-European security agreements based on the Helsinki Accords, the Charter of Paris for a New Europe, and the OSCE. Many American and European leaders cautioned that NATO expansionism would revive the East-West division of Europe and possibly start another Cold War. Yet, the new dividing lines also revived an ideological divide as all subsequent tensions were largely interpreted through the heuristics of a wider struggle between democracy and authoritarianism. Diplomacy degenerated, arms treaties collapsed, and the security dilemma intensified.

Chapter seven analyses how Ukraine became a pawn on the European chessboard between 1991 and 2014. Ukraine was destined to become the centre of a proxy conflict between a liberal hegemony and a Westphalian world order as Ukraine is a divided country in a divided Europe. Nation-building in post-Soviet Ukraine has been troubled by the lack of unifying narratives and identity. The ethnic, cultural, and linguistic connectivity between Ukrainians and Russians became a double-edged sword as the closeness eroded the distinctiveness required for full sovereignty. While Eastern Ukrainians commonly defined relations with Russians as a "fraternal bond," Western Ukrainians tend to interpret the shared history as imperialism that diluted and undermined the development of a distinctive Ukrainian identity. Russia placed its support behind the Eastern Ukrainians and the West backed the Western Ukrainian nationalists due to competing visions of a regional order and world order in terms of the distribution of power and values.

Chapter eight outlines the Ukrainian Civil War sparked by the Western-backed coup in February 2014. Russia's annexation of Crimea and support for Donbas brought the liberal hegemonic order under great strain. Hegemony, liberal values, and international law required a principled rejection of Russia's incursion. Yet, the hegemonic order was supported by backing far-right nationalists that would purge the Russian-friendly elements in society and set Ukraine on a path to war. The new government in Kiev suppressed the Russian language, culture, and the Orthodox Church while it also purged the media and opposition parties, including the arrest of the opposition leader. Meanwhile, the West used the UN-approved Minsk Agreement to buy time to arm and train Ukraine which was becoming a de facto member of NATO.

Chapter nine explores the Russian invasion of Ukraine in February 2022 and the proxy war that ensued. NATO's reluctance to prevent the war, the sabotage of peace negotiations after the Russian invasion, and the continued escalations are indicative of the failure of world order and what is at stake. NATO's objective to weaken Russia as a strategic rival and send a clear signal to China could bring new energy to liberal hegemony, while a Russian victory could restore a balance of power system. As the war dragged on, the geostrategic objective of weakening Russia no longer harmonised with the goal of "helping Ukraine," and NATO began to display its intent more overtly to "fight to the last Ukrainian."

Chapter ten analyses the emergence of the Eurasian world order that intensified because of the Ukraine War. Russia, China, and other Eurasian states had already diversified their economic connectivity and aspired for a multipolar system for several years as the international distribution of power shifted. Yet, the war demonstrated the urgency of decoupling from the economic dependence on the West and it collapsed the normative justification of liberal hegemony. Irrespective of the military outcome, the war revealed multipolar realities as the world outside NATO did not accept the West's narrative, did not join sanctions, and instead accommodated Russia economically and politically. Eurasian states are spearheading the transition to a multipolar Westphalian world order with Eurasian characteristics. Western maritime powers lose their competitive advantage to Eurasian land powers as new autonomous centres of power emerge that reject liberal universalism in favour of civilisational distinctiveness.

It is concluded that the world is entering a period of disorder as the world is between liberal hegemony and multipolarity. States that adapt to the multipolar realities will thrive and those that resist the necessary adjustments will contribute to war.

2.

The Modern Westphalian World Order: Power and Legitimacy

WORLD ORDER refers to the world's commonly accepted rules and behaviour. The distribution of power and the legitimacy of the system determine and uphold the rules of world governance. A commonly accepted set of rules based on an international distribution of power and the source of legitimacy constantly changes and must be recalibrated. World order is commonly reorganised after great disruptions as the former conditions enabling it have come to an end and states seek something new.

The concept of world order and its actual existence is a relatively recent phenomenon as the various regions of the globe had until the last few centuries been organised largely independently of each other. The European regional order of Westphalia laid the foundation for world order due to centuries of European dominance at the time when the world became interconnected. The expanding capacity of global interactions increases the complexity of a world order.

How are rules established and upheld in an international system defined by international anarchy—i.e., the absence of a global government? The world order has been based on either a hegemon functioning as a world government or a balance of power imposing constraints on states. To what extent can and should each entity of power enjoy sovereignty? Is international anarchy mitigated by enhancing human freedoms to create more civilised interactions between peoples, or does idealism obscure the imperative of prioritising the primacy of balancing power relations between states?

The modern world order is the consequence of the balance of power and deterrence that are designed to constrain states, although world order also refers to the common interests that incentivise cooperation and unity among states in the pursuit of shared goals. Raymond Aaron argued that world order was the answer to the question: "Under what conditions would men (divided in so many ways) be able not merely to avoid destruction, but to live together relatively well on one planet?"[2] Hedley Bull similarly described world order as "those patterns or dispositions of human activity that sustain the elementary or primary goals of social life among mankind as a whole."[3]

This chapter first explores the Peace of Westphalia as the origin of the modern world order, which organised the international system under a balance of power between sovereign states. Following the Industrial Revolution, the balance of power was increasingly expressed through geoeconomics as a balance of dependence. The number of great powers in the system and the avoidance of permanent alliances were critical conditions for the functioning of the balance of power. Second, the chapter addresses how the Peace of Westphalia resolved anarchy at the national level by establishing the state as the highest sovereign with delineated territorial borders, and yet the international system became defined by anarchy due to the absence of a higher sovereign. The extent to which justice can be increased without unravelling order has largely defined the evolution of the world order. Universalism brings with it the legacy of both justice and imperialism by eschewing the principle of sovereignty. Last, world order is continuously challenged by the temptation to transcend the international anarchy by establishing hegemony and unifying humanity under universal values.

The Peace of Westphalia: A Balance of Power among Sovereign Equals

The Peace of Westphalia of 1648 is commonly treated as the beginning of the modern world order. It recognises the sovereign state

---

2 S. Hoffmann, "Report of the Conference on Conditions of World Order: June 12–19, 1965, Villa Serbelloni, Bellagio, Italy," *Daedalus* (1966), 456.

3 H. Bull, *The Anarchical Society: A Study of Order in World Politics* (Bloomsbury Publishing, 2012), 20.

as the highest sovereignty and main powerholding entity, and peace is ensured by a balance of power among the sovereign equals. The Peace of Westphalia followed a European order based on hegemony that ended with the disintegration of the Holy Roman Empire. There had been a desire to overcome the anarchy of the international system by establishing a hegemon as a successor to the Roman Empire and Charlemagne, but religious and political fragmentation prevented any one power from dominating.

In most regions of the world, a regional hegemon emerged to mitigate the anarchy and to restore order. The Holy Roman Empire was widely recognised as the legitimate successor of the former Roman Empire as the Catholic Church continued to recognise its emperors as Roman emperors. While the Roman Empire collapsed in 476, the Holy Roman Emperors continued to claim the role of universal monarchs holding legitimate jurisdiction across all Christian territory. However, the decline of the Holy Roman Empire resulted in sovereignty becoming an increasingly complex topic due to overlapping land rights and authorities.[4] These disruptive claims continued until the 17th century although the Holy Roman Empire was only dissolved in 1806. The distribution of power no longer favoured hegemony and the Reformation had ended the source of its legitimacy as concerned governance over protestants. It is common to recognise the Peace of Westphalia in 1648 as ending much of the power of the Roman Emperor.

The Thirty-Year War from 1618 to 1648 began with religious fragmentation but evolved into a great power rivalry. The Protestant Reformation challenged the universal authority of the Catholic Church, which intensified the competition for claiming sovereignty over the people and the social norms that would dictate the way of life. Fragmentation led to overlapping claims of sovereignty due to the rivalry of local princes, which was exacerbated by the intervention of the Catholic Church as a supernational institution. The Catholic Hapsburg Empire fought the Protestant German princes who were supported by France, Sweden, and Denmark. Any pretence of unity based on a shared faith, morality and universalism diminished as

---

4 R. Asch, *The Thirty Years War: The Holy Roman Empire and Europe 1618-1648* (London: Palgrave Macmillan, 1997).

Catholic France supported Protestant Sweden to balance the power of the Catholic Habsburgs, who held the title of Holy Roman Emperors.

None of the conflicting sides were able to impose a decisive victory as the various actors sought to preserve their self-determination by pursuing a power equilibrium prohibiting the reassertion of a hegemon. Former assumptions about universality had been further shattered by the destructive war, and a common agreement was thus needed to accommodate the pessimism concerning the international system. As aptly argued by Kissinger, "Paradoxically, this general exhaustion and cynicism allowed the participants to transform the practical means of ending a particular war into general concepts of world order."[5]

The Peace of Westphalia was a series of agreements that concluded the Thirty Years War, a total war which at the time was the longest and most destructive war in European history. It thus established a new international system of multiplicity rather than hegemony, based on a balance of power among sovereign equals. The conflicts deriving from overlapping sovereignty were resolved by making the state, with clearly defined physical borders, the highest sovereign in the international system. Rival authorities such as the church were integrated under the authority of the state as the highest sovereign:

> The end of the Thirty Years War brought with it the final end of the medieval Holy Roman Empire. Authority for choosing the religion of the political unit was given to the prince of that unit and not to the Hapsburg Emperor or the Pope. No longer could one pretend there was religious or political unity in Europe. Authority was dispersed to the various kings and princes, and the basis for the sovereign state was established.[6]

The religion of the prince became the state religion, and the principle of sovereignty meant that foreign states could not intervene in the domestic affairs of other states to support the rights of minorities. To ensure that sovereign states were not threatened by the hegemonic

5 H. Kissinger, *World Order* (New York: Penguin Press, 2014), 26.

6 B. Russett and H. Starr, *World Politics: The Menu for Choice*, (San Francisco: Freeman, 1981), 47.

ambitions of any expansionist state, the leading powers were committed to balancing each other. For the next four centuries, the Peace of Westphalia shaped the world order with the concept of sovereignty at the centre.

The Westphalian world order was put to the test, reaffirmed, and strengthened by the Treaty of Utrecht in 1713, which ended the War of Spanish Succession. One of the key objectives of the treaty was to ensure that the settlement preserved the balance of power in Europe by preventing any one state from becoming dominant. Ensuring the security of opponents was recognised to be a critical step toward achieving lasting peace and stability in Europe. To ensure stability, it was required to guarantee the security of all states participating in the order. This principle was a departure from the traditional approach to international security in which the victors in a conflict could punish and subjugate the defeated side. Thus, the order aimed to replace conquest and domination with constraints and cooperation. This principle was largely embraced with the establishment of the Concert of Europe in 1815 as France was included as an equal participant, despite being defeated in the Napoleonic Wars.

The shift from one centre of power to several equal centres of power required a new approach to international order. While a hegemonic system that relies and is based on universal social norms and values as the source of its legitimacy to govern, a balance of power system must accept greater multiplicity which is then reflected in international rules and law. A hegemonic system based on sovereign inequality utilises a legal framework that legitimises the hierarchy of superior and subordinate states, while a system based on a balance of power requires sovereign equality among the key participants. What could replace the common religious identity and morality that had organised the European system? In a system of multiplicity, how can many states of localised order be entangled without causing conflict?

The Peace of Westphalia laid the foundation for codifying sovereign equality under international law by shifting from substantive to procedural agreements. In the past, Europe had largely been based on substantive law in which states would act according to accepted social norms. Substantive law can result in arbitrary decision-making and social norms can be interpreted inconsistently as the strongest powers do not impose self-constraints. In an international system of states with different religious and social norms, the use of substantive law becomes a hegemonic project in which the most powerful state seeks to impose its social norms and system on the rest. In contrast, procedural law establishes a set of uniform rules. The Peace of Westphalia was thus unique at its time as the negotiations were to a large extent done by bureaucrats and lawyers as opposed to the monarchs referencing universal values.

The concept of sovereign equality demanded procedural law, and this made the Westphalian system attractive and subsequently spread across the international system. According to Kissinger:

> The genius of this system, and the reason it spread across the world, was that its provisions were procedural, not substantive. If a state would accept these basic requirements, it could be recognized as an international citizen able to maintain its own culture, politics, religion, and internal policies, shielded by the international system from outside intervention. The ideal of imperial or religious unity—the operating premise of Europe's and most other region's historical orders—had implied that in theory only one center of power could be fully legitimate. The Westphalian concept took multiplicity as its starting point and drew a variety of multiple societies, each accepted as a reality, into a common search for order.[7]

The Westphalian Geoeconomic Balance of Dependence

The Industrial Revolution made it more difficult to manage a balance of power, while concurrently fuelling the belief that the necessity for a balance of power can be transcended. In the capitalist economy, there is a natural trend towards the concentration of technology, wealth, and power.

There is also a greater ability to act as a benign hegemon by delivering common goods to the international system. An economic hegemon can facilitate a more efficient international division of labour by

7 H. Kissinger, *World Order*, 27.

producing the leading technologies, facilitating reliable transportation corridors, and managing the common international trade/reserve currency. The hegemon's ability to deliver these common goods reduces the incentives for the rest of the world to disrupt a liberal international economy. Economic hegemony thus incentivises the embrace of economic liberalism: "If economic capabilities are so concentrated that a hegemon exists, as in the case of Great Britain in the late 19th century and the USA after World War II, an 'open' or 'liberal' international economic order will come into being."[8] Countries reluctant to open their markets can be coerced to do so.

However, under a benign hegemon, the costs of providing collective goods enable weaker economies to exploit the large economy, and the asymmetries will gradually even out.[9] Eventually "the differential growth in the power of various states in the system causes a fundamental redistribution of power in the system."[10]

When the economic hegemon is confronted with a dilemma about how to respond to the rise of new centres of power, it can either accommodate the rise of new powers and return to a balance of power or abandon its role as a benign hegemon by abusing its administrative role in the international economy by means of economic coercion to impede the rise of rivals. The more rivals that are suppressed, the greater incentive the rising powers will have to collectively counterbalance the shared adversary.[11] Hence, when the economic hegemony is weakened and challenged, "the liberal order is expected to unravel and its regimes to become weaker, ultimately being replaced by mercantilist arrangements in which strategic autonomy and national sovereignty are elevated above market forces.[12]

It was widely assumed that the Industrial Revolution had displaced militaristic zero-sum mercantilism with positive-sum industrial

---

8 J.G. Ruggie, "International regimes, transactions, and change: Embedded liberalism in the postwar economic order," *International Organization* 36, no. 2 (1982): 381.

9 D. Snidal, "The limits of hegemonic stability theory," *International Organization* 39, no. 4 (1985).

10 R. Gilpin, *War and Change in World Politics* (Cambridge: Cambridge University Press, 1981), 13.

11 S.P. Huntington, "The Lonely Superpower," *Foreign Affairs* 87, no. 2 (1999): 35–49.

12 J.G. Ruggie, 381.

economics. It was believed that it was no longer necessary for a state to enrich itself by plundering the territory and wealth of another; wealth could be created from technological advancement and prosperity is intensified by economic interdependence. However, Friedrich List cautioned that liberal economics must adapt to the political realities of the international anarchy in which states compete over relative gain for survival:

> As long as the division of the human race into independent nations exists, political economy will as often be at variance with cosmopolitan principles… a nation would act unwisely to endeavour to promote the welfare of the whole human race at the expense of its particular strength, welfare and independence.[13]

The underlying rationality of relative gain to survive in an anarchic international system merely reformed mercantilism towards neo-mercantilism and geoeconomics. Interdependence entails losing some autonomy and gaining influence, although economic interdependence is never completely symmetrical as one side will always be more dependent than the other. Under asymmetrical interdependence, the more powerful and less dependent side will retain more autonomy and gain more influence.

States therefore seek to skew the symmetry of economic interdependence to maximise their autonomy and influence. Neomercantilism, or geoeconomics, is largely about making one's state less reliant on other states while making others more dependent on your state. Hirschman noted that asymmetrical economic interdependence translates into political power:

> The power to interrupt commercial or financial regulations with any country, considered as an attribute of national sovereignty, is the root cause of the influence or power position which a country acquires in other countries, just as it is the root cause of the "dependence on trade."[14]

---

13 F. List, *Outlines of American Political Economy, in a Series of Letters* (Philadelphia: Samuel Parker, 1827), 30.

14 A. Hirschman, *National Power and the Structure of Foreign Trade* (Berkeley: University of California Press, 1945), 16.

States subsequently seek to control the areas of the international economy that are difficult to diversify as the lack of competition produces greater wealth and can be used to exert political influence. Geoeconomic dominance is obtained by "develop[ing] exports in articles enjoying a monopolistic position in other countries and direct trade to such countries."[15]

Monopolies that are economically profitable and that create political influence can be divided into three categories: (1) strategic industries, (2) physical connectivity, and (3) financial power. Strategic industries include high-tech industries as they are required for economic efficiency, and natural resources as they are finite. Physical connectivity refers to control over the transportation corridors and infrastructure, such as the Suez Canal, which are required for reliable access to international markets. Financial power denotes the international reserve/trade currencies, banks and payment systems used.

In geoeconomics, the "balance of dependence" mirrors the balance of power logic.[16] According to the assumptions of political realism, sustainable and mutually beneficial cooperation can exist when there is a balance of dependence and a consensus to preserve the status quo. When the balance of power is disrupted by wars, technological innovation, or state collapse, the unbalanced state will expand as states do not constrain themselves. However, the international system naturally gravitates back towards equilibrium as expansionist impulses by the unconstrained state are collectively balanced by the other great powers.

Geoeconomics or neomercantilism similarly creates an incentive to restore a balance of dependence. An economic hegemon converts economic dependence into political power, which incentivises other states to reduce economic dependence on the hegemon by increasing self-sufficiency and diversifying economic connectivity. Defensive neo-mercantilism (or geoeconomics) "meant the shaking off of commercial dependence on foreigners which was continually becoming more oppressive."[17] Neo-mercantilism has subsequently

15 Ibid., 34.

16 G. Diesen, *Russia's Goeconomic Strategy for a Greater Eurasia* (London: Routledge, 2017).

17 G. Schmoller, *The Mercantile System and its Historical Significance*, (London: Macmillan, 1897), 76.

been considered to be benign or defensive when protectionism was used to defend political sovereignty, the labour force or the welfare state force.[18] The weaker states in a dyad seek to reduce economic dependence, although there are limitations on economic autarky as excessive self-reliance reduces prosperity and power. The solution is thus self-reliance in strategic industries and the diversifying of economic partnerships to avoid excessive dependence on any one state or region. The international system subsequently gravitates towards a balance of dependence.

International law can exist when there is a balance of power as this incentivises states to accept constraints in foreign policy flexibility in return for reciprocity and thus predictability. In contrast, under a hegemon, there is an incentive for the hegemon to abandon mutual constraints and instead impose rules and norms that support sovereign inequality. List subsequently recognised that a balance of dependence was required for a harmonious international system:

> The highest ultimate aim of rational politics is… the uniting of all nations under a common law of right, an object which is only to be attained through the greatest possible equalisation of the most important nations of the earth in civilisation, prosperity, industry and power, by the conversion of the antipathies and conflicts that now exist between them into sympathy and harmony.[19]

Balance of Power versus Permanent Alliances

Collective security arrangements aiming to preserve a balance of power have proven vulnerable to alliance systems. History demonstrates that peacetime alliances challenge loyalty towards the inclusive collective security arrangement. Case in point, efforts by Bismarck to develop peacetime alliances against France at the end of the 19th century undermined the Concert of Europe, the preserver of the balance of power.

---

18 Buzan, B., "Economic structure and international security: The limits of the liberal case," *International Organization* 38, no. 4 (1984): 608.

19 F. List, *The National System of Political Economy* (London: Longmans, Green & Company, 1841), 96.

The balance of power in the international system mimics the function of checks and balances in domestic politics. The U.S. Constitution was created with a focus on checks and balances to ensure that the concentration of power did not corrupt and hollow out its institutions.[20] The legislative, executive, and judicial branches are intended to balance each other; even within the legislative branch, the two houses can balance each other. The assumption is that if one power wins by overwhelming the others, then everyone loses. Similarly, as states do not constrain themselves, a hegemon is likely to overextend itself and thus exhaust both legitimacy to govern in the international system, and its resources expended to enable that. A balance of power thus presents checks and balances to prevent the emergence of a hegemon, which also makes cooperation and multilateralism necessary as no state or region can act unilaterally.

The balance of power is a central component of modern diplomacy and arms treaties which aim to ensure that no single country or group of countries can gain excessive advantage and dominate. A central tenet of arms treaties is proportional disarmament to ensure that the balance of power is not disrupted. Case in point, the Washington Naval Treaty of 1922, also known as the Five-Power Treaty, agreed to prevent an arms race by limiting naval construction. The governments of the U.S., UK, Italy, France, and Japan agreed to a proportionate reduction of military capabilities to prevent an arms race without disrupting the balance of power.

A multipolar balance of power also encourages innovation as each centre of power must compete to develop new technologies and innovative solutions to problems and governance. In ancient Greece, the competition between city-states was the source of a diversity of ideas and a vitality that elevated Greek civilisation. Greek city-states were reluctant to integrate and pursue universalism because that would entail losing the diversity of philosophy, wisdom, and leadership that incentivised experimentation and advancement.

A balance of power is rarely reached between two states in isolation. Alliance theory developed to a large extent within the context of the balance of power theory, posting that two or more states would ally against another state to constrain expansionist or hegemonic ambitions.

20 H. J. Morgenthau, *Politics among Nations: The Struggle for Power and Peace* (New York: Alfred A. Knopf, 1948), 128.

Alliances can have a positive effect in terms of restoring equilibrium, although alliances that outlive their purpose can cause disruptions to the balance of power and thus international stability by pursuing collective hegemony. The ability of states to act in accordance with the balance of power logic is undermined when loyalties to military alliances are prioritised above the higher objective of preserving an equilibrium.

British Prime Minister Lord Palmerston famously stated: "We have no permanent allies, we have no permanent enemies, we only have permanent interests." This sentiment has since been repeated by Henry Kissinger and other realists who subscribe to the assumption that alliances are a means to an end, with a balance of power as the condition for stability. Morgenthau opined that the role of the balancer was to preserve the peace by ensuring there are no disruptions to the equilibrium: "The balancer is not permanently identified with the policies of either nation or group of nations. Its only objective within the system is the maintenance of the balance, regardless of the concrete policies the balance will serve."[21] Advocating a balancing role for the U.S. after the Cold War, Buzan recommended a "swing power" strategy in which the U.S. must be "engaged in several regions but not permanently wedded to any of them."[22]

The pragmatism of preserving the balance of power can appear to be crude as it is premised on ideological neutrality. Rationality is defined as acting in accordance with the balance of power logic to maximise security; this requires states to adjust to changes in the distribution of power. Kissinger subsequently argues that: "The Peace of Westphalia did not mandate a specific arrangement of alliances or a permanent European political structure."[23]

Pragmatic alliances are designed to preserve stability by upholding equilibrium, while permanent alliances can distort the balance of power. Alliances incentivise the creation of counter-alliances to restore an equilibrium, and the consequence is fewer and larger entities of power that do not have the flexibility to restore a balance of

---

21 Ibid., 143.

22 B. Buzan, "The Security Dynamics of a 1+4 World," in E Aydinli and JN Rosenau (eds.), *Globalization, Security, and the Nation State: Paradigms in Transition* (Albany: State University of New York Press, 2005), 193.

23 H. Kissinger, *World Order*, 27.

power. Booth and Wheeler refer to the "Mitrany paradox" where the construction of new institutional superpowers to enhance peace results in fewer, larger, and less compatible entities of power.[24] John Herz similarly cautioned that military alliances could replace a state's right to make war with a duty to make war.[25]

A distinction should be made between inclusive versus exclusive institutions. Inclusive security institutions tend to develop security *with* other member states, while exclusive security institutions usually pursue security *against* non-member states. While alliances counter common adversaries, a security community is committed to peaceful change by pre-empting disputes between member states.[26]

Multipolarity and the Number of Great Powers

The number of states in the international system greatly impacts the ability to preserve the balance of power. More major powers in the international system enable greater flexibility to rebalance the system and dissuade any ambitions for hegemony.

Since the Peace of Westphalia, the number of states with somewhat equal power has been reduced dramatically. The reduction of great powers according to Morgenthau has "deprived the balance of power of much of its flexibility and uncertainty and, in consequence, of its restraining effect upon the nations actively engaged in the struggle for power."[27]

After the Napoleonic War, there were only eight great powers left: Great Britain, France, Russia, Austria, Prussia, Spain, Portugal, and Sweden. By the end of the Second World War, there were only two great powers, which organised the international system according to a zero-sum manner with the prospect of hegemony within grasp for one if its adversary could be defeated. In an international system of three or more great powers, the conflicting sides must accept more constraints as aggression and expansionism are punished by rebalancing.

---

24 K. Booth and N. J. Wheeler, *The Security Dilemma: Fear, Cooperation and Trust in World Politics* (Basingstoke: Palgrave Macmillan, 2008), 188–89.

25 J. H. Herz, "Power politics and world organization," *The American Political Science Review* 36, no. 6 (1942): 1046–47.

26 E. Adler and M. Barnett, *Security Communities* (Cambridge: Cambridge University Press, 1998).

27 H. J. Morgenthau, *Politics among Nations,* 271.

Conflict is discouraged if the confrontation between state A and state B could leave state C as the victor in terms of relative power. Bipolarity incentivises a zero-sum logic as the loss of one side will be the gain for the other. General Charles de Gaulle thus cautioned in July 1946 that the balance of power would not function under the bipolar distribution of power:

> It is certain indeed that, with respect to what it was before this thirty-year war the face of the world has altered in every way. A third of a century ago we were living in a universe where six or eight great nations, apparently equal in strength, each by differing and subtle accords associating others with it, managed to establish a balance everywhere in which the less powerful found themselves relatively guaranteed and where international law was recognized, since a violator would have faced a coalition of moral or material interests, and where, in the last analysis, strategy conceived and prepared with a view to future conflicts involved only rapid and limited destruction.[28]

Charles de Gaulle famously envisioned France or a united Europe under French leadership to perform the role of a third centre of power to hold the balance of power and thus impose greater restraints and curb the expansionist impulses of the U.S. and Soviet Union:

> Who then can re-establish the equilibrium, if not the old world, between the two new ones? Old Europe, which, during so many centuries was the guide of the universe, is in a position to constitute in the heart of a world that tends to divide itself into two, the necessary clement of compensation and understanding.[29]

The failure to achieve an independent role made Europe a vassal of the U.S., about which French President Emmanuel Macron would lament more than 75 years later. After the Cold War, Europe was similarly faced with a dilemma of either pursuing parity with the U.S. in

28 Ibid., 353.
29 Ibid., 354.

a bid for the collective hegemony of the West or developing an autonomous role in a multipolar system. Russia hoped the EU would be an independent centre of power and represent the "good West" by being able to accommodate Russia and other centres of power. However, the EU eventually pursued collective hegemony with the U.S. by aligning itself within NATO, which serves as the principal institution to project U.S. hegemony in Europe. Such an intended unipolar system can only sustain itself by preventing the rise of other centres of power, thus reverting to the zero-sum logic of the Cold War.

The Politics of Order under International Anarchy

International anarchy refers to the absence of a centralised or overreaching authority in the international system that can regulate the behaviour of states. The Peace of Westphalia ended the anarchy within the borders of the state by eradicating overlapping sovereignties and establishing one supreme sovereign that monopolised the use of violence. Nonetheless, the international system became defined by international anarchy due to the absence of a world government exercising monopoly on the use of force. Subsequently, each state must ensure its own security and survival through the development of military power and alliances. The resultant international anarchy is the source of conflict. In an effort to establish order in the international anarchy, states aim to develop the rules of the game that are acceptable globally—a world order.

The international anarchy creates a security dilemma as states can either reduce their military power and be vulnerable to foreign aggression or enhance their military power and thus undermine the security of other states, forcing them to similarly enhance their militaries. A security paradox subsequently ensues as states' defensive intentions propel them towards conflict.[30] Mitigating the security dilemma requires solutions that also enhance the security of opponents. Conflict resolution to ensure lasting peace therefore requires that the losing side is protected from retaliation.

In 1651, three years after the Peace of Westphalia, Thomas Hobbes published Leviathan, which laid the foundation for realist theory. Hobbes argued that the natural condition or state of nature was the

30 K. Booth and N. J. Wheeler, *The Security Dilemma.*

war of all against all, in which men would accrue power and weapons to fight each other for survival. A strong government monopolising the use of force was thus a necessary evil to end the anarchy. However, in the international realm, there was no higher sovereign, and the state of nature was thus one of endless war.

Neorealist theory builds on the basic assumptions of Hobbes, who suggests that states do not constrain themselves. Constraint and thus peace are therefore dependent on a balance of power as states must balance each other. Under a balance of power, international rules and laws can develop as balanced states are willing to limit flexibility in their foreign policy in return for reciprocity and thus predictability. The durability of international law, therefore, rests upon the international distribution of power and adheres to the principle of sovereign equality.

John Locke presented a liberal theory about human nature and society as an alternative to the theoretical assumptions of Thomas Hobbes. Believing that human nature is defined by tolerance and reason, Locke was more optimistic about the possibility of peace to be achieved by enhancing human freedoms. The social contract theory of Locke assumes that sovereignty derives from the will of the people, in which the government is granted authority, and legitimacy to the extent it protects the rights of the people. If the government breaks the social contract by violating natural rights, the legitimacy of the state's authority is revoked. Locke is subsequently considered the father of liberal theory, which assumes that international anarchy can be mitigated or transcended by advancing liberal values, interdependence, and common rules of governance.

Immanuel Kant's 1795 *Perpetual Peace* reflected the liberal ideals of the American and French Revolutions, which viewed world order in terms of the link between all people in a community of humanity. The interests of humankind are largely common and universal; this deviates drastically from the zero-sum nature of relations between states. The ideas of Kant laid the foundation for democratic peace theory that assumes democracies do not go to war against each other, which then suggests that security can be promoted as a positive-sum game by pursuing common liberal values and good governance. It views the existence of international institutions of justice as an indicator of world order.[31]

International relations theory largely builds on the competing assumptions of Hobbes and Locke about human nature and the state. International anarchy serves as the point of departure in international relations theory, which presents rival assumptions about human nature and why states act the way they do. Liberal theory aspires to transcend the international anarchy of international relations, while realist theory cautions against ignoring the international anarchy and the realism of international relations. It assumes that international anarchy can be mitigated by developing democracy, international institutions, and international law to externalise the benign nature of humanity.

Realist theory considers human nature to be inherently self-interested and competitive, and preserving the balance of power is the main priority to ensure that states are constrained. While both liberal and realist scholars view the elevation of human freedoms as a positive development, the realists caution that idealist illusions about the possibility of transcending the balance of power logic obscure the primacy of power and thus cause extremely destructive policies.

Order versus Justice

Order manifests itself as sovereignty and a balance of power while justice refers to moral ideas about how the world is organised. Order tends to favour and be constrained by the status quo and justice refers to progress that requires readjustments. The order-justice nexus outlines the opposing yet mutually dependent ideals of order and justice. Without order there cannot be justice, and in the absence of justice there cannot be order. Thus, ideologies favouring advancing human freedoms are deeply critical of sovereign absolutism and the pragmatism of preserving a power equilibrium to constrain states.

The definitions of world order differ in terms of the expectation to deliver greater justice. Order must inevitably address justice as the two concepts are intimately connected. On one hand, order can be seen as a prerequisite for justice: a society that lacks order may be unable to establish and enforce the rules and thus fail to deliver justice.

---

31 J. M. Rochester, *International Institutions and World Order: The International System as a Prismatic Polity* (Sage Publications. 1975).

On the other hand, systems devised to uphold complete order by suppressing basic human freedoms eventually stagnate and contribute to the breakdown of order.

Based on the assumption that justice is required for order, normative considerations are imperative for the legitimacy of a world order. Mendlovitz and Weiss argue that a "world order inquiry involves the use of relevant utopias culminating in the statement of the investigator's preferred world."[32] World order must therefore aim to "significantly reduce the likelihood of international violence and create minimally acceptable conditions of worldwide economic well-being, social justice, ecological stability, and participation in decision-making processes."[33]

The competing theoretical assumptions about how the world works have created a realist versus a liberal understanding of world order, which conflict in terms of what should be prioritised:

> The term "world order' is used in two very different ways in the discussions of world politics. Realists, in the tradition of Richard Nixon and Henry Kissinger, see international politics occurring among sovereign states balancing each others' power. World order is the product of a stable distribution of power among the major states. Liberals, in the tradition of Woodrow Wilson and Jimmy Carter, look at relations among peoples as well as states. They see order arising from broad values like democracy and human rights, as well as from international law and institutions such as the United Nations.[34]

The competing theoretical assumptions also produce conflicting perspectives on the rise of non-state actors as a new source of power and authority. Realist assumptions assume that order depends on preserving the sovereignty of the state as the foundation of the Westphalian order, while liberal theory expects that limiting the power

32 S. Mendlovitz and T. Weiss, "The Study of Peace and Justice: Toward a Framework for Global Discussion," in L.R. Beres and H. Targ (eds.), *Planning Alternative Future* (New York: Praeger, 1975), 157.

33 Ibid.

34 J. S. Nye, "What new world order?," *Foreign Affairs* 71, no. 2 (1992): 84.

of the state can reduce the zero-sum power competition in the international system.

Liberal theory assumes that the emergence of non-state actors such as international institutions, multinational corporations, and international civic society created a more benign world order as the international system becomes less state-centric. The opposing realist view is that less power to the state may entail less protection for people as international institutions may undermine the sovereignty of the state that represents the national interests of its inhabitants. For example, profit-driven corporations have become multinational with the ability to sidestep domestic interests and regulation, and civil society organisations may empower a loud minority over a quiet majority or even be manipulated by foreign powers. The realist concept of a rational state entails maximizing security by mobilising its resources to act in accordance with the balance of power logic. Ceding power to non-state actors subsequently prevents the state from acting rationally, i.e., in accordance with its interests. Furthermore, it enables rival states to extend their influence by establishing influence over international institutions, multinational corporations, and civil society organisations.

Justice is commonly associated with the issue of human freedoms, which can be promoted in a manner that undermines the sovereignty of the state. In December of 1948, Moscow abstained as UN members signed the Universal Declaration of Human Rights (UDHR); it feared the West would use human rights as a weapon to interfere in Soviet Union's domestic affairs to weaken them. However, Moscow still cited the Universal Declaration of Human Rights to lecture the U.S. about the treatment of the African American minority and other American human rights abuses. In more modern times, the U.S. has similarly expressed support for the International Court of Justice (ICJ) to arrest war criminals of adversarial states, although the U.S. has not signed the charter and even threatened to invade Den Haag in the Netherlands to liberate any Americans that might be arrested. The world order is thus fiercely committed to preserving one's own sovereignty yet pursuing justice in other states.

Human security, in which the individual is the referent object to be protected, entails providing individuals with security from the threat of actions taken by their own government. Elevating human security to the extent that it undermines state sovereignty is thus a call for enhancing justice at the expense of order. The concept of human security challenges sovereignty as the foundational pillar of world order by contesting the state's monopoly on the use of violence within its own borders. A key argument for human security is, again, that without justice there can be no order. But the dilemma is: while African states argued that apartheid in South Africa was unjust in how it jeopardised the order of the region, in more recent years many African states have expressed their apprehensions about "human rightism," conceptualised as a Western instrument of power to legitimise another civilising mission on their continent.

Furthermore, Western states attempt to monopolise the right to suspend sovereignty in defence of other peoples as they recognise that the order that presently favours them would quickly unravel if countries such as China or Russia could also defend ethnic Chinese or Russians in neighbouring states, or the sovereignty of other peoples, elsewhere. The West's support for human security is therefore, to a large extent, conditioned on its hegemony in order to ensure it remains their exclusive prerogative. Human security can be a genuine aspiration or an instrument in the pursuit of power interests, and at worst humanitarian crisis can be instigated to invite self-serving military interventions.

A more just world order can be harmonised with state sovereignty if it occurs within the framework of an inclusive international institution, primarily the UN as the arbiter of international law. The UN introduced the concept of the Responsibility to Protect (R2P) in the early 2000s, presenting sovereignty as both a right and a responsibility. If the state fails to live up to the responsibility of defending human rights of its people, then the international community could be enabled to temporarily suspend its sovereignty. R2P was proposed to represent a balance between order and justice as humanitarian interventions must be authorised by the UN Security Council to ensure the practice is not abused and does not erode order. However, R2P was operationalised against countries such as Libya in service of strategic Western interests, leading to massive disorder, not just within the state to which it was addressed, but to states in the vicinity. Western states claim the right to sideline the UN due to the "threat" of a Russian or

Chinese veto. This is a claim to further enhance justice, although it unravels the foundation of the existing order.

The debate about removing the veto powers of the permanent members of the UN Security Council is similarly a suggestion to recalibrate the balance between order and justice. It is commonly argued that the veto power of the permanent members of the UN Security Council are unjust and must be suspended, although that was what enabled the UN to become a stable and durable institution capable of providing order as it reflected the then-existing international distribution of power. The most powerful states in the international system were endowed with special powers in the UN Security Council, which ensured that the most powerful states in the international system had an incentive to preserve the authority of the UN. Pursuing a more just UN by cancelling the privileges of the great powers in the UN Security Council would reduce the value of the UN to the great powers and make them more reliant on hard power to defend their security interests. In the subsequent absence of order, there would also be no justice.

Universalism, Morality and Exceptionalism

World order includes a set of values and morality that must be followed as a condition for membership in the community of sovereign states. Since the Peace of Westphalia, these values have largely been defined and dictated by the West and subsequently, the non-Western world has not always qualified for full sovereignty.

Adherence to values determines the extent to which states are to be regarded as "civilised," which has, through history, been conditioned on religion, culture, enlightenment, secularism, constitutionalism, democratisation, industrialisation, stage of development, and form of government. Western-centrism created a strong "us" versus "them" division to the extent of fuelling a sense of exceptionalism. In a relationship between a superior and an inferior, the former can set the conditions for representation and membership of the community of sovereignty states:

> As the sense grew of the specifically European character of the society of states, so also did the sense of its

> cultural differentiation from what lay outside: the sense that European powers in their dealings with one another were bound by a code of conduct that did not apply to them in their dealings with other and lesser societies.[35]

Ideologies of elevating humanity and introducing greater morality into the world order are vulnerable to unravelling order. When it is assumed that international anarchy can be transcended with what is believed to be universal values, it is common to externalise evil by only finding the sources of evil in the "other." This undermines the balance of power principle that all people and states must be constrained and balanced, as the fundamental condition for peace in accordance with realist theory. The sources of peace within human nature and states are usually attributed to one's own characteristics, thus morally elevating one's own above the rest because of the presumed superiority of one's own race, culture, religion, values, or form of government.

Practical considerations and compromise are important for successful diplomacy aimed at pursuing stability and peace. Idealism can produce a sense of moral superiority and self-righteousness that can damage diplomatic relationships. Conviction of one's own inherent goodness can manifest itself in destructive "moral crusades" and "nationalist universalism."[36] The assumption that the internal characteristics of certain people and states determines their proclivity for peace or war implies that peace is not achieved through mutual constraints. Rather, peace requires that the virtuous civilise or convert the "other" to the correct faith, values, race, or form of government. If this fails, then the alternative is to contain or defeat the other.

If it is recognised that the world is divided by conflicting interests, then peace is created by placing ourselves in the shoes of the opponent and pursuing compromise. However, if conflicts are defined by good versus bad values, then empathy and compromise become tantamount to appeasement and betrayal of sacred values that can ensure peace. Morgenthau cautioned against the dark side of universal ideals and values:

---

35 H. Bull, *The Anarchical Society,* 32.

36 K. Booth and N. J. Wheeler, *The Security Dilemma,* 98.

> The moral code of one nation flings the challenge of its universal claim with Messianic fervor into the face of another, which reciprocates in kind. Compromise, the virtue of the old diplomacy, becomes the treason of the new; for the mutual accommodation of conflicting claims, possible or legitimate within a common framework of moral standards, amounts to surrender when the moral standards are themselves the stakes of the conflict. Thus the stage is set for a contest among nations whose stakes are no longer their relative positions within a political and moral system accepted by all, but the ability to impose upon other contestants a new universal political and moral system recreated in the image of the victorious nation's political and moral convictions.[37]

The international system becomes most dangerous under "pure conflict" when the possibility for compromise is absent, and the winner takes all.[38] Ideologies are vulnerable to extremism as the promise of perpetual peace as an end can legitimise violent and non-compromising means:

> Idealistic diplomacy slips too often into fanaticism; it divides states into good and evil, into peace-loving and bellicose. It envisions a permanent peace by the punishment of the latter and the triumph of the former. The idealist, believing he has broken with power politics exaggerates its crimes.[39]

The impulse in human nature to introduce order into chaos creates a proclivity to embrace ideologies of internationalism that aim to overcome the international anarchy. Idealist internationalism envisions that the embrace of universal ideals that advance human freedom will transcend the anarchy of the international system, thus replacing the Westphalian system of sovereign states under a balance of power. By linking an ideal to an entity of power, political idealism can aspire

---

37 H. J. Morgenthau, *Politics among Nations,* 256.

38 T. C. Schelling, *The Strategy of Conflict*, (London: Harvard University Press, 1980), 3.

39 R. Aron, *Peace and War: A Theory of International Relations* (Garden City, Doubleday, 1966), 584.

for hegemony as a direct revision of the world order. Idealism can paradoxically also encourage violent means if it presupposes that the difference between the current flawed world and perpetual peace can be bridged by destroying an adversary. The promise of perpetual peace justifies perpetual war.

Cosmopolitanism and universalism are largely defined by Socrates' announcement that he was a citizen of the world. The sentiment represents genuine benign ideals about shared humanity and an aspiration to make the entire globe into one large community. However, these same ideals underpinned Alexander the Great's "brotherhood of man" and "the unity of mankind" as he expanded his empire to the East. Universalism often comes with the promise to unify all people under common faith, norms, or values to elevate world order beyond mere power politics. Universalism also offers a potent argument against moral, cultural, or civilizational relativism as some values and norms can be objectively argued to be superior to others. Albeit universalism can also be used for power politics by inviting dominance over others.

The Enduring Appeal of Hegemony

Over the past centuries, there have been several revisionist efforts to alter the foundation of the world order by abandoning the balance of power between sovereign equals and replacing it with hegemony. The attraction of hegemony is that it proposes to overcome the international anarchy caused by the absence of an overarching authority. With one centre of power that advances universal values, it is believed that it is possible to restore another Pax Romana, the 200-year-long period in Roman history viewed as a golden age. Under hegemony, the Romans imposed relative peace in their part of the world and prosperity.

Aspiring hegemons seek to undo the balance of power which is commonly accompanied by a desire to mitigate the international anarchy and advance an ideal of human freedom. Hegemonic stability theory posits that the existence of a dominant global power can temper the international anarchy.[40] A benign hegemon can be conceptualised as acting as a responsible administrator of the international system by

40 C. P. Kindleberger, *The World in Depression, 1929–1939* (Berkeley, University of California Press, 1986).

providing public goods such as security, trade, and monetary stability. The mere presence of the hegemon can mitigate the international anarchy and dissuade great power rivalry. Furthermore, by being a force for good, the hegemon is not challenged. Kissinger therefore argued:

> Empires have no interest in operating within an international system; they aspire to be the international system. Empires have no need for a balance of power. That is how the United States has conducted its foreign policy in the Americas, and China through most of its history in Asia.[41]

Hegemonic aspirations typically coexist with and are legitimised by ideologies promising to elevate human freedoms. Hegemony requires both power and legitimacy as it implies a "coherent conjunction or fit between a configuration of material power, a prevalent collective image of world order (including certain norms) and a set of institutions which administer the order with a certain semblance of universality."[42]

Idealism and liberal theory emphasise the importance of values and principles to shape human behaviour and the international system. Idealism can inspire progress and positive change, although it can also undermine the balance of power. During the Thirty Years War (1618-1648) in Europe, the various armies pursued hegemony based on the view that their morality and universalism that had to be imposed on the entire continent. The consequence was total war.

Hegemony is characterised by the dominance of the ruling elites through a combination of coercion and consent. Hegemony "manifests itself in two ways, as 'domination' and as 'intellectual and moral leadership'."[43] When the slaves internalise and accept their subordinate role in society, the hegemon can rely on consent instead of coercion. Hegemonic discourse normalises hegemonic power relations between the master and the slave, or the enlightened state and the uncivilised

---

41 H. Kissinger, *Diplomacy* (New York, Touchstone, 1994), 21.

42 R.W. Cox, "Social Forces, States and World Orders: Beyond International Relations Theory," in R.O. Keohane (ed.), *Neorealism and Its Critics* (New York, Columbia University Press, 1986), 223.

43 A. Gramsci, *Selections from the Prison Notebooks of Antonio Gramsci* (New York, International Publishers, 1971), 57.

state as consent from the uncivilised reduces the reliance on coercion. The hegemon achieves consent to its dominance by depicting it as being in the service of universal ideals for all peoples.[44]

In an international order premised on universal ideals, the inferior state must either accept a subject-object relationship as a civilisational student or be regarded as a barbaric threat to civilisation that must be contained or defeated. Either way, the inferior state does not obtain a seat at the table. And as the saying goes, if you don't have a seat at the table, you're likely on the menu.

Liberal hegemonies praise hegemonic rule as another stable Pax Romana and paint a dark picture of the alternatives. While hegemony can mitigate the anarchy of the international system and the subsequent conflicts, the preservation of hegemony demands the suppression of rival power. Thus, a hegemonic international system naturally gravitates back towards a Westphalian equilibrium as the other states in the system seek to balance the hegemon. Economically, the emergence of multipolarity weakens economic liberalism as the rising powers seek economic autonomy while the hegemon will increasingly rely on economic coercion.

Under a balance of power, states must be prudent and make rational priorities to survive, whereas a dominant state is vulnerable to hubris and delusions about its own superiority and invincibility. While the costs of the mistakes it makes can be absorbed, the hegemon incrementally overextends itself as the accumulation of the costs of misadventure eventually grows towards a breaking point. Resources are transferred from the core to the periphery to preserve the empire, and domestic issues are insufficiently addressed, with economic inequality fuelling social and political instability. On the other hand, economically weaker states become increasingly willing to endure economic hardship in order to shed dependence on the hegemon.[45] In the "imperial lifecycle," empires become wealthy and powerful as they expand and extract wealth from the wider world; although in the process they contribute to the development of new centres of power which eventually challenge their empire.[46]

---

44 Ibid., 181–82.

45 A. Hirschman, "Beyond asymmetry: critical notes on myself as a young man and on some other old friends," *International Organisation*, vol.32, no.1, 1978.

46 J. Rapley and P. Heather, *Why Empires Fall: Rome, America, and the Future*

When people are born into wealth they tend to be deprived of a sense of necessity, often resulting in their complacency. Affluence also tends to decouple power and authority from competence, which produces systemic distrust and anti-intellectualism among the public. Economic determinism makes money the core indicator of value, and society becomes subservient to the economy. Nationalism and culture are degraded from an instrument of unity and shared purpose to a mere tool by the powerful to obtain and prolong their power, calling for the return to a glorious past or an unattainable future.

In the study of civilisations, the "universal state" is commonly associated with decadence. The "universal state" or "universal empire" denotes political supremacy or hegemony like Rome in which the dominant state is subverting efforts by others to collectively balance.[47] In his important work on civilisations, Quigley observed that like a star, the hegemon shines the brightest when it has already begun to die:

> When a universal empire is established in a civilisation, the society enters upon a "golden age." At least this is what it seems to the periods that follow it. Such a golden age is a period of peace and of relative prosperity. Peace arises from the absence of any competing political unity within the area of the civilization itself, and from the remoteness or even absence of struggles with other societies outside. Prosperity arises from the ending of internal belligerent destruction, the reduction of internal trade barriers, the establishment of a common system of weights, measures, and coinage, and from the extensive government spending associated with the establishment of a universal empire. But this appearance of prosperity is deceptive. Little real economic expansion is possible because no real instrument of expansion exists. New inventions are rare, and real economic investment is lacking… A period of acute economic depression, declining standards of living, civil wars between the various vested

of the West (Dublin: Penguin, 2023).

47 J. A. Toynbee, *Study of History* (Oxford, Oxford University Press, 1946).

interests, and growing illiteracy. The society grows weaker and weaker.[48]

Conclusion

Understanding the competing theoretical assumptions of world order is imperative to an assessment how the contemporary world order came to be and the direction in which it will likely evolve. The dichotomy of hegemony versus a balance of power influences the extent to which sovereign equality, universal values and collective security can be organised. The international distribution of power and legitimacy for the system dictates the rules managing relations under international anarchy. Theories on world order should encourage critical thinking and exploration of different perspectives on world affairs to promote a deeper understanding of international relations. The theories on world order help identify potential risks and opportunities. They are not just academic exercises; they are essential tools for comprehending, navigating, and shaping the complex social, economic, and political connectivity.

48 C. Quigley, *The Evolution of Civilisations: A Historical Analysis*, (Indianapolis, Liberty Press, 1961), 158–59.

3.

The Rise of the Western-Centric World Order

THE WORLD became increasingly Western-centric in the early 16th century onward and Europe's Westphalian regional order of 1648 thus laid the foundation for world order. European politics were defined by the tensions between an order based on hegemony versus a balance of power. While there was largely a balance of power between sovereign equals in Europe, the wider world was defined by the collective hegemony of Europe and the subsequent sovereign inequality. Since the Napoleonic Continental System challenged Britain as a maritime power, the power struggle in the world was to a large extent defined by the maritime powers pursuing hegemony by instigating divisions between the continental powers. While a balance of power was consistent with the Westphalian world order, Britain as an island state could use a balance of power in continental Europe to dominate.

Britain developed a hegemonic position due to its advantage in the Industrial Revolution, control over the seas, and subsequent financial power. The concentration of economic power in an island state also made Britain inclined to promote a world order based on political and economic liberalism. Nationalism, democratisation and other organising ideas and universal values were linked to—and to a certain extent corrupted by—the intense power struggle in the West. The U.S. eventually succeeded Britain as a more powerful de facto island state, and was able to prevent land powers in Europe and Eurasia from coming together and cooperating independently from the U.S. Subsequently, the world order evolved according to Western characteristics.

Rise of the West: Military Supremacy to Establish Mercantilist Empires

The Western-centric world order can only be said to have begun at the end of the 15th century when Western maritime powers obtained control of the maritime transportation corridors that connected the world. In 1492, Columbus crossed the Atlantic and connected Europe with the Americas. In 1498, Vasco da Gama circled Africa and reached India. The Europeans established a network of trade posts and colonies around the world based on international trade. The Portuguese established the first trade post empire in the early 16th century by opening trading posts along the African coast and in India. The Spanish similarly established colonies in Latin America, and the Dutch became powerful in Southeast Asia with the mercantilism of the Dutch East India Company.

The world was subsequently already Western-centric when a new political order was established with the Peace of Westphalia in 1648. The British copied the model of the Dutch East India Company and established colonies across the world from India, and North America to Africa. The Industrial Revolution further assisted European empires in cementing their dominance over the world in the 19th century.

Diplomacy and war among the great European powers thus revolved around seeking peace and stability among the European empires, while between them carving up the rest of the world in the struggle for the world product vis-à-vis other European empires. The competition between European empires did not need to result in direct confrontation, as they instead competed by extending their control of overseas resources, markets, and by colonizing or replacing indigenous populations. An enduring format for world order was thus established, a Westphalian system of sovereign equality among Western states and collective hegemony with sovereign inequality as the foundation for order in the wider world.

The five centuries of political, economic and civilisational dominance of Europe and the wider West was based on the military superiority established in the 16th and 17th centuries. To a large extent, "the 'rise of the West' depended upon the exercise of force, upon the fact that the military balance between the Europeans and their adversaries overseas was steadily tilting in favour of the former, which was the key to the Westerners' success in creating the first truly global empires between 1500 and 1750."[49] While the Western narrative tends to suggest its predominance was due to its ideals, the rest of the world identifies military superiority as the source of its power. Huntington argues:

> For four hundred years, intercivilizational relations consisted of the subordination of other societies to Western civilization... The immediate source of Western expansion, however, was technological: the invention of the means of ocean navigation for reaching distant peoples and the development of the military capabilities for conquering those peoples... The West won the world not by the superiority of its ideas or values or religion (to which few members of other civilizations were converted) but rather by its superiority in applying organized violence. Westerners often forget this fact; non-Westerners never do.[50]

Military superiority was instrumental in asserting economic, cultural, and political dominance, and thus to define and uphold the world order. An uncontested hegemon failed to establish itself in modern Europe largely because of the geographical makeup. The maritime powers in Western Europe could expend their excess energy and compete indirectly by taking to the sea and developing colonies. As the European system was not closed, aspiring hegemons could be countered by maritime powers from the West or the Russian land power in the East that could introduce large amounts of resources into the fight.[51]

British-French Struggle for Hegemony

Britain and France competed for hegemony in the 18th century and the early 19th century through colonial expansion and control

49 G. Parker, *The Military Revolution: Military innovation and the rise of the West, 1500-1800*, Cambridge, Cambridge University Press, 1996), 4.

50 S. P. Huntington, *The Clash of Civilizations and the Remaking of World Order* (New York, Simon and Schuster, 1996), 51.

51 W. R. Thompson, "Dehio, long cycles, and the geohistorical context of structural transition," *World Politics* 45, no. 1 (1992): 129.

over the seas. The rivalry between Britain and France culminated in the Seven Years' War (1756-1763) in which the opposing alliances led by Britain and France fuelled a global conflict. This conflict included French support for American secession from Britain during its war for independence. The absolute monarchy of France, which would shortly thereafter experience its own revolution, supported the American anti-monarchy rebellion to weaken its British opponent, although the British-French rivalry for hegemony continued until 1815 with the defeat of Napoleon.

The 1789 French Revolution's introduction of nationalism threatened to disrupt the Westphalian balance of power by revising the concept of sovereignty. While the Peace of Westphalia built a system based on the rule of sovereign princes, nationalism represented the transition to sovereign nations. Before the emergence of nationalism, the international system largely consisted of a few great empires and kingdoms. The rulers of these entities were given the title of "sovereign," which meant possessing supreme power. The American Revolution and the French Revolution shifted the focus of world order toward greater justice, which entailed greater emphasis on the internal governance of states as monarchies were replaced. Then, the world order that focused on the rights of states as sovereign entities was reformed as the "rights of man" was deemed a key principle of justice.

The French Revolution in the final years of the 18th century launched a new idea of concentrating power in the nation as a way to organise society and the international system. The Westphalian principle of sovereignty was preserved, although sovereignty (supreme power) was transferred from the monarch to the people. While the kings claimed a divine right to rule under a mandate from God, the nation obtained legitimacy from the common political identity of the collective. This had a profound impact on governance as it introduced democracy since the political leadership was viewed as *representing* the people. Nationalism became a force for freedom since it provided no legitimacy for asserting sovereignty over other peoples. This is why nationalism became a powerful force during de-colonisation in the 20th century.

Nationalism also changed the relations between states as nations became the main entities of power in the international system. Immanuel Kant, a liberal philosopher, believed that the transition of sovereignty from monarchs to the people could deliver perpetual peace as heretofore princes had accrued the spoils of war while the people paid an immeasurable cost. Kant's perpetual peace thus inspired the influential democratic peace theory, a liberal theory suggesting that democracies do not go to war with each other, since they are controlled by the people, who will not see war as in their interest. The prospect of liberating other peoples from the monarchs and creating world peace based on the brotherhood of nations gave rise to idealist internationalism, resulting in the Napoleonic Wars. Nationalism also became a force for freedom among colonised people that assisted in unravelling the vast European empires.

Those who disputed the assumed peaceful nature of humanity cautioned that nationalism could also be an instrument to mobilise people for war. Nationalism affords a powerful collective identity that generates immense loyalty, which can be used to subvert rationality. By organising nations into hierarchies, nationalism can give rise to crude ethnic tribalism and elevate some nations above others. The primordial human instinct of dividing people into the in-group of "us" versus the out-group of "them" can be manipulated by governments through appeals to nationalism. Presenting the in-group/out-group relationship as friends versus enemies lays the foundation for mass violence and war, with fascism originating from the radicalisation of "us" versus "them."[52] The nation inevitably creates a powerful groupthink with the belief that we must be correct and righteous if everyone among us believes the same thing. The American historian, Robert Roswell Palmer, argued that in 1793 "The wars of kings were over; the wars of peoples had begun."[53]

Furthermore, transferring sovereignty to the people does not imply that the political leadership becomes demoted to being mere servants of the people. Democracies are more inclined to use manipulation and propaganda due to the need for constructing social cohesion and consent for policies. When the public is the sovereign and the source of legitimate power, there is an even greater incentive to

---

52 J. Stanley, *How Fascism Works: The Politics of Us and Them* (New York: Penguin Books, 2018).

53 S. P. Huntington, *The Clash of Civilizations and the Remaking of World Order*, 52.

manipulate public opinion.[54] The idea that the political leadership must guide the uninformed and ignorant masses was expressed by Neville Chamberlain in 1923: "The new electorate contains an immense mass of ignorant voters, of both sexes, whose intelligence is low and who have no power of weighing evidence."[55]

Nationalism created an unrivalled collective identity in terms of harnessing the loyalties of people. George Kennan argued that "nationalism has developed into the greatest emotional-political force of the age. In the Western world, and in part elsewhere as well, all other forms of collective self-identification, including those based on religion or class or dynastic loyalties, have been swept before it."[56] Exploring group psychology and its impact on the individual, Walter Lippman asserted that "the fierce power of national feeling is due to the fact that it rises from the deepest sources of our being."[57]

The nation-state also proved to be a powerful political entity as it responded to deep instincts in human nature. Sociologists have devoted much focus to the duality of humankind caused by instincts formed over thousands of years and the relatively recent emergence of rationality as an organising principle. Human beings seek *gemeinschaft* (community) as the natural habitat in which collective identities are formed that enjoy high social capital. The community consists of close-knit communities such as the family, tribe, and clan that are based on informal social bonds and trust. Humans have developed instincts to form these collective identities based on kinship to ensure shared security, a sense of belonging, meaning, morality, and even a form of immortality by reproducing the group. Yet, humankind also gravitates towards *gesellschaft* (society), which represents larger, complex, industrial, and cosmopolitan societies that are more efficient, competitive, and based on rational formal ties and contracts.[58]

---

54 W. Lippman, *Public Opinion* (San Diego:, Harcourt, Brace & Co, 1922); E. Bernays, *Propaganda* (New York: Liveright, 1928).

55 P. M. Taylor, *British Propaganda in the Twentieth Century: Selling Democracy* (Edinburgh: Edinburgh University Press, 2019), 91.

56 G. F. Kennan, *Around the Cragged Hill: A Personal and Political Philosophy* (New York, Norton, 1993), 76–77.

57 W. Lippman, *The Stakes of Diplomacy* (New Brunswick: Transaction Publishers, 1932), 66–67.

58 F. Tönnies, *Community and Society* (New York: Dover Publications, 1957).

The success of the nation-state is attributed to its ability to bridge the community and society. George Kennan recognised that: "Man, to the degree that he tries to shape his behavior to the requirements of civilization, is unquestionably a cracked vessel. His nature is the scene of a never-ending and never quite resolvable conflict between two very profound impulses."[59] Max Weber similarly recognised that the human struggle between reason and the instinctive had to be resolved by establishing a balance. The nation is a powerful political entity as it bases its sovereignty on its collective identity entailing a common history, tradition, ethnicity, religion, culture, language, and other key shared characteristics of the collective. Yet, the nation-state also emerged as a powerful vessel for liberalism and the rights of the individual.

Napoleon's Continental System

The Napoleonic Continental System was a geoeconomic initiative by France originating in 1806 to unite Europe against the British economy and thus claim leadership in Europe. Napoleon aimed to shift the balance away from economic dependence on Britain via an economic blockade by continental Europe. The Continental System produced a geostrategic logic of British maritime power vis-à-vis European land powers.

The continental system was a political intervention to develop European industries, transportation corridors and financial instruments independent of Britain. British control over the seas created blockades and maritime restrictions that severed France from its colonial vassals, which therefore incentivised new transportation corridors on continental Europe to redirect trade within the European market.[60] Napoleon became the first European leader to call for developing "the United States of Europe" and he wrote: "I wished to found a European system, a European Code of Laws, a European judiciary; there would be but one people in Europe."[61] While France sought hegemony by

---

59 G. F. Kennan, *Around the Cragged Hill: A Personal and Political Philosophy* (New York: Norton, 1993), 17.

60 E. Heckscher, *The Continental System* (Oxford: Clarendon Press, 1922), 93.

61 P. Ingram, *Napoleon and Europe* (Cheltenham: Stanley Thornes Publishers Ltd., 1998), 49.

integrating continental Europe, the British strategy relied on dividing continental Europe along a balance of power to preserve its dominant position as a maritime power.

The Continental System did not provide Russia with necessary economic connectivity to prosper due to heavy reliance on trade with Britain and its economy suffered greatly under the blockade. Furthermore, tsarist Russia grew increasingly uncomfortable with the extensive territorial control France demanded across Europe to uphold the system and its revolutionary mission to uproot the monarchy.[62] In the absence of economic incentives, the geoeconomic region had to be held together through coercion. Russia withdrew from the Continental System in 1810, and Napoleon responded with a disastrous invasion.

Russia's victory over Napoleon destroyed an aspiring hegemon and restored a balance of power. The defeat of France resulted in Europe's first collective security institution as the Congress of Vienna delivered the Concert of Europe, lasting from 1815 to 1914. The organisation, based on the Westphalian world order, was structured to preserve peace through a balance of power to prevent any single power from dominating Europe. The pragmatism of the system was defined by the ad hoc alliances to respond to specific disruptions to the balance of power. Recognising that peace relied on a balance of power rather than the destruction of rivals, the Concert of Europe included the defeated state, France. However, Britain was able to use the balance of power in continental Europe to divide and rule from the maritime periphery. Russia's defeat of Napoleon ended the French-British rivalry and thus made a French-British partnership against Russia possible.

The French Revolution challenged the rule of the monarchs by transferring sovereignty to the people, an idea that spread throughout the rest of Europe. Even though France was defeated, the liberal ideals had taken root and Europe was eventually swept by revolutions in 1848 based on the ideals of nationalism and liberal reforms.

---

62 M. Broers, P. Hicks and A. Guimera, *The Napoleonic Empire and the New European Political Culture* (New York, Springer, 2012).

Pax Britannica: Liberal Imperial Hegemony

Britain's imperial century ran from 1815 to 1914, with the Victorian era often referred to as Pax Britannica, a "British Peace," that was seen to provide relative stability and prosperity. During this century, Britain could shape the rules that governed economics and politics. Europe was largely administered from the maritime periphery. Britain's head start in the Industrial Revolution, supported by state intervention, led to an immense disruption in the balance of power as Britain could establish core-periphery relations with continental Europe. Britain became the dominant producer, world trader, shipper, and banker:

> An entire world economy was thus built on, or rather around, Britain, and this country therefore temporarily rose to a position of global influence and power unparalleled by any state of its relative size before or since, and unlikely to be paralleled by any state in the foreseeable future. There was a moment in the world's history when Britain can be described, if we are not too pedantic, as its only workshop, its only massive importer and exporter, its only carrier, its only imperialist, almost its only foreign investor; and for that reason its only naval power and the only one which had a genuine world policy. Much of this monopoly was simply due to the loneliness of the pioneer, monarch of all he surveys because of the absence of any other surveyors.[63]

The UK played a significant role in shaping the international political system and contributing to the development of democracy and free market capitalism. As an island state with naval supremacy, Britain's principal strategy was to take responsibility for upholding the Westphalian balance of power in Europe, while ensuring its leading position in the world. As a maritime power on the periphery of continental Europe, Britain pursued an offshore balancing strategy in which its resources were preserved by avoiding direct military involvement and instead manoeuvring other states to balance each other. As long as

---

63 E. J. Hobsbawm, *Industry and Empire: An Economic History of Britain since 1750* (London: Weidenfeld and Nicolson, 1968). xi.

Britain could create divisions within Europe with constant tensions, the Europeans would prioritise balancing each other rather than collectively balance the British hegemon. During peacetime, the offshore balancer can act as a benign hegemon and only enter wars towards the end of a conflict when the outcome is more predictable and other states have exhausted their blood and treasury. The main reason for influencing the outcome of a war is to ensure that the post-war outcome entails a balance of power that does not challenge the interests of the hegemon. Once the conflict is over, the offshore balancer departs to avoid being perceived as an intrusive occupier. The failure to withdraw may result in the regional powers collectively balancing the offshore balancer instead of each other.[64] Morgenthau similarly hailed the role of Britain in preserving the Westphalian world order:

> Thus, it has been said of the outstanding balancer in modern times, Great Britain, that it lets others fight its wars, that it keeps Europe divided in order to dominate the continent, and that the fickleness of its policies is such as to make alliances with Great Britain impossible.... It has, therefore, been called the "arbiter" of the system who decides who will win and who will lose. By making it impossible for any nation or combination of nations to gain predominance over the others, it preserves its own independence as well as the independence of all the other nations.[65]

Britain, as the hegemon, had a proclivity for promoting political liberalism. As an island state without land borders, Britain was less reliant on a large standing army during peace times. Lacking adequate military power that could be turned against its own population, the government had less negotiating power vis-à-vis their population, leading to acceptance of more limitations on its power. This strengthened the foundation for liberal democratic governance. Alexander Hamilton argued that Britain could not have advanced liberty if it had been a European continental power as it would probably have become

---

64 J. J. Mearsheimer and S. M. Walt, "The Case for Offshore Balancing: A Superior U.S. Grand Strategy," *Foreign Affairs* 95, no. 4 (2016), 78.

65 H. J. Morgenthau, *Politics among Nations*, 143.

"a victim to the absolute power of a single man."[66] The power of the representative British Parliament vis-à-vis the Monarch was also imperative for advancing land rights and enclosures, which intensified the efficiency of the agricultural industry and facilitated the Industrial Revolution.

Britain was thus further incentivised to introduce and promote a liberal, international economic system to cement its industrial and financial leadership and control over the seas. Britain's mature industries (high quality, low cost) could outcompete the infant industries (low quality, high cost) of Europe and North America. Under a system of free trade, Britain could saturate the manufactured goods markets in Europe and thus prevent the continent from industrialising. The result would be hegemony through asymmetrical interdependence, as Britain would be the sole producer of manufactured goods while the Europeans and Americans could compete over producing agricultural products. Reliable access to British-controlled transportation corridors negated the need for foreign powers to contest the dominance of the British navy over the seas, and a liberal, international economy naturally gravitated towards the banks and currency of the hegemon.

Free trade thus became known to many as a hegemonic or imperial policy. Economic liberalism was an instrument to prevent competing states from industrialising and thus deprive Britain of its comparative advantage.[67] The repeal of the Corn Laws in 1846 had the explicit purpose of creating an international division of labour, with Britain producing manufactured goods and continental Europe producing agricultural goods. A British MP proclaimed the benefit of free trade: "Foreign nations would become valuable Colonies to us, without imposing on us the responsibility of governing them."[68] David Ricardo explained that his concept of *comparative advantage* is the "principle which determines that wine shall be made in France and Portugal, that corn shall be grown in America and Poland, and that hardware and other goods shall be manufactured in England."[69]

---

66 A. Hamilton, *The Federalist: On the New Constitution, Written in 1788*, Hallowell, Masters, Smith & Company, 1857), 37.

67 D.A. Irwin, "Political Economy and Peel's Repeal of the Corn Laws," *Economics & Politics* 1, no.1 (1989): 41–59.

68 B. Semmel, *The Rise of Free Trade Imperialism* (Cambridge: Cambridge University Press, 1970), 8.

69 D. Ricardo, *On the Principles of Political Economy and Taxation* (London,

Friedrich List denounced free trade as the economic strategy of a hegemon by "kicking away the ladder" to economic greatness:

> It is a very common clever device that when anyone has attained the summit of greatness, he kicks away the ladder by which he has climbed up, in order to deprive others of the means of climbing up after him. In this lies the secret of the cosmopolitical doctrine of Adam Smith, and of the cosmopolitical tendencies of his great contemporary William Pitt, and of all his successors in the British Government administrations. Any nation which by means of protective duties and restrictions on navigation has raised her manufacturing power and her navigation to such a degree of development that no other nation can sustain free competition with her, can do nothing wiser than to throw away these ladders of her greatness, to preach to other nations the benefits of free trade, and to declare in penitent tones that she has hitherto wandered in the paths of error, and has now for the first time succeeded in discovering the truth.[70]

A paradox emerged as the benign British hegemon required great military power to hedge against the risks of disruptions in international trade. Karl Polanyi notes how the British economic hegemony was forced to trust in the endurance of the international distribution of labour:

> International free trade involved no less an act of faith. Its implications were entirely extravagant. It meant that England would depend for her food supply upon overseas sources; would sacrifice her agriculture, if necessary, and enter on a new form of life under which she would be part and parcel of some vaguely conceived world unity of the future; that this planetary community would have to be a peaceful one, or, if not would have to be made safe for Great Britain by the power of the Navy; and that the English

John Murray, 1821), 139.

70 F. List, *The National System of Political Economy* (London: Longmans, Green & Company, 1841), 295–96.

nation would face the prospects of continuous industrial dislocations in the firm belief in its superior inventive and productive ability. However, it was believed that if only the grain of all the word could flow freely to Britain, then her factories would be able to undersell all the world. Again, the measure of the determination needed was set by the magnitude of the proposition and the vastness of the risks involved in complete acceptance. Yet less than complete acceptance spelled certain ruin.[71]

Return to a Multipolar Balance of Power: New Centres of Power

New centres of power emerged that embraced economic nationalist policies to assert their autonomy from the British. The U.S., Japan and Germany all outgrew the British-led system, causing an economic and military challenge that unravelled British hegemony.

The U.S. developed the American System in the early 19th century, based on the economic ideas of Alexander Hamilton and Henry Clay. As economic independence was considered a requirement to preserve political independence, the economic policies of the American System replaced free trade with what was termed fair trade. The three-pillared American system entailed the development of economic independence through (1) a domestic manufacturing base for technological and industrial sovereignty, (2) the creation of physical economic connectivity through infrastructure projects such as roads, canals, ports (and later railroads), and (3) a national bank to issue a uniform currency for financial independence. The rapid industrialisation and economic independence of the U.S. through economic nationalist policies prevented Britain from converting the American mid-West and Central America into dependencies.[72] Under protectionist policies and the principle of fair trade, U.S. economic power grew rapidly throughout the 19th century.[73] But then, much like

---

71 K. Polanyi, *The Great Transformation,* (Boston, Beacon Press, 1944), 87.

72 J. Gallagher and R. Robinson, "The Imperialism of Free Trade," *The Economic History Review* 6, no.1, (1953, pp.1-15, p.10.

73 M. Hudson, *America's Protectionist Takeoff, 1815-1914: The Neglected American School of Political Economy*, (New York, Islet, 2010.

its British counterpart, the U.S. began to advocate for free trade in the 20th century once it established a dominant position.

Friedrich List was a great advocate of the American System as the "English national economy is predominant; American national economy aspires only to become independent."[74] Yet, as the U.S. became increasingly powerful, List predicted that the rise of the U.S. would compel Britain to align itself with the other Europeans to restore a balance of power and thus "accustom herself betimes to the idea of being only the first among equals."[75] A balance of power in Europe was required as "the natural necessity which now imposes on the French and Germans the necessity of establishing a Continental alliance against the British supremacy, will impose on the British the necessity of establishing a European coalition against the supremacy of America."[76]

The rise in U.S. industrial power was complemented by the growing control over maritime transportation corridors. The annexation of Texas in 1845, and then California in 1848, made the U.S. a continental power connected from the Atlantic to the Pacific. Given the absence of any powers in the Americas capable of challenging U.S. regional hegemony, the U.S. became a virtual island state protected from all sides. The Monroe Doctrine was formulated by U.S. Secretary of State Richard Olney in 1895 as a claim for hegemony in the Western hemisphere: "The United States is practically sovereign on this continent, and its fiat is law upon the subjects to which it confines its interposition."[77]

The U.S. became a major maritime power in the late 19th century in accordance with the naval strategy of Alfred Thayer Mahan. Victory in the American-Spanish War of 1898 awarded the U.S. with colonies, and a maritime empire was constructed as it acquired Hawaii, the Philippines, Guam, Puerto Rico, Wake Island, American Samoa and the Virgin Islands. The U.S. coerced Panama's secession from Colombia in 1903 to construct the strategic Panama Canal over

74 F. List, *Outlines of American Political Economy, in a Series of Letters*, Philadelphia, Samuel Parker, 1827, p.12.

75 F. List, *The National System of Political Economy* (London: Longmans, Green & Company, 1841), 111.

76 Ibid.

77 G. Smith, "The Legacy of Monroe's Doctrine," *The New York Times*, 9 September 1984.

which the U.S. claimed sovereignty until 1979, thus connecting the Pacific with the Atlantic. The future emergence of U.S. global dominance meant that the Americans would replace Britain's control over maritime transportation corridors and assume the responsibility for advancing liberal democracy:

> To the degree that the story of world power politics in the last few centuries has a single overarching plot, that plot is the long and continuing rise of the maritime system as its center shifted from the United Provinces to the United Kingdom to the United States.... Throughout modern times, the English-speaking world has been in the vanguard of humanity's march deeper and deeper into the world of democratic capitalism.[78]

The American System of economic nationalism also spread to Japan. The Japanese had witnessed how the British Empire defeated China in the Opium Wars (1839–1842 and 1856–1860) to impose the conditions of trade and extract commercial privileges such as favourable tariffs, exemptions from local laws, and acquisition of strategic territory for trade. Recognising that economic independence was a condition for political independence, Japan imported the ideas of Alexander Hamilton and Henry Clay. E. Peshine Smith, a second-generation economic nationalist and advocate of the American System, served as an advisor to the Japanese Emperor in the 1870s following the Meiji restoration. Among other foreign economic advisors, Peshine Smith sought to bring the American System of Manufacturers to Japan.[79] It was the ability of Japan to avoid excessive dependence on more powerful and advanced economies that enabled it to pursue such a successful capitalist development.[80] Much like its American counterparts, the successful policies of the Japanese enabled it to preserve its autonomy and emulate European empire-building. Britain

---

78 W. R. Mead, *God and gold: Britain, America, and the making of the modern world*, (New York, Vintage, 2008.

79 E.S. Reinert and A.M. Daastøl, "The Other Canon: the history of Renaissance economics," in E.S. Reinert (ed.), *Globalization, Economic Development and Inequality: An Alternative Perspective*. (Edward Elgar Publishing, 2007), 38.

80 E.H., Norman, *Japan's Emergence as a Modern State*, (New York: University of British Columbia Press, 1940.

had more pressing adversaries to deal with, and even eventually provided critical material support to Japan in defeating Russia in 1905.[81]

The rise of Germany in the second half of the 19th century also reveals how the emergence and growth of new centres of power can disrupt the world order. Bismarck, as the Chancellor of the newly unified German Empire, pursued a realpolitik approach to advance the interests of Prussia and strengthen the German nation. The unification of Germany in 1871 created a powerful state that altered the balance of power. By provoking the French to launch the Franco-Prussian War in 1870, Bismarck created a common enemy needed to overcome the opposition of the southern German states to create a common German empire. After the war, Bismarck aimed to permanently weaken and isolate France by forming alliances against it with other European powers during peacetime. This undermined the principle of collective security through multilateralism to preserve the balance of power. Rather than toppling the balance of power, Bismarck seemingly sought to establish a new balance of power capable of accommodating Germany.

The geography of Germany made it more difficult to establish a new balance of power on the continent. The German Customs Union (Zollverein), lasting from 1834 to 1919, sought to restore a more benign version of the Napoleonic Continental System under which the Germans had prospered. Otto von Bismarck, much like Alexander Hamilton, opined that free trade was a hegemonic policy and subsequently established tariffs in 1879 to enable the development of German infant industries.[82] In 1871, Britain produced twice as much steel as Germany, but by 1893 German steel production had surpassed British production, and by 1914, German steel production was twice that of the British.

Germany had outgrown a British-led Europe and under the leadership of Wilhelm II, there was a growing recognition that Germany was too limited by its territory. Max Weber argued in 1895 that Germany's success relied on "the amount of elbow-room we conquer" and the

81 P. Towle, "British Assistance to the Japanese Navy during the Russo-Japanese War of 1904–5," *The Great Circle* 2, no.1, 1980, pp.44-54.

82 H.J. Mackinder, *Democratic Ideals and Reality: A Study in the Politics of Reconstruction* (London: Constable, 1919), 100.

ability to ensure "the German flag waves on the surrounding coasts."[83] However, Germany's connectivity with the international markets was obstructed, leading to the beginning of the construction of the Berlin-Baghdad Railway in 1903 as a land corridor to connect with seaports on the Persian Gulf, although it was opposed and obstructed by the British, French and Russians. Similarly, the German efforts to develop reliable maritime corridors supported by a navy led to an arms race with the British.

After Napoleon's Continental System, a German-Russian alliance was recognised as the principal threat to the rule of the UK and the U.S. as maritime powers. Dominance thus required maintaining divisions in Europe:

> The oversetting of the balance of power in favour of the pivot state, resulting in its expansion over the marginal lands of Euro-Asia, would permit the use of vast continental resources for fleet-building, and the empire of the world would then be in sight. This might happen if Germany were to ally herself with Russia.[84]

World Wars and a World Order Organised Around Ideology

Liberal ideals about world order assumed that economic interdependence and globalisation would reduce the incentives for war and create peace among nations turned out to fail. Case in point, Norman Angell's renowned book *The Great Illusion*, first published prior to the First World War in 1909, presented the thesis that war is no longer a rational way to accumulate wealth or achieve lasting national security.[85] He argued that economic interdependence, globalization, and the complex nature of modern industrial economies made conquest and military aggression counterproductive. The costs of waging war and

83 M. Weber, "The national state and economic policy (Freiburg address, Inaugural lecture, Freiburg, May 1895)," *Economy and Society* 9, no.4, (1980), 436; 445.

84 H.J. Mackinder, "The Geographical Pivot of History," *The Geographical Journal* 170, no.4, (1904), 436.

85 N. Angell, *The Great Illusion: A Study of the Relation of Military Power to National Advantage*, (London:, W. Heinemann, 1913.

occupying foreign territories far outweighed any potential benefits, especially in an era where economic ties were becoming increasingly interconnected. Yet, the ability to elevate world order beyond power politics failed.

The Concert of Europe had begun to weaken towards the end of the 19th century as peacetime alliances merged and contested with the principle of indivisible security. The Triple Alliance and the Triple Entente subsequently became alternative sources of loyalty. The century-old Concert of Europe came to an end with the outbreak of the First World War, leaving Germany devasted and humiliated, Britain and France impoverished with their dominant empires never to be recovered, and the Russian Empire replaced by the Soviet Union.

The Treaty of Versailles was designed to cement the defeat and perpetuate the weakness of Germany. The extreme punishment of Germany that violated the Westphalian balance of power principle had partly been the result of Woodrow Wilson's ideological approach to the war in which it was contended that good fought against evil in a "war to end all wars." The refusal to facilitate a new balance of power in Europe contrasted with the Vienna Congress's lesson of including France after its defeat in the Napoleonic Wars.

The League of Nations, established after the First World War in 1919 as a successor to the Concert of Europe, established an international system that dealt with the issue of sovereign inequality. Rather than having states be either completely sovereign or completely subservient to another state, the League of Nations created a spectrum by establishing a system of mandates. The League of Nations largely failed due to its lack of authority, given the low participation among the great powers, its weak enforcement mechanisms, and the emergence of alternative power structures.

If Germany had not instigated another world war, another such war might have been unleashed by other states as evidenced by the competition for primacy on the seas between the U.S. and Britain. U.S. determination to preserve regional dominance produced the "War Plan Red" in the late 1920s, war plans to invade Canada to prevent the British from using Canadian ports. Woodrow Wilson wrote in 1920:

> It is evident to me that we are on the eve of a commercial war of the severest sort, and I am afraid that Great Britain

> will prove capable of as great commercial savagery as Germany has displayed for so many years in her competitive methods.[86]

On the other side of the Atlantic, British Vice-Admiral Sir Osmond Brock observed that "The late war has removed Germany as a possible enemy, but the other effect of the war has been that the United States has become our rival for the carrying trade of the world."[87] Winston Churchill similarly argued in 1927 that even though it was "quite right in the interests of peace to go on talking about war with the United States being 'unthinkable,' everyone knows that this is not true."[88]

The continued rivalry between expanding industrial powers became a key issue for the development of Marxist ideology. Case in point, in 1934 Leon Trotsky published in *Foreign Affairs*:

> One of the main causes of the World War was the striving of German capital to break through into a wider arena. Hitler fought as a corporal in 1914–1918 not to unite the German nation but in the name of a supra-national imperialistic program that expressed itself in the famous formula "to organize Europe".... But Germany was no exception. She only expressed in a more intense and aggressive form the tendency of every other national capitalist economy.... The United States represented the most perfect type of capitalist development. The relative equilibrium of its internal and seemingly inexhaustible market assured the United States a decided technical and economic preponderance over Europe. But its intervention in the World War was really an expression of the fact that its internal equilibrium was already disrupted.[89]

---

86 G. W. Baer, *One Hundred Years of Sea Power: The U.S. Navy, 1890–1990* (Stanford: Stanford University Press, 1996), 85.

87 C. Bell, *The Royal Navy, Seapower and Strategy Between the Wars* (London: Palgrave, 2000), 51.

88 C. Bell, "Thinking the Unthinkable: British and American Naval Strategies for an Anglo-American War, 1918–1931," *The International History Review* 19, no. 4 (1997): 790.

89 L. Trotsky, "Nationalism and Economic Life," *Foreign Affairs* 12 (1934):

In 1940, Leon Trotsky believed the U.S. would eventually become as menacing as Germany:

> For Germany it was a question of "organizing Europe." The United States must "organize" the world. History is bringing mankind face to face with the volcanic eruption of American imperialism.... Under one or another pretext and slogan the United States will intervene in the tremendous clash in order to maintain its world dominion.[90]

The German question had not been resolved with the First World War and the Treaty of Versailles. Germany was still a rising industrial power without reliable access to markets in the wider world, which could be hampered by the British dominance of the seas. There were several potential solutions to this problem.

German General Haushofer argued in favour of constructing a Eurasian parentship with Russia, China, India and Japan to counter the oppressive divide-and-conquer hegemonic strategy of Britain and the U.S. as maritime powers.[91] Haushofer was deeply inspired by the geostrategies of Mackinder, Ratzel, and Kjellén and recognised that a cooperative initiative was required by Eurasian powers to overcome the British and U.S. strategy of controlling the seas and dividing land powers. Haushofer opposed a war with Britain as it would merely weaken all Europeans and enable the U.S. to replace Britain to dominate the seas. Haushofer believed it was necessary to look to the Pacific Ocean for cooperation with Asian states to balance the maritime powers:

> By a dreadful decision, with consequences of utmost gravity for those who made it, the ocean-embracing cultural and economic powers of our own race have expelled us from their midst. They have left us in no doubt about the fact that

397; 401.

90 L. Trotsky, *Manifesto of the Fourth International on the Imperialist War and the Proletarian World Revolution: Writings of Leon Trotsky 1939-40* (New York: Pathfinder, 1940), 227.

91 K. Haushofer, *Geopolitik des pazifischen Ozeans: Studien über die Wechselbeziehungen zwischen Geographie und Geschichte*, Berlin Kurt, Vowinckel, 1924.

> only their destruction and decomposition will create another life for us who are now mutilated and enslaved. Thus they have forced us to search for comrades of destiny who are in a similar situation. We see such companions of disaster in the 900 million southeast Asiatics.[92]

Haushofer wrote in 1935 that Germany had to make a strategic choice: "Does she want to be a satellite of the Anglo-Saxon powers and their super-capitalism, which are united with the other European nations against Russia, or will she be an ally of the Pan Asiatic union against Europe and America?."[93] Haushofer believed that "the geo-political future will belong to the Russian-Chinese bloc," thus both Germany and Japan could be partners in this new centre of power and thus avoid being subordinated by British-American power.[94] Haushofer had significant influence over Hitler's strategic thinking, although Hitler was also deeply influenced by racists and anti-Bolshevik ideology that made him favour conquest to dominate Eurasia rather than cooperate with it.[95] Inspired by the American continental state that had been constructed by casting aside what he termed the inferior races, Hitler argued: "In the East a similar process will repeat itself for a second time as in the conquest of America."[96]

From a War of Nations to a War of Ideology

The First World War also unleashed an ideological struggle that dictated the organising principle of society and the international system. Ideologies can be defined as "systems based upon a single opinion that proved strong enough to attract and persuade a majority of people and broad enough to lead them through the various experiences and situations of an average modern life."[97]

92 H. W. Weigert, "Haushofer and the Pacific," *Foreign Affairs* 20, no. 4 (1942), 736.

93 Ibid., 740.

94 Ibid., 741.

95 H. H. Herwig, *The Demon of Geopolitics: How Karl Haushofer" Educated" Hitler and Hess* (London:, Rowman & Littlefield, 2016), 186.

96 W. W. Beorn, *The Holocaust in Eastern Europe: at the Epicenter of the Final Solution* (London, Bloomsbury Publishing, 2018), 61.

97 H. Arendt, *The Origins of Totalitarianism,* (New York: Harcourt Inc, 1951), 159.

Liberal ideology also transformed world order, as evident by the Wilsonian expectations about the contributions of democracy to human progress and reimagining the international system. The teleology based on Immanuel Kant's "Perpetual Peace" bore similarities to Georg Hegel's view that the French Revolution was bringing about the end of history. Like the internationalist claim by the French Revolutionaries and the Bolsheviks to defend the freedom of other peoples, U.S. President Wilson embraced a militaristic and interventionist interpretation of human security. Convinced that political realism was responsible for destructive wars, liberal ideology influenced the U.S. transition from regarding and presenting itself as a passive beacon of democracy to be emulated, to taking on an active missionary duty to make the world "safe for democracy." The efforts to introduce more morality into international politics also produced a Manichean view where competition under a balance of power was interpreted as a conflict between good and evil. This contributed to its reluctance to reach a compromise with Germany in the First World War, and instead pursue excessively punitive conditions for German surrender that violated the balance of power principle and contributed to the onset of another world war. Kenneth Waltz compared the U.S. ideological mission of democratisation with the British "White Man's Burden" and the French a "Civilising Mission," and "In like spirit, we say that we act to make and maintain world order."[98]

Unfettered capitalism transformed nation-states. Polanyi argues that the failure to manage industrial capitalism and thereby succumbing to unregulated markets over the past century had given birth to communism and fascism: "Fascism, like socialism, was rooted in a market society that refused to function."[99] Arendt similarly observed that capitalist imperialism had enabled communists and fascists to offer alternative visions of how to organise the world economy and the international system.

Capitalism itself began to transform in a fascist direction after the First World War with Germany leading the way. The relationship between the state, industry, and the public was transformed in Weimar, Germany. Mass inflation, followed by deflation, contributed to the

---

98 K. N. Waltz, *Theory of International Politics* (New York, McGraw-Hill, 1979), 200.

99 K. Polanyi, *The Great Transformation* (Boston, Beacon Press, 1944), 239.

destruction of incomes, property values, and savings, while large industry could repay their debts, transition away from old equipment and rebuild. Subsequently, large and specialised industries emerged that made Germany a leader in technology and manufacturing. These industries had much greater power vis-à-vis the public, and were more closely aligned with the government in a corporatist approach, which served to integrate economic interests with national interests. The fascist political economy subsequently emphasised strong state control and intervention in the economy, which included the nationalisation of strategic industries. The partnership between the state and private industry created an overwhelming power and made the individual a loyal servant of the nation through radical nationalism and militarism.

This economic revolution pre-dated Hitler, although the ascendance of the Nazis mixed its political economy with xenophobia, militarism, and race theory.[100] The international division of labour was thus envisioned to be organised by race as Eastern Europeans would be used for hard manual labour, while Germanic peoples would be placed higher in global value chains. While the Nazis could be defeated, the fascist political economy would inevitably spread as it was more competitive: "unless England and the United States follow the foot-steppes of Germany, they can never expect to rival her in technical production and distribution."[101]

The dilemma of international capitalism was that large industries were required to compete in international markets, while such powerful corporations would obtain political influence domestically. The solution was a fascist political economy, as large national champions were aligned with national interests. As the 19th century came to an end, the historian Brooks Adams had similarly predicted that massive industrial growth in the U.S. would create the future need for a powerful administrative state capable of harmonising state interests with the market, which would result in the government becoming "a gigantic corporation whose business is to materially benefit its members."[102]

---

100 W.E.B. Du Bois, "Neuropa: Hitler's New World Order," *The Journal of Negro Education* 19, no.3, 1941.

101 Ibid., 383.

102 B. Adams, *America's Economic Supremacy* (New York, Macmillan, 1900), 80.

During the Second World War, Du Bois recognised how great a challenge it would be for the U.S. to embrace the fascist political economy in the future as political freedoms and democracy were dependent on "economic anarchy" that limited the power of the state.[103] Alexis de Tocqueville similarly argued in the early 19th century that the democratic spirit was stronger in America than in France because there was less concentration of capital in America, which suggests that the concentration of economic power would erode U.S. democracy.[104] Despite the risks of pursuing a fascist political economy, Du Bois advocated that the U.S. should aspire to be a benign industrial democracy as the alternative would be the rule of authoritarian states in Europe. The rise of U.S. industrial power after the Second World War might have subsequently assisted in organising the capitalist world under U.S. control, although the concentration of capital aligned with state interests incrementally undermined its democratic system.

The Cold War: Westphalian World Order and Hegemonic Regional Order

The Cold War era produced a dual system—a world order based on a Westphalian balance of power and hegemonies within the capitalist and communist worlds. The common world order developed under the stewardship of the UN focused on sovereignty, self-determination, and deterrence, while the U.S. and the Soviet Union established primacy consistent with their respective ideologies of human freedom. The binary distribution and ideological rivalry produced a zero-sum geopolitical struggle for global influence and supremacy.

The United Nations—as the successor of the League of Nations—was established as the principal arbiter of international law. Its distribution of power reflected the balance of power, which would ensure the support of the great powers. The UN played a crucial role in maintaining stability and resolving disputes, laying the groundwork for a new era of multilateral diplomacy. The UN Charter was largely organised around the sovereign nation-states, which made it challenging for the Europeans to preserve their colonies. Yet, by implementing

103 W.E.B. Du Bois, "Neuropa: Hitler's New World Order," 386.

104 T. Piketty, *Capital in the Twenty-First Century* (Harvard University Press, 2014), 188.

the colonial trusteeship, the UN accommodated the principle of sovereign inequality, although this principle was gradually eliminated as the European empires dissolved.

The Second World War exposed the inherent flaws of colonial rule and sparked the decolonisation movement. Colonised nations, inspired by the principles of self-determination and independence, demanded freedom from imperial powers. Many African and Asian countries gained independence during the post-war period, leading to a significant realignment of global power dynamics. The European Westphalian system of sovereign nation-states was thus gradually expanding to encompass the entire world. There were 51 original member states when the UN was established in 1945, and by 2023 the UN consisted of 193 sovereign states.

The American and Soviet superpowers both pushed the principle of self-determination that unravelled the world order that had been defined largely by the rule of European empires. The U.S. had emerged as the leading Western power at the peace conference in 1919 that followed the defeat of Germany and pursued a world order based on self-determination and non-intervention. The liberal ideology of human freedoms aligned with the objective of dismantling the European empires that obstructed the continued rise of U.S. industrial power.

The Soviet communist ideology of human freedom similarly sought to dismantle the European capitalist empires, which also aligned with its power interests as it did not have any colonies to lose. While the decolonisation process took decades, the new world order became less and less favourable to colonisation and more supportive of national self-determination in the third world. However, the withdrawal of European empires created a vacuum and thus new arenas for a competition for influence between the two remaining superpowers.

The Hegemony of the United States in the Capitalist World

The Cold War provided the ideal condition for the U.S. to establish liberal hegemony in the capitalist world, consisting of three major geoeconomic regions: North America, Western Europe and Japan. The Second World War had devastated Western Europe and East

Asia, enabling the U.S. to assert hegemony in these two regions by constructing the trans-Atlantic and Asia-Pacific regions as hierarchical economic regions. The U.S. objective was therefore to integrate former geoeconomic rivals under its leadership—Britain, Germany, France and Japan.[105]

Geoeconomic rivalry was mitigated by the Cold War. The Soviet Union and China, as the primary rivals of the U.S. during the Cold War, were communist states largely decoupled from international markets, thus the balance of power was maintained primarily by military power. Geoeconomic competition among allies was similarly mitigated by the military threat from the East and the security dependence on the U.S. NATO became a military instrument to balance the Soviets and maintain U.S. hegemony in Europe. Lord Ismay, the first Secretary-General of NATO, famously expressed the purpose of the military alliance as "to keep the Americans in, the Russians out, and the Germans down." Preserving the militarised dividing lines thus became an important condition for U.S. power. The same approach was assigned to Japan, as the U.S. sabotaged the peaceful settlement of the territorial dispute between the Soviet Union and Japan in 1956 by threatening to annex Okinawa if Tokyo would cede the Southern Kuril Islands to Moscow. Maintaining divisions and tensions ensured that Japan would remain reliant on U.S. security guarantees, making Soviet-Japanese relations hostage to Soviet-U.S. relations.[106]

A liberal international capitalist system emerged as the U.S. established primacy in all three pillars of geoeconomic power—strategic industries, transportation corridors and financial instruments. These were the three pillars of the American System that had ensured U.S. economic and political independence from the British in the early 19th century, which had evolved into instruments of hegemony.

The first pillar of strategic industries was firmly under U.S. control as it became the factory of the world. The U.S. had experienced technological advancements, the rise of large corporations, and the creation of a large wartime industry that could be converted into

---

105 T. Nierop and S. De Vos, "Of Shrinking Empires and Changing Roles: World Trade Patterns in the Postwar Period," *Tijdschrift Voor Economische en Sociale Geografie* 79, no. 5 (1988).

106 J. D. Brown, *Japan, Russia and Their Territorial Dispute: The Northern Delusion* (New York Routledge, 2016).

commercial production. In contrast, the industries, infrastructure and populations of the other capitalist states had been devastated by war. Furthermore, the U.S. asserted control over key natural resources to fuel its industrial power as the European empires began to crumble. Case in point, a 1945 memorandum draft to President Truman explained: "In Saudi Arabia, where the oil resources constitute a stupendous source of strategic power, and one of the greatest material prizes in world history, a concession covering this oil is nominally in American control."[107] States tend to be distrustful and pursue protectionism after wars, yet the Marshal Plan financed the reconstruction of Western Europe in return for removing protectionist measures against U.S. industries.

The second pillar of physical connectivity was achieved as maritime transportation increasingly came under the control of the U.S. Navy to ensure its primacy on the seas. The U.S. established a network of naval bases and stations in strategic locations worldwide. Furthermore, a naval strategy with a focus on the importance of aircraft carriers to project power across the globe made the seas even more important. The economic imperative of controlling sea lanes also increased as innovations such as the shipping container in 1956 radically increased international trade, enabling exporters to become competitive in markets of non-complex items such as clothing. The immense pressure on the British, French, and Israelis to abandon their control over the Suez Canal in 1956 demonstrated that the U.S. was prepared to use economic coercion against its allies.

The third pillar of financial instruments also reached hegemonic status at Bretton Woods in 1944. The U.S.-led International Monetary Fund (IMF) and the World Bank were established to influence economic development and to extract political power via this prerogative. The U.S. was also able to establish the U.S. dollar as the sole international reserve/trade currency. It had significantly increased its gold reserves during the Second World War due to Europe's payment for war-related supplies and assistance. This enabled the U.S. to peg the dollar to gold at a fixed rate, with other major currencies then pegged to the U.S. dollar. In the early 1970s, U.S. financial control expanded further with the development of SWIFT (Society for Worldwide

107 U.S. State Department, "Memorandum by the Under Secretary of State (Acheson) to the Secretary of State," *U.S. State Department*, 9 October 1945.

Interbank Financial Telecommunication), an international messaging system for banks that gave the U.S. extraterritorial reach as users of the dollar and SWIFT could then be and were subjected to unilateral U.S. sanctions. A system of U.S. hegemony and unilateralism thus emerged parallel to the norms established by international law.

Yet, the concentration of economic power enabled the U.S. to act as a benign hegemon.[108] Both Truman and Eisenhower considered trade concessions to allies as preferable to aid, which resulted in generous trade agreements with the Europeans. A report by the U.S. Senate Finance Committee in 1976 outlined the costs of being a benign hegemon:

> Throughout most of the postwar era, U.S. trade policy has been the orphan of U.S. foreign policy. Too often the Executive has granted trade concessions to accomplish political objectives. Rather than conducting U.S. international economic relations on sound economic and commercial principles, the executive has set trade and monetary policy in a foreign aid context.

The dominant strategy during the Cold War was one of containment. The focus was to dominate the world's oceans to control the vast Eurasian landmass from the periphery while ensuring that divisions persisted among the Eurasian land powers, the aim being that no one state or group of states could challenge U.S. hegemony. The lessons of the threat from the Napoleonic Continental System persisted as dominance by the maritime hegemon depended on splitting the Germans from the Russians, the Russians from the Chinese etc. Much like its British predecessor, the U.S. recognised that its hegemony would depend on maintaining divisions and a balance in Europe and Eurasia.

Containment has relied on partnerships with the UK and Western Europeans to control the western periphery of Eurasia, and to "adopt a similar protective policy toward Japan" on the eastern periphery of Eurasia.[109] Thereafter, a strong presence in the Middle East was

108 D. A. Baldwin, *Economic Statecraft* (Princeton: Princeton University Press, 1985), 46.

109 N. J. Spykman, *America's Strategy in World Politics: The United States and the Balance of Power* (New Brunswick: Transaction Publishers, 1942), 470.

required as the southern periphery of Eurasia. The German question was seemingly resolved as the European Community and NATO became the two main pillars that anchored Germany within the collective West; this resolved Germany's problem of reliable access to foreign markets for its industrial rise. In 1978, Chancellor Helmut Schmidt acknowledged a need to "clothe" Germany in the European mantle:

> It is all the more necessary for us to clothe ourselves in this European mantle. We need this mantle not only to cover our foreign policy nakednesses, like Berlin or Auschwitz, but we need it also to cover these ever-increasing relative strengths, economic, political, military, of the German Federal Republic within the West. The more they come into view, the harder it becomes to secure our room for manoeuvre.[110]

Besides ensuring that Germany and the Soviet Union remained divided, the U.S. also had to divide the Soviet Union and China. Influenced by Mackinder, Kissinger's ability to decouple China from the Soviet Union in the 1970s was a duplicate of the policy to divide Germany and Russia. Kissinger, therefore, defined U.S. strategy as continuing the British policy of dominance at sea by dividing Europe and Eurasia:

> For three centuries, British leaders had operated from the assumption that, if Europe's resources were marshaled by a single dominant power, that country would then resource to challenge Great Britain's command of the seas, and thus threaten its independence. Geopolitically, the United States, also an island off the shores of Eurasia, should, by the same reasoning, have felt obliged to resist the domination of Europe or Asia by any one power and, even more, the control of *both* continents by the same power.[111]

---

110 Bundesbank, "EMS: Bundesbank Council meeting with Chancellor Schmidt (assurances on operation of EMS) [declassified 2008]," *Bundesbank Archives*, N2/267, 30 November 1978.

111 H. Kissinger, *Diplomacy*, 50–51.

U.S. National Security Council reports from 1948 and beyond framed the containment policies in the language of Mackinder's heartland theory.[112] As outlined in the U.S. National Security Strategy of 1988:

> The United States' most basic national security interests would be endangered if a hostile state or group of states were to dominate the Eurasian landmass—that area of the globe often referred to as the world's heartland. We fought two world wars to prevent this from occurring.[113]

The two regional orders of U.S. liberal hegemony in the Western world and an inclusive Westphalian system under the UN eventually began to harmonise under a common world order. Signed in 1975, the Helsinki Accords represented a significant diplomatic agreement that sought to bridge the divide between capitalist and communist blocs during the Cold War. The Helsinki Accords addressed key principles associated with the Westphalian system, such as the recognition of state sovereignty, the principle of non-interference and the indivisibility of security, and common values such as human rights as the foundation for diplomacy and the avoidance of war. The Helsinki Accords inspired Gorbachev's vision of a "Common European Home" and contributed to the end of the Cold War in 1989. Thereafter, a new world order based on the Helsinki Accords laid the foundation for the Charter of Paris for a New Europe in 1990, which called for the building of a new Europe that included the "ending of the division of Europe," affirming that "security is indivisible and the security of every participating State is inseparably linked to that of all the others," and introduction of a new era of human rights, democracy and rule of law. When the Soviet Union and the communist system collapsed in December 1991, the prospect of constructing a new world order arose.

---

112 J. L. Gaddis, *Strategies of Containment: A Critical Appraisal of Postwar American National Security Policy* (New York Oxford University Press, 1982), 57–58.

113 The White House, "National Security Strategy of the United States" (April 1988), 1.

Conclusion

The emergence of a common world order developed under a Western-centric international distribution of power, and the West dictated the values and conditions for membership in the community of states. Technology transformed military and economic power, while legitimacy shifted from a hierarchy of nations to ideology. The Western-centric system began by controlling the world's maritime transportation corridors, enabling the maritime hegemon to dominate by creating divisions among the land powers.

Understanding the evolution of the Western-centric world order is imperative to grasping its foundation and resilience. The end of the Cold War resolved many problems and presented the possibility of constructing a more stable world order, yet key challenges remained. It required reinventing relations with former adversaries that began to embrace economic statecraft, while capitalist allies were more likely to return to geoeconomic rivalry in the absence of a unifying threat. The world was still based on the dominance of a maritime power that required enduring divisions on the vast Eurasian continent. The sustained dominance of the U.S. underpinned the preservation of the liberal international economic system and the prevalence of liberal ideals.

Creating a new world order after the Cold War required a critical reflection on the socio-economic and political foundations of the requisite power and rules to govern the world. Yet, Washington was awash with hubris from its ideological victory. Seduced by the prospect of fundamentally transcending history, the U.S. was confident in its inherent benevolence as the world's only remaining superpower and convinced that liberalism was the silver bullet for organising the economic system and society.

4.

Pax Americana: The New World Order of Liberal Hegemony

THE END of the Cold War aroused great optimism about the possibility of creating a more benign world order. The zero-sum military rivalry with nuclear weapons and proxy wars across the world had come to an end, and the collapse of communism seemingly finished the ideological rivalry that had defined the conflicts of the 20th century. The world was subsequently at a crossroads as the new world order could either be a Westphalian system based on the balance of power and sovereign equality or on liberal hegemony in which the world would align under U.S. leadership and liberal democratic values. The balance of power system was burdened with the pessimism of perpetual conflict, while the project of expanding the trans-Atlantic system to the entire world came with the promise to transcend power politics and deliver perpetual peace.

The end of the Cold War implied that there were incentives in terms of both power and ideology to establish a new world order based on U.S. hegemony. The trans-Atlantic region established after the Second World War had already been based on U.S. hegemony and liberal democratic values, which had proven to offer unprecedented peace and prosperity within the West. The end of the Cold War also removed the power balance and constraints on U.S. power. However, the existence of the Soviet Union had legitimised the extension of U.S. power around the world to counter its influence, and without an enemy to defend the world against, U.S. hegemony was left without a new mission to justify its existence. The objective then became an acknowledged hegemonic peace by preventing the emergence of rivals. U.S. Secretary of State Madeleine Albright termed America the "indispensable nation." The U.S. convinced itself that its military, economic supremacy, and superior values were a necessary and sufficient condition for peace and stability.

This chapter first explores the theoretical assumptions behind the arguments for and against constructing Pax Americana. Second, a liberal case for sovereign inequality is outlined as a feature of liberal hegemony. Last, the liberal imperialism of Pax Americana has followed the model of idealist internationalism in which the aspiration to transition to a more benign world instead legitimised belligerent means and hegemony.

Fukuyama versus Huntington

In the early 1990s, two theories about the future of humanity dominated the discourse. The first prediction was Francis Fukuyama's *The End of History* thesis which expected that all countries would eventually adopt the same socio-economic and political system as the world united under liberal democratic values and U.S. leadership. The battle for ideologies was over and it was believed that no country could become a formidable power, and thus a challenger, unless they pursued the liberal democratic path of the U.S. Pursuing economic competitiveness in the world economy would create interdependence, an open society would unleash democratic reforms, and integration into common institutions would result in states and their populations internalising the shared norms and values. As liberal theory assumes that economic interdependence, democracy, and shared institutions create peace, Fukuyama believed that the Cold War had a profound impact on the world order it signalled:

> What we may be witnessing is not just the end of the Cold War, or the passing of a particular period of post-war history, but the end of history as such: that is, the end point of mankind's ideological evolution and the universalization of Western liberal democracy as the final form of human government.[114]

---

114 F. Fukuyama, "The End of History?," *The National Interest* 16 (1989): 3–18.

The competing forecast was largely based on the theoretical assumptions presented in Samuel Huntington's *The Clash of Civilizations and the Remaking of World Order*, which expected states would separate into distinctive civilisational blocs.[115] Individualism, democracy, and human rights, Huntington argued, were not universal, but reflections of culture rooted in Western Christendom. Rather than the world being organised around the U.S. and liberal values, the world order would increasingly be defined by de-centralisation as cultural identities, economic systems, and military alliances would be organised along civilisational lines. Humans organise in groups and the largest tribe is civilisation; people would thus become more aware of their distinctive civilisational identities. Huntington cautioned against "the 'Single Alternative Fallacy.' It is rooted in the Cold War assumption that the only alternative to communism is liberal democracy and that the demise of the first produces the universality of the second."[116]

Subsequently, two different recommendations emerged in terms of the ideal world order to be pursued. Fukuyama expected that the advancement of Western universalism was the source of perpetual peace, while Huntington believed the West could only thrive if it abandoned its universalist aspirations. Huntington envisioned a more chaotic world as Western hegemony would eventually come to an end and unleash a clash of civilisations. The dominant power of the West would continue to decline relative to other states and regions, which would compel the non-Western world to make a choice: "Some [will] attempt to emulate the West, others—especially Confucian and Islamic societies—attempt to expand their own economic and military power to resist and to 'balance' the west."[117] Such a rivalry would manifest itself as a struggle between culture and civilisations.

The work by Fukuyama has been immensely influential on the West's post-Cold War policies. It created a metanarrative, a big story about the West's central role in advancing democracy and

115 S. P. Huntington, *The Clash of Civilizations and the Remaking of World Order*, (New York: Simon and Schuster, 1996).

116 S. P. Huntington, "If Not Civilizations, What? Paradigms of the Post–Cold War World," *Foreign Affairs* 72, no. 5 (Nov.-Dec. 1993): 191.

117 S. P. Huntington, "The West and the Rest," *Prospect Magazine*, 20 February 1997.

capitalism—which eventually triumphed decisively over all competing ideas and ideologies. Realist theory can explain the attractiveness of Fukuyama's theory as a reflection of a balance of power—the West was not balanced after the Cold War and thus there were systemic incentives to embrace ideas and theories that justified exceptionalism, sovereign inequality, and expansion. Furthermore, politicians and other decision-makers have a proclivity towards idealism as it is more appealing to believe they can fundamentally transform the world rather than to acknowledge that all human beings and states need constraints.

Washington's decision to pursue Pax Americana according to the views of Fukuyama convinced Russia that the world ahead would follow the predictions of Huntington's clash of civilisations. In Russia, the debate between Fukuyama's end of history versus Huntington's clash of civilisations has deeper roots, going back to the domestic rivalry between the Westernisers and the Slavophiles that began in the 1840s. The Westernisers were followers of Peter the Great's effort to Europeanise Russia insofar as the West was leading a universal path to modernity. The assumption was that the world would eventually unify at a common end. In contrast, the Slavophiles represented a conservatism that rejected universalism, insisting Russia needed to pursue organic change and development based on its distinctive orthodox culture. In the 1990s and early 2000s, Russia pursued the path of the Westernisers which entailed an effort to adopt the socio-economic and political system of the West. However, the West could not accommodate Russia under Pax Americana as it would remain a threat merely due to its capabilities as an independent pole of power. As Russia's Westernisers lost their political platform, universalism was increasingly rejected, and the discourse of civilisational distinctiveness became increasingly prevalent. As Putin would eventually conclude: "No civilisation can take pride in being the height of development."[118]

Constructing Pax Americana

The prevailing argument in Washington called for Pax Americana as a world order based on liberal hegemony. The U.S. had established a peaceful and prosperous trans-Atlantic region during the Cold War,

118 V. Putin, "Valdai International Discussion Club meeting," *President of Russia*, 27 October 2022.

and the objective was to expand this format as the foundation for a new world order. A precedent was seen to have been established as both Germany and Japan had been transformed under U.S. hegemony from imperial militaristic aggressor states into peaceful democracies.

However, the U.S. influence on Germany and Japan should be attributed to an alliance system that depended on a shared adversary in Russia. As Latin America has suffered greatly under U.S. hegemony, Waltz argued that "how we have behaved in our own backyard over a long period of time provides a clue of how we are likely to wield unbalanced power in the future."[119]

The term "unipolar moment" was coined by Charles Krauthammer to outline the historically unique international distribution of power after the Cold War.[120] Krauthammer acknowledged being at the crossroads of replacing bipolarity with either multipolarity or unipolarity—arguing that turbulent times would return and contrasted unipolarity with irresponsible isolationism:

> Only a hopeless utopian can believe otherwise. We are in for abnormal times. Our best hope for safety in such times, as in difficult times past, is in American strength and will—the strength and will to lead a unipolar world, unashamedly laying down the rules of world order and being prepared to enforce them.[121]

Krauthammer recognised that multipolarity would eventually reassert itself in the future, although a temporary peace could be ensured by embracing the unipolar moment. A weakness in the logic is that the U.S. would voluntarily reform the unipolar world order into a multipolar world order once the international distribution of power changed. It was more probable that by developing a security strategy based on global primacy, any threat to the hegemon would be met with force. Obsessed with past glories, the U.S. would refuse to accept a diminished role in the world and instead aim to turn back the clock to restore its greatness.

---

119 K. N. Waltz, "The New World Order," *Millennium* 22, no. 2 (1993): 188.
120 C. Krauthammer, "The Unipolar Moment," *Foreign Affairs*, 1 January 1990.
121 Ibid., 33.

However, many Americans favoured dismantling the U.S. empire after the Cold War and returning to a more modest position in the international system with a demilitarised foreign policy, in which the U.S. would be one among many great powers, while others aspired for global hegemony. From the former perspective, unipolarity is inherently temporary as it requires the hegemon to transfer resources from the core in order to hold on to the periphery, while the suppression of rising power incentivises collective balancing. In contrast, by abandoning the superpower status the U.S. could preserve its strength by focusing on domestic social, economic, industrial, and political challenges. As Walter Lippmann famously wrote in 1965:

> A mature great power will make measured and limited use of its power. It will eschew the theory of a global and universal duty, which not only commits it to unending wars of intervention, but intoxicates its thinking with the illusion that it is a crusader for righteousness.[122]

The concept of a benign hegemon is problematic as power corrupts. In 1821, U.S. Secretary of State John Quincy Adams cautioned against going "in search of monsters to destroy" as "the fundamental maxims of her policy would insensibly change from liberty to force. She might become the dictatress of the world." Francois Fenelon, who died in the early 18th century, similarly observed that no country with overwhelming power would be able to act with restraint and moderation for more than a short time.[123] President Kennedy specifically denounced the aspiration of Pax Americana in his influential speech at the American University on 10 June 1963:

> What kind of peace do I mean? What kind of peace do we seek? Not a Pax Americana enforced on the world by American weapons of war. Not the peace of the grave or the security of the slave. I am talking about genuine peace, the kind of peace that makes life on earth worth living, the kind that enables men and nations to grow and to hope and

122 Congressional record, Proceedings and Debates of the 89th Congress, Volume 111, Part 7 (28 April 1965 to 10 May 1965): 8786.

123 K. N. Waltz, "The New World Order," *Millennium* 22, no. 2 (1993), 188.

> to build a better life for their children--not merely peace for Americans but peace for all men and women—not merely peace in our time but peace for all time.

The Liberal Case for Sovereign Inequality: Redividing the Garden and the Jungle

Universalism is commonly associated with a hegemonic world order. Under the higher sovereignty of the Catholic Church, the Roman Emperor could exercise his authority over other entities. In contrast, the Westphalian preservation of cultural and civilisational distinctiveness becomes a defence of sovereign equality as no state or civilisation can claim to be superior to others.

Yet, while the Peace of Westphalia established sovereign equality among the Europeans; beyond Europe it was a hegemonic order based on sovereign inequality. An international system of European dominance legitimised sovereign inequality that reflected the relationship between superiors and inferiors. The Westphalian order has, to some extent, been paradoxical as a European system based on the absolute sovereignty of states accepted the violation of the sovereignty of non-European states. The Westphalian order provided a rules-based approach to international affairs, yet the rules did not apply equally to all.

The Western-centric world order over the past centuries has been defined by a balance of power in Europe and the exercise of collective hegemony in the wider world. This produced a dual system that emerged based on sovereign equality in Europe, while the rest of the world was organised within an imperial structure based on sovereign inequality. With civilisation as viewed by the Europeans set the condition for sovereignty, so-called barbaric peoples were not deemed fit to qualify for self-governance.

The British orientalist Rudyard Kipling used the analogy of the jungle versus the garden to describe the world of international affairs, in which civilised and barbaric peoples do not have the same claim to sovereignty. The garden represents the order of the civilised where nations abide by rules and norms, engage in diplomacy, and cooperate for the greater good. The jungle, on the other hand, represents an anarchic and chaotic world, a dangerous and unpredictable place in which only the strongest survive. Sovereign inequality as order can only exist within civilisation, while only the law of the jungle prevails outside the garden. The metaphor depicts sovereign inequality as remediable, insofar making it the duty of the virtuous gardener to then cultivate the jungle and make it into a garden. Kipling thus wrote about "The White Man's Burden" in which colonisation as a civilising mission was a righteous responsibility to spread order. The American concept of "Manifest Destiny" similarly suggested that the expansionist push to the West to colonise new territory was a duty to spread civilisation. Primitive races were believed to not qualify for sovereignty. John Stuart Mill argued:

> Despotism is a legitimate mode of government in dealing with barbarians, provided the end be their improvement, and the means justified by actually effecting that end. Liberty, as a principle, has no application to any state of things anterior to the time when mankind have become capable of being improved by free and equal discussion.[124]

The West's efforts to challenge the principle of sovereign equality in the Westphalian world order after the Cold War can be explained through both liberal and realist theories. From the liberal perspective, the end of the Cold War's ideological rivalry and the emergence of a liberal consensus presented an opportunity to develop a common world order in which liberal ideals were elevated. From the realist perspective, the end of the Cold War's bipolar division of power and the emergence of unipolarity enabled the collective West to construct a hegemonic order based on sovereign inequality.

The emergence of peace studies after the Cold War made a liberal case for a positive-sum approach to security. While traditional state-centric security under international anarchy results in a security dilemma as the increasing of one state's security can diminish the security of another, enhancing human security by promoting democracy and human rights as an intrinsic part of security was argued to be a format for positive-sum security. However, human security

---

124 J. S. Mill, *On Liberty and Other Writings* (Cambridge: Cambridge University Press, 1989), 13.

undermined state security as the principle of sovereignty was weakened and militaristic interpretations of human security prevailed.

Liberalism that prioritises progress will in turn demand clear hierarchies, setting different rules for the civilised and the barbarian; now the distinctions are between the liberal democratic and what is deemed authoritarian. Exceptionalism is thus a feature of liberalism as claiming superiority over an inferior adversary is required to legitimise a system of inequality. The promotion of civilising missions and democracy implies the rejection of sovereign equality.

After the colonial era, a new subject-object relationship was formed as the civilising mission was replaced by a mission of development and modernisation. After the Cold War, human rights and democratisation became the new rationale for enforcing the international hierarchy between the superior and inferior.[125] Sovereignty was transformed from a right to a responsibility with regard to political structures and social norms, justifying the West infringing the sovereignty of other states if they were accused to violate human rights.

Washington asserted that its overwhelming power and moral superiority gave it a special responsibility in terms of defending universal liberal values such as democracy and human rights. Making the case for the unilateral use of military force, U.S. Secretary of State Madeleine Albright argued in 1998 in favour of U.S. exceptionalism: "If we have to use force, it is because we are America; we are the indispensable nation. We stand tall and we see further than other countries into the future, and we see the danger here to all of us."[126] In *The Pentagon's New Map,* Barnett uses the term "the gap" to revive the principle of sovereign inequality between the core that consists of economically developed regions of the world under U.S. leadership that are deserving of full sovereignty, and the underdeveloped interior at the gap.[127]

Paradoxically, democracy and human rights were no longer values used to criticise and constrain power; instead, they were used

---

125 M. E. Latham, *The Right Kind of Revolution: Modernization, Development, and U.S. Foreign Policy from the Cold War to the Present* (New York: Cornell University Press, 2011).

126 B. Herbert, "In America; War Games," *The New York Times*, 22 February 1998.

127 T. P. Barnett, *The Pentagon's New Map; War and Peace in the Twenty-First Century* (New York: Penguin, 2004).

to enable the use of power. Case in point, Germany's brutal history in the Second World War used to be cited as a reason for it to exercise constraint, while in the post-Cold War era, it was suggested that Germany's history of committing genocide gave it a special responsibility to prevent it from occurring in other places. Foreign Minister and vice-chancellor Joschka Fischer argued that he had learned two things in his childhood: "never another war" and "never another Auschwitz," although supposedly in Kosovo "these two maxims came into conflict, and I had to give up the notion of never another war."[128] In 2000, Fischer argued that European integration had made Westphalia and the balance of power principle obsolete: "The core of the concept of Europe after 1945 was and still is a rejection of the European balance-of-power principle and the hegemonic ambitions of individual states that had emerged following the Peace of Westphalia in 1648."[129]

The Westphalian world order based on mutual constraints was increasingly denounced as an immoral system as it obstructed the West from acting as a force for good. In his famous Chicago speech in April 1999, the *Doctrine of the International Community*, British Prime Minister Tony Blair legitimised the invasion of Yugoslavia by promoting the wider objective of transcending the principle of absolute sovereignty. Blair insisted: "We are all internationalists now, whether we like it or not" as globalisation had made the world more interdependent.[130] The speech is widely considered to have foreshadowed the decision to invade Iraq four years later. In 2004, Blair justified that invasion by denouncing Westphalia:

> So, for me, before September 11th, I was already reaching for a different philosophy in international relations from a traditional one that has held sway since the treaty of Westphalia in 1648; namely that a country's internal affairs are for it and you don't interfere unless it threatens you, or breaches a treaty, or triggers an obligation of alliance. I did

---

128 Spiegel, "Berlin Reverts to Old Timidity on Military Missions," *Spiegel International*, 26 March 2013.

129 J. Fischer, "From Confederacy to Federation: Thoughts on the Finality of European integration," *Speech at the Humboldt University*, Berlin, 12 May 2000.

130 T. Blair, "Doctrine of the International Community," *Speech in Chicago*, 22 April 1999.

> not consider Iraq fitted into this philosophy, though I could see the horrible injustice done to its people by Saddam.[131]

While not contesting the sovereignty of Western states, Blair referred to limited sovereignty in the context of "regimes that are undemocratic and engaged in barbarous acts."[132] The language implied reviving the former imperial system of endowing civilised states with sovereignty while deeming barbaric peoples incapable of upholding the responsibility of sovereignty.

Senior British diplomat Robert Cooper who served as special advisor to Blair and assisted in the development of the post-Westphalian doctrine of liberal internationalism was even more explicit in reviving imperial designs for the new world order. Cooper argued in favour of "the new liberal imperialism" because, throughout history, "order meant empire. Those within the empire had order, culture and civilisation. Outside it lay barbarians, chaos and disorder. The image of peace and order through a single hegemonic power centre has remained strong ever since."[133] The world, therefore, needed one set of rules for the garden and another for the jungle. The West could be civilised among each other in the garden, although when engaging with barbarians in the jungle a new set of rules was required:

> Among ourselves, we keep the law but when we are operating in the jungle, we must also use the laws of the jungle… we need to revert to the rougher methods of an earlier era—force, pre-emptive attack, deception, whatever is necessary to deal with those who still live in the nineteenth century world.[134]

The decline of U.S. dominance in the world spurred concerns that the entire world order based on liberal hegemony was coming to an end. Robert Kagan's book *The Jungle Grows Back* was published in 2018 and was a warning against the U.S. abandoning its responsibility

---

131 Guardian, "Full text: Tony Blair's Speech," *The Guardian*, 5 March 2004.

132 T. Blair, "Doctrine of the International Community," *Speech in Chicago*, 22 April 1999.

133 R. Cooper, "The New Liberal Imperialism," *The Guardian*, 7 April 2002.

134 Ibid.

to lead the world. Borrowing Kipling's analogy of the garden versus the jungle, Kagan warned that if the United States were to withdraw from its role as the "gardener" of the international order, the jungle of power politics would return with a vengeance. Therefore, global primacy is a responsibility resting on the shoulders of the U.S. Robert Kagan is the husband of Victoria Nuland, who had a central role in toppling Ukrainian President Yanukovich in February 2014.

Similar analogies were revived in Europe as the EU foreign policy chief Josep Borrell warned that relative decline meant that the civilised world could be overrun by barbarians. Borrell used Kipling's analogy to infer the need for sovereign inequality, now making it the moral duty of the gardener to intervene in the jungle to ensure that the jungle would not invade the garden:

> Europe is a garden. We have built a garden… The rest of the world—and you know this very well, Federica—is not exactly a garden. Most of the rest of the world is a jungle, and the jungle could invade the garden. The gardeners should take care of it, but they will not protect the garden by building walls. A nice small garden surrounded by high walls in order to prevent the jungle from coming in is not going to be a solution. Because the jungle has a strong growth capacity, and the wall will never be high enough in order to protect the garden. The gardeners have to go to the jungle. Europeans have to be much more engaged with the rest of the world. Otherwise, the rest of the world will invade us.[135]

The Liberal Imperialism of Pax Americana

Idealist internationalism envisions that the embrace of universal ideals that advance human freedom will transcend the anarchy of the international system, thus replacing the Westphalian system of sovereign states constrained by a balance of power. By linking an ideal to

---

135 J. Borrell, "The Gardeners have to go to the Jungle. Europeans have to be much more Engaged with the Rest of the World. Otherwise, the Rest of the World will Invade Us," *European Union External Action*, 13 October 2022.

a powerholding entity, political idealism can aspire to achieve hegemony by undertaking a direct revision of the world order.

Idealism, often paradoxically, has an acceptance for the greater use of violence if the current flawed world and perpetual peace can be bridged by destroying an adversary. Both the French Revolution and Bolshevik Revolution aimed to elevate human freedoms by toppling the world order based on a balance of power and sovereign equality and replacing it with a hegemonic state that would promote universal ideals.

The liberal, international order after the Cold War was similarly a revisionist effort to transform the international system by making a break with the international anarchy of the past. The expectation that liberal democracies would de-militarise international relations after the Cold War was soon disappointed as democratic peace theory instead legitimised new wars by the notion of advancing liberal ideals with military power. Western democracies are less capable of recognising that they, themselves, pose a threat to others, as "citizens of democratic states tend to think of their countries as good, aside from what they do, simply because they are democratic." Similarly, "democratic states also tend to think of undemocratic states as bad, aside from what they do, simply because they are undemocratic."[136] Ideological fundamentalism suggests that actors are assigned the role of enemies due to their ideological identity rather than their actual behaviour in the international system. Similarly, ideological fundamentalism diminishes the ability to recognise that one's own policies and actions may threaten others as one's own political identity is held to be intrinsically positive and a force for good.[137]

Liberal democracies tend to demand higher authority in the international system with the argument that they are more representative of their people. The argument against relativism is reasonable to some extent as one can question if, for example, the North Korean government should have equal representation in the international system when it does not adequately represent its people. Yet, it is almost always the authoritarian governments that reject Western domination

---

136 K. N. Waltz, "Structural Realism after the Cold War," *International Security* 25, no. 1 (2000): 11.

137 K. Booth and N. J. Wheeler, *The Security Dilemma: Fear, Cooperation and Trust in World Politics* (Basingstoke: Palgrave Macmillan, 2008), 331.

which are punished, suggesting the case for liberal exceptionalism is a veil for power politics. Nonetheless, liberal democracies implicitly demand an international aristocracy in which the enlightened few will rule for the benefit of the collective.

Coercion: Belligerent Means for Benign Ends?

The idealist internationalism of Pax Americana initially aspired for the rest of the world to align itself under liberal democratic values and U.S. leadership as prescribed by Fukuyama's *End of History* thesis. Yet, recognising that the world does not make the required transition to liberal democracy and subordination to U.S. leadership, the hegemon embraces the principle of belligerent means for benign ends.

The French, Soviets, and the collective West considered themselves to be altruistic by taking on the burden of guiding the world towards universal ideals and peace. Sovereignty is diluted as human freedoms are elevated above state security. In 1792, the French National Convention declared that France would "come to the aid of all peoples who are seeking to recover their liberty." The Bolsheviks similarly announced in 1917 "the duty to render assistance, armed, if necessary, to the fighting proletariat of the other countries."[138] The liberal hegemony of the West claimed similarly responsibility for ensuring the democratic and humanitarian rights of other peoples via an increasingly militaristic and interventionist interpretation of human security.

From the perspective of liberal theory, the elevated role of the liberal ideals of freedom is central to developing a world order. Under the presidency of Woodrow Wilson, the U.S. began to abandon its position as a passive beacon of democracy to be emulated, and instead sought to take on an active missionary responsibility to make the world "safe for democracy." From a realist perspective, the growing missionary duty of the U.S. represented a direct threat to the world order based on a balance of power. The ideals of liberal internationalism that elevate democracy and human rights as a central theme in international politics similarly have a tradition of both pacification and imperialism. Doyle cites Reagan's genuine belief in a "crusade for

---

138 Ibid., 170.

freedom" to explain why liberal internationalism carries with it two legacies, both pacification and imperialism.[139]

The U.S. and the Soviet Union declared the Cold War to be over at the Malta Summit in December 1989, and cooperation appeared to replace competition as the Soviets did not block the U.S. from attacking Iraq. In the speech announcing the first U.S. attack on Iraq in January 1991, President George H.W. Bush proclaimed it signified a new world order:

> We have before us the opportunity to forge for ourselves and for future generations a new world order—a world where the rule of law, not the law of the jungle, governs the conduct of nations. When we are successful—and we will be—we have a real chance at this new world order, an order in which a credible United Nations can use its peacekeeping role to fulfil the promise and vision of the U.N.'s founders.[140]

Bush Senior did not recognise any contradictions between U.S. leadership and the primacy of the UN. While he secured UN support for launched the First Gulf War based on an argument requiring that the sovereignty of Kuwait be protected, later that month, Bush emphasised in his State of the Union address that the superior power and values of the U.S. had given Washington the "burden of leadership" and "Among the nations of the world, only the United States of America has both the moral standing and the means to back it up. We're the only nation on this Earth that could assemble the forces of peace."[141]

After the collapse of the Soviet Union in December 1991, the balance of power became even more skewed. Merely one month after the collapse of the Soviet Union, in January 1992, President Bush triumphantly declared the new role of the U.S.:

---

139 M. W. Doyle, "Kant, Liberal Legacies, and Foreign Affairs," *Philosophy & Public Affairs* 12, no. 3 (1983).

140 G. Bush, "Address to the Nation Announcing Allied Military Action in the Persian Gulf," *The American Presidency Project*, 16 January 1991.

141 G. Bush, "Address Before a Joint Session of the Congress on the State of the Union," *The American Presidency Project*, 29 January 1991.

> By the grace of God, America won the Cold War… the Cold War didn't end, it was won…We are the United States of America, the leader of the West that has become the leader of the world, and as long as I am president, I will continue to lead in support of freedom everywhere.[142]

The historical revisionism of declaring victory in the Cold War had immense implications. When Gorbachev and Bush declared the Cold War to be over at the Malta Summit in December 1989, it had been recognised that diplomacy had been the instrument to usher in a common peace. Bush had even instructed his administration to not treat the fall of the Berlin Wall as a victory, as the negotiated end of the Cold War meant "there were no losers, only winners."[143] Declaring victory after the collapse of the Soviet Union had several implications: there was a winner and a loser, peace had not been achieved through negotiations but through military power by exhausting the Soviets, and the U.S. as the victor could subsequently dictate the new world order. Former U.S. Ambassador to the Soviet Union, Jack Matlock, had contributed to negotiating an end to the Cold War and warned how "mythmaking began almost as soon as the Soviet Union fell."[144] Bolstered by the new interpretation of history, the U.S. advanced further into a militaristic culture that celebrated peace through dominance and victory over adversaries.

The U.S. derision of diplomacy was strengthened in the Cuban missile crisis in 1962. Nuclear war was averted when a diplomatic agreement was reached in which the U.S. would remove its Jupiter missiles from Turkey in return for the Soviet Union removing its missiles from Cuba. Instead of celebrating the diplomacy that prevented a nuclear war, the U.S. conditioned the agreement on it being kept a secret. Washington lied to its own public and allies. For two decades, the U.S. public believed that the Cuban missile crisis was solved with

---

142 G. Bush, "Address Before a Joint Session of the Congress on the State of the Union," *The American Presidency Project*, 28 January 1992.

143 S. F. Cohen, *Soviet fates and lost alternatives: from Stalinism to the new Cold War* (Colombia, Columbia University Press, 2009), 160.

144 J. F. Matlock, *Superpower Illusions: How Myths and False Ideologies Led America Astray—and How to Return to Reality* (New Haven: Yale University Press, 2010), 3.

an aggressive and uncompromising stance resulting in victory as Moscow had to back down.

President Bush was convinced that the rest of the world would align under benign U.S. leadership as they did not fear the U.S. would abuse its immense power. Yet, debates in France about American imperialism after the first Gulf War included the remark by one politician who stated: "Now that the Soviet Union no longer holds the United States in check, American imperialism imposes the greatest threat to the world."[145]

The sentiment among the neo-conservatives in Washington was that before there could be lasting peace, the U.S. had to clean up the remnants of Soviet allies. After the first Gulf War, U.S. Under-Secretary of Defence Paul Wolfowitz lamented that Saddam Hussein had been allowed to remain in power, and that the U.S. should take advantage of its limited time of global dominance:

> With the end of the Cold War, we can now use our military with impunity. The Soviets won't come in to block us. And we've got five, maybe 10, years to clean up these old Soviet surrogate regimes like Iraq and Syria before the next superpower emerges to challenge us.[146]

The incentive to impose U.S. hegemony on the world meant that Washington favoured military solutions over negotiations and compromises. Abraham Maslow famously wrote in 1966: "If the only tool you have is a hammer, it is tempting to treat everything as if it were a nail." Under a doctrine of military supremacy, all conflicts are believed to have a military solution. In the lead-up to the first Gulf War, officials in Washington discussed the "nightmare scenario" of Iraq making sufficient concessions to break up the coalition against it, which would deprive the U.S. of the *casus belli* for an invasion. Waltz recalls how "Bush worked very effectively to thwart those who were trying to promote compromise and a peaceful settlement," which

145 K. N. Waltz, "The New World Order," *Millennium* 22, no. 2 (1993): 189.

146 J. Sachs, "Ending America's War of Choice in the Middle East," *Horizons: Journal of International Relations and Sustainable Development*, no.11 (2018): 25.

included sabotaging the peace initiatives of the French, Russians, and Arabs.[147]

A similar formula was followed in Yugoslavia. The U.S. contributed to instigating and intensifying the conflict by removing the Kosovo Liberation Army (KLA) from its list of terrorist groups to use it as a proxy against Yugoslav authorities. Following the escalation of the conflict, Washington and NATO began their diplomatic initiative supported by the threat of war. Belgrade was presented with a dilemma of accepting a complete surrender of sovereignty or facing a war with NATO. Appendix B of the Rambouillet proposal demanded complete surrender and NATO occupation of Yugoslavia:

> NATO personnel shall enjoy, together with their vehicles, vessels, aircraft, and equipment, free and unrestricted passage and unimpeded access throughout the FRY [Federal Republic of Yugoslavia] including associate airspace and territorial waters. This shall include, but not be limited to, the right of bivouac, maneuver, billet, and utilization of any areas or facilities as required for support, training, and operations.

George Kenney, a former State Department Yugoslav desk officer, reported in *The Nation* that a senior U.S. State Department official had boasted that the U.S. "deliberately set the bar higher than the Serbs could accept" as the Serbs "need some bombing, and that's what they are going to get."[148] Henry Kissinger confirmed that Washington had deliberately placed unacceptable demands on Yugoslavia as "an excuse to start bombing."[149] The Serbian National Assembly rejected the surrender of their sovereignty and suggested instead a diplomatic solution that would formalise Kosovo's autonomy, which would be organised under the supervision of the OSCE and the UN. Washington and NATO rejected this offer and insisted that diplomatic efforts had been exhausted as Belgrade was unwilling to compromise. John Norris, the Director of Communications for U.S. Deputy Secretary

---

147 K. N. Waltz, "The New World Order," 189.

148 G. Kenney, "Rolling Thunder: the Rerun," *The Nation*, 14 June 1999.

149 H. Kissinger, "Interview with Henry Kissinger," *The Daily Telegraph*, 28 June 1999.

of State, Strobe Talbott, acknowledged that the war over Kosovo was primarily about geopolitical restructuring and not humanitarianism: "it was Yugoslavia's resistance to the broader trends of political and economic reform—not the plight of Kosovar Albanians—that best explains NATO's war."[150]

A decade after the first Gulf War, the neoconservative agenda gained wind in its sails following the terrorist attacks on September 11, 2001. In his memoirs, U.S. General Wesley Clark wrote that after the terrorist attacks, he was presented with a memo from the Office of the Secretary of Defence explicitly outlining the U.S. strategy to "take out seven countries in five years."[151] After attacking Iraq, the U.S. would then invade Syria, Lebanon, Libya, Somalia, Sudan, and then finish off with Iran. Bush Junior was likely convinced that the idea that the U.S. was using belligerent means to pursue such benign ends as the objective of spreading democracy was likely genuine. In a 2003 address, Bush imagined that the brutal invasion would result in the proliferation of democracy across the region: "Iraqi democracy will succeed—and that success will send forth the news, from Damascus to Tehran, that freedom can be the future of every nation."[152]

The mentality of moral righteousness whereby the world could be transformed through military force was commonplace despite presenting a cartoonish picture of the world. The good versus evil heuristics was displayed in *An End to Evil* by Richard Perle and David Frum, in which the U.S. was framed as a virtuous world policeman to advance U.S. interests: "when it is in our power and our interests, we should toss dictators aside with no more compunction than a police sharp shooter feels when he downs a hostage-taker."[153] In the years that followed the U.S. attack on Iraq, the U.S. and NATO pursued wars against Libya, Syria, Yemen, and continued its occupation of Afghanistan for 20 years. Yet, as new

150 J. Norris, *Collision Course:. NATO, Russia, and Kosovo* (foreword by Strobe Talbott) (Westport: Praeger, 2005), xxiii.

151 W. K. Clark, *A Time to Lead: For Duty, Honor and Country* (New York: Palgrave Macmillan, 2007), 231.

152 "In Bush's Words: Iraqi Democracy Will Succeed," *The New York Times*, 6 November 2003.

153 D. Frum and R. Perle, *An End to Evil: How to Win the War on Terror* (New York: Random House Publishing Group, 2003), 114.

centres of power inevitably emerged, the "small wars" were replaced with the preparation for larger wars by shifting focus to Russia and China.

Redividing the World

Another stage of idealist internationalism is the recognition that pursuit of power is an end in itself. The demand for hegemony rests on the assumption that internationally hierarchic structures are required to defend its ideals. The French, Soviets, and NATO/EU members considered themselves the champions of universal ideals that could only be defended with a hegemonic international distribution of power. The internationalist ideals "become subservient to a primarily 'national' cause, or rather, the maintenance of the regime of one specific 'big power'."[154] The term "Titoism" illustrates the Soviet rejection of alternate communist power structures to its "federalistic ideology."[155] Similarly, liberal democracies demand hierarchies justified by ideology and thus often reject multilateralism in inclusive international institutions. John Herz argued in 1942 that the stronger the democracy at the national level, the more likely a country is to reject an international democracy in order to protect its democratic values and prerogatives from the rule of the international majority.[156] The ideals of human freedoms were, in all instances, based on idealist internationalism, while the political realities resulted in these values being linked to hegemony.

The Wolfowitz doctrine for global primacy was outlined less than two months after the collapse of the Soviet Union. The leaked *Defense Planning Guidance* (DPG) of February 1992 outlined a hegemonic world order. The endurance of the hegemony therefore relied on preventing future rivals from emerging: "Our first objective is to prevent the re-emergence of a new rival… we must maintain the mechanisms for deterring potential competitors from even aspiring to a larger regional or global role."[157] The DPG also warns against

154 J. H. Herz, "Idealist Internationalism and the Security Dilemma," *World Politics* 2, no. 2 (1950): 171.

155 Ibid., 172.

156 J. H. Herz, "Political Ideas and Political Reality," *Western Political Quarterly* 3, no. 2 (1950).

157 DPG, "Defense Planning Guidance," Washington, 18 February 1992.

allies becoming too independent and thus advocated that allies such as Germany and Japan should not rearm, but be integrated into a U.S.-led system. The paper recognised that "it is of fundamental importance to preserve NATO as the primary instrument of Western defence and security, as well as the channel for U.S. influence and participation in European security affairs."[158]

In 2002, the *U.S. Security Strategy* explicitly linked national security to global dominance as the objective to "dissuade future military competition" should be achieved by advancing and maintaining "the unparalleled strength of the United States armed forces, and their forward presence."[159] The pursuit of global primacy was also encapsulated in the U.S. full spectrum dominance concept, which aspires for dominance of American power is all spheres: land, sea, air, space, cyberspace and information space. Linking hegemony to liberal values, U.S. National Security Advisor Condoleezza Rice dismissed multipolarity as a threat to liberalism: "Multi-polarity is a theory of rivalry; of competing interests—and at its worst—competing values."[160]

Former U.S. National Security Advisor Zbigniew Brzezinski produced an influential strategy for advancing and preserving unipolarity. Brzezinski outlined a grand strategy of ensuring "that no Eurasian challenger emerges, capable of dominating Eurasia and thus of also challenging America."[161] Using the language of traditional imperialists, Brzezinski advocated that the U.S. "prevent collusion and maintain security dependence among the vassals, to keep tributaries pliant and protected, and keep the barbarians from coming together."[162] Translated into layman's language, George Friedman from Stratfor, also known as the shadow CIA, put it this way: the U.S. must "keep Eurasia divided among as many different (preferably mutually hostile) powers as possible."[163]

158 Ibid.

159 G. W. Bush, "The National Security Strategy of the United States of America," *The White House*, 1 June 2002.

160 C. Rice, "Remarks by Dr Condoleeza Rice, Assistant to the President for National Security Affairs," at the International Institute for Strategic Studies, London, United Kingdom, 16 June 2003.

161 Z. Brzezinski, *The Grand Chessboard: American Primacy and Its Geopolitical Imperatives* (New York: Basic Books, 1997), xiv.

162 Ibid., 40.

163 G. Friedman, "The Geopolitics of the United States, Part 1: The Inevitable Empire," *Stratfor*, 4 July 2014.

Washington offered patronage to key regional powers in return for allegiance to the U.S.-centric system.[164] Europe was organised under the trans-Atlantic partnership that excluded and limited the influence of Russia, Asia was sustained as a U.S.-led region under what is termed the Indo-Pacific Region to limit the influence of China, while partnerships with Israel and Arab states contained Iran. While the rimlands of the Eurasian continent were secured by establishing these partnerships, the U.S. also aimed to penetrate the heart of Eurasia. The U.S. developed the "Silk Road" concept in the 1990s that would integrate Central Asia under U.S. leadership with a view to severing relations between Russia and Central Asian states.

The perpetuation of U.S. hegemony demands the recreation of Cold War dividing lines and conflicts that ensured adversaries were weakened, while allies remained dependent and obedient. The U.S. converts security dependence into geoeconomic and political loyalties. The challenge of the system is that excessive peace reduces the influence of the U.S. in allied states, while excessive tensions incentivise adversaries to decouple geoeconomically from the U.S.

The Europeans' aspiration for ever-more autonomy was expressed ambiguously under the goal of "strategic autonomy" and "European sovereignty." Jacques Delors, the French president of the European Commission, advocated strengthening the UN and European autonomy to balance U.S. power. Increasingly, the Europeans were developing their independent foreign policy in the form of energy deals with Russia, technology and infrastructure cooperation with China, and were even resisting U.S. efforts to reimpose sanctions on Iran. Concurrently, U.S. allies in Asia and around the world made China their largest trading partner. Distrust and tensions between the allies and adversaries were required to ensure allies remained dependent and loyal, while also containing Russia, China, and any other rival. Even before the Soviet Union had collapsed, Cumings observed: "Although the Cold War has ended, the two pillars of postwar American foreign policy—global hegemony and allied containment—remain largely intact."[165]

---

164 P. J. Katzenstein, *A World of Regions: Asia and Europe in the American Imperium* (London: Cornell University Press), 2005.

165 B. Cumings, "Trilateralism and the New World Order," *World Policy Journal* 8, no.2 (Spring, 1991), 195.

Concurrently, both China and Russia became increasingly concerned that the U.S. continued its containment policies. Russia considered it necessary to punch above its weight to balance an expansionist NATO and EU that marginalised its role in Europe, while China enjoyed more stability and could bide its time through its "peaceful rise" to grow in strength for as long as possible without attracting unwanted attention from the West.

The U.S. pursued military containment through NATO expansion in Europe and its "pivot to Asia" to strengthen the regional containment policies that then U.S. Secretary of State John Foster Dulles defined in 1952 as the two island chains.[166] The first island chain "locks in" the Sea of Japan, the East China Sea and the South China Sea with an encirclement stretching from Japan, Ryukyu Islands, Taiwan, Philippines and towards Malaysia and Indonesia, where the U.S. controls the strategic Strait of Malacca. The second island chain stretches from Japan, the Northern Mariana Islands, Guam, Micronesia and Palau before reaching Indonesia.[167] To strengthen its island chain containment strategy, the began to U.S. incrementally abandon the One-China Policy that had been the foundation for stability and peace since the late 1970s. The One-China Policy recognised that Taiwan is part of China, and President Jimmy Carter had committed the U.S. to only cooperate with Taiwan in economics and culture. Washington's incremental push for Taiwan's secession effectively cancelled the entire peace with China.

Economic containment similarly aims to maintain asymmetrical dependence on the U.S. by constraining the economic influence of rivals. In 2012, Secretary of State Hillary Clinton referred to the Transatlantic Trade and Investment Partnership (TTIP) with the Europeans as an "economic NATO."[168] Arguing in favour of the Trans-Pacific Partnership (TPP), President Barack Obama wrote an op-ed in the *Washington Post*:

> America should write the rules. America should call the shots. Other countries should play by the rules that America

---

166 J. F. Dulles, "Security in the Pacific," *Foreign Affairs* 30, no.2 (1952).

167 Q. Xu, "Maritime geostrategy and the development of the Chinese navy in the early twenty-first century," *Naval War College Review* 59, no.4 (2006): 46–67.

168 B. Oreskes, "Moscow wary of TTIP talks," *Politico*, 9 May 2016.

> and our partners set, and not the other way around. That's what the TPP gives us the power to do… The United States, not countries like China, should write them.[169]

However, Washington would need to reform the geoeconomic architecture to maintain system dominance as the relative power if the U.S. declines and new poles of power emerge. Containing both Russia and China would likely incentivise the two Eurasian giants to converge to de-Americanise technologies, industries, transportation corridors, banks, trade/reserve currencies, and payment systems. To divide the two rivals, it would be necessary for the U.S. to accommodate Russia as the weakest to contain China as the larger power. Even anti-Russian hawks such as Brzezinski, who contributed with key ideas for cementing unipolarity, recognised that Washington would have to eventually create an "expanded West" that included Russia to ensure the Russians and Chinese would balance each other.[170]

The U.S. is faced with a dilemma as its dominant position in the international system wanes. The U.S. can either accept a more modest role in the international system by facilitating a multipolar system to accommodate the new centres of power, or it could weaponize its administrative control over the international economy. Washington would choose the latter, thus creating incentives for the rest of the world to gradually reduce their excessive dependence on the U.S.

Conclusion

The liberal hegemonic world order of Pax Americana aspired to transcend power politics and create a more benign world order. Yet, idealist internationalism tends to result in radical power politics as ideals and the institutions and policies intended to serve them are degraded to mere instruments of power politics to advance a national cause. The social contract between the population of the world and the world's policeman subsequently began to collapse as the effort to

---

169 Obama, B., "President Obama: 'The TPP would let America, not China, lead the way on global trade'," *The Washington Post*, 2 May 2016.

170 Z. Brzezinski, Z., *The Choice: Global Domination or Global Leadership* (New York: Basic Books, 2009).

use peaceful means to achieve benign ends instead created belligerent means to sustain hegemony.

Liberal hegemony maintains its peaceful ideological identity within the collective West as if it were a fundamental break with history. However, for states beyond the West, the concept of a benign liberal hegemon increasingly resembles the continuation of traditional Western imperialism. Once again, the world is divided into civilised states with sovereignty versus uncivilised states with limited sovereignty, with the gardeners claiming the authority to use military means when operating in the jungle. As new centres of power emerged, they predictably rejected liberal hegemony as propping up a disorderly and unjust world order.

5.

Decline of the West and the Liberal World Order

THE DECLINE of liberal hegemony included the deterioration of relative power and legitimacy. Hegemony tends to become unsustainable as the costs of an empire become unaffordable and its legitimacy collapses. The liberal hegemonic order had predictable problems. Preserving unipolarity exhausted U.S. economic resources, challenged the norms of state sovereignty, and the reliance on coercion undermined legitimacy. The ideology of Pax Americana eventually came under great strain as the narrative of the eventual triumph of capitalism and democracy began to falter.

The famous historian, Richard Hofstadter, remarked that the U.S. has the misfortune of being an ideology rather than having one. The U.S. was founded on a revolution based on liberal ideals, and its global hegemony was legitimised by liberal values. Hubris following the ideological victory of the Cold War contributed to the neoliberal consensus in which economic and political liberalism became a uniform solution to the world. The central role of liberalism in the American experiment creates a proclivity for exceptionalism, and deviation from the liberal consensus threatens to unravel liberal hegemony and even abandon the fundamental ideas of America.

This chapter analyses why the liberal hegemonic world order threatens to unravel the West itself as it necessitates the excesses of liberalism, which laid the intellectual foundation for replacing international law with the rules-based international order. Accordingly traditional diplomacy conflicted with the objective to "socialise" other states. The excesses of liberalism fuelled a neoliberal economic system of unfettered markets, degraded social and political cohesion, and subsequently gave rise to an authoritarian and undemocratic liberalism. It also contributed to cultural decline, enabled the corruption of global civil society, and even allowed market forces to manipulate the military and policymaking. Worse, the U.S. has, to some extent, become an irrational actor as its political squabbles at the national level influence its foreign policy in a manner that undermines its security.

The Rules-Based International Order Replaces International Law

International human rights law introduced a set of rules focused on the rights of the individual to elevate justice, yet the attempt to realise these rights often contradicts the state-centric foundation that defines international law. The choice of which principles to follow in terms of human security or state security is only consistent in terms of aligning with power interests. Justice that is unevenly applied is not justice, instead, it is a weapon of the powerful. International law has been systematically dismantled since the 1990s and replaced with the arbitrary "rules-based international order" that does not consist of any uniform rules.

The process of constructing alternative sources of legitimacy to facilitate the principle of sovereign inequality began with NATO's illegal invasion of Yugoslavia in 1999 without a UN mandate. The violation of international law was justified by liberal values and the legitimacy of the UN Security Council was contested by arguing it could be circumvented as Russia and China threatened to veto NATO since they did not share the liberal values of the West.

The efforts to establish alternative sources of authority continued in order to gain legitimacy for the invasion of Iraq. Former U.S. Ambassador to NATO Ivo Daalder co-authored an article with James Lindsay in 2004 calling for the establishment of an "Alliance of Democracies" as the focal point of U.S. foreign policy.[171] A similar proposal suggested that a "Concert of Democracies" should be established in which liberal democracies could act in the spirit of

---

171 I. Daalder and J. Lindsay, "An Alliance of Democracies," *The Washington Post*, 23 May 2004.

the UN without being constrained by authoritarian states.[172] During the 2008 presidential election, these concepts manifested themselves more forcefully in politics as Republican presidential candidate Senator John McCain argued in favour of establishing a "League of Democracies." In December 2021, the U.S. organised the first "Summit for Democracy," which similarly sought to divide the world into liberal democracies versus authoritarian states. The envisioned world order would align the liberal democracies under U.S. leadership and legitimise interference into the domestic affairs of states deemed authoritarian. The White House outlined sovereign inequality in the language of democracy as Washington pursued "a targeted expansion of U.S. support for democracy around the world," while framing the defence of the West's sovereignty as the defence of democracy.[173] These initiatives manifested themselves as the "rules-based international order."

The rules-based international order created a two-tiered system of legitimate versus illegitimate states. The paradox of liberal internationalism is that liberal democracies often demand that they dominate international institutions in order to defend democratic values from the control of the majority. Yet, a durable and resilient international system capable of developing common rules is imperative to have international governance and resolve disputes among states.

The concept of the rules-based international order is commonly treated as a synonym of international law, or it is merely defined as international law plus humanitarian law. Yet, the rules of the rules-based international order are never explicitly stated and are nowhere to be found. Under the veil of obscure semantics, the rules-based international order represents a drastic revision of international law.

International law in accordance with the UN is based on the Westphalian principle of sovereign equality as "all states are equal." In contrast, the rules-based international order is a hegemonic system based on sovereign inequality, using international humanitarian law selectively to enable exceptions in international law reserved

172 G. J. Ikenberry and A. M. Slaughter, *Forging a World of Liberty Under Law: U.S. National Security in the 21st Century* (Princeton: The Princeton Project on National Security, 2006).

173 The White House, "Summit for Democracy Summary of Proceedings," 23 December 2021.

for U.S.-aligned liberal democracies. Such a system of sovereign inequality follows the principle from George Orwell's *Animal Farm* that stipulates "all animals [states] are equal but some animals [states] are more equal than others." The collective West has the prerogative to interfere in the domestic affairs of other states under the banner of promoting democracy, to topple governments under the guise of supporting democratic revolutions, and even to invade other states under the concept of humanitarian interventionism.

Humanitarian law introduces principles that conflict with state-centric international law, and the rules-based international system enables the collective West to select the principles that correspond with their power interests. Case in point, while the principles of state sovereignty and territorial integrity as enshrined in international law, the principle of self-determination is part of humanitarian law. On one hand, in Kosovo, the West promoted self-determination as a normative right of secession that had to be prioritised above territorial integrity. On the other hand, in South Ossetia and Crimea, the West insisted that the sanctity of territorial integrity as stipulated in the UN Charter must be elevated above self-determination. The term rules-based international order thus covers up the reality of the "might is right" principle as dominant states decide which rules to apply.

Instead of resolving conflicts through diplomacy and uniform rules, there is an incentive to manipulate, moralise and propagandise as international disputes are decided by a tribunal of public opinion. In 1999, the U.S. and UK especially presented false accusations about war crimes to make interventionism legitimate. British Prime Minister Tony Blair told the world that Yugoslav authorities were "set on a Hitler-style genocide equivalent to the extermination of the Jews during the Second World War. It is no exaggeration to say that what is happening is racial genocide."[174]

The rules-based international order fails to establish common unifying rules of how to govern international relations, which is the fundamental function of world order. Both China and Russia have denounced the rules-based international order as a dual system to facilitate double standards. Chinese Vice Foreign Minister, Xie Feng, asserted that the rules-based international order introduces the "law

174 N. Clark, "Fools no more," *The Guardian*, 19 April 2008.

of the jungle" insofar as universally recognised international law is replaced by unilateralism.[175] Russian Foreign Minister Sergey Lavrov similarly criticised the rules-based international order for creating a parallel legal framework to legitimise unilateralism:

> The West has been coming up with multiple formats such as the French-German Alliance for Multilateralism, the International Partnership against Impunity for the Use of Chemical Weapons, the Global Partnership to Protect Media Freedom, the Global Partnership on Artificial Intelligence, the Call for Action to Strengthen Respect for International Humanitarian Law—all these initiatives deal with subjects that are already on the agenda of the UN and its specialised agencies. These partnerships exist outside of the universally recognised structures so as to agree on what the West wants in a restricted circle without any opponents. After that they take their decisions to the UN and present them in a way that de facto amounts to an ultimatum. If the UN does not agree, since imposing anything on countries that do not share the same "values" is never easy, they take unilateral action.[176]

Diplomacy Replaced with Socialisation

The collective hegemony of the West does not require diplomacy in terms of seeking mutual understanding and compromise. Diplomacy includes placing oneself in the shoes of the opponent and pursuing opportunities for finding common ground, building trust, and addressing shared challenges. However, while competing security interests are solved by mutual understanding and compromise, the proliferation of superior values requires the other side to make unilateral adjustments.

Compromising on liberal democratic values that can deliver perpetual peace is regarded as signifying a dangerous return to the

175 "U.S. 'rules-based intl order' is 'law of the jungle' to contain others: Chinese vice FM tells U.S. envoy," *Global Times*, 26 July 2021.

176 S. Lavrov, "Foreign Minister Sergey Lavrov's remarks at the 29th Assembly of the Council on Foreign and Defence Policy (CFDP)," The Ministry of Foreign Affairs of the Russian Federation, 2 October 2021.

era of power politics. For example, NATO's decision in the 1990s to begin expanding eastwards was framed as advancing the zone of democracy and peace, thus any opposition to expansion of a military bloc could be dismissed as a rejection of democracy. Yeltsin's pro-Western foreign minister, Andrey Kozyrev, complained about the reinvention of diplomacy: "Some people in the West have actually succumbed to the fantasy that a partnership can be built with Russia on the principle of 'if the Russians are good guys now, they should follow us in every way.'"[177] Russia was therefore presented with a dilemma as it could either accept NATO expansionism as a common good or be considered a "counter-civilisational force" that would have to be contained.[178] Similarly, the EU considers it necessary to acquire more power vis-à-vis Russia due to the need to pressure Russia into accepting one-sided adaptions.[179]

The diplomacy of the hegemon organises states into a subject-object / teacher-student relationship in which the superior West must socialise the inferior other. Rather than being labelled dominating or oppressive, the hegemon can claim benevolence and virtue by portraying its actions as selflessly taking on the responsibility of civilising the other. The relationship between NATO and partners such as Russia is commonly framed in a pedagogic teacher-student relationship where unilateral concessions are expected from the student.[180] The EU-Russia relationship was similarly conceptualised as a teacher-student relationship.[181]

An undiplomatic pedagogic language is applied which categorises the policies of other states as "good behaviour" or "bad behaviour" depending on states' preparedness to follow the directions of the hegemon. Bad behaviour is "punished" and good behaviour is "rewarded," while compromising risks that the student learns the wrong lesson.

177 A. Kozyrev, "Russia and the U.S: Partnership Is Not Premature, It Is Overdue," *Current Digest of the Russian Press* 46, no. 6 (1994).

178 M. C. Williams and I. B. Neumann, "From Alliance to Security Community: NATO, Russia, and the Power of Identity," *Millennium* 29, no. 2 (2000).

179 H. Haukkala, "The European Union as a Regional Normative Hegemon: The Case of European Neighbourhood Policy," *Europe-Asia Studies* 60, no. 9 (2008): 1601–1622.

180 A. Gheciu, "Security institutions as agents of socialization? NATO and the 'New Europe'," *International Organization* 59, no.4 (2005): 973–1012.

181 I. B. Neumann, *Uses of the Other: The "East" in European Identity Formation* (Manchester: Manchester University Press, 1999).

Any compromise is perceived as meaning that the West as a "force of good" is surrendering values that can deliver perpetual peace. The U.S. therefore has a tendency of "thinking of any concession to Russia as 'appeasement,'" while caution is tantamount to cowardice.[182] In an alarming development in the West, the concept of Russia's nuclear deterrent is reinvented as "nuclear blackmail" and therefore rejected.

Shared institutions for diplomacy are also degraded by the teacher-student format as participation and inclusion in various forums become mere rewards by "legitimising" the counterpart for good behaviour, rather than establishing a forum to resolve common challenges. When conflicts arise, common institutions and diplomacy are suspended to punish and deprive the counterpart of legitimacy. Case in point, the NATO-Russia Council was established to build trust and manage relations, yet negotiations were largely absent as NATO members agreed on common positions before meeting the Russian counterpart. This was done to enable them to negotiate from a position of strength; and once a NATO consensus had been reached there was very little room for manoeuvre to make any changes based on Russian requests. Once the first major conflict arose, the 2008 Georgian War, NATO responded by punishing Russia by suspending it from formal contact in the NATO-Russia Council.

The Exhaustion and Decline of Economic Liberalism

The market requires restraint at both the domestic and the international level. At the national level, unfettered markets concentrate economic power to the extent it undermines societal and political stability. Thus, the political Left has traditionally sought to redistribute wealth and the political Right has attempted to protect traditional community and family values from becoming a mere appendage to the market.

At the international level, economic liberalism is historically promoted by the dominant economy seeking to position itself as a trustworthy and benign hegemon capable of administrating the international economy. However, the costs of providing collective goods

---

182 D. Deudney and G. J. Ikenberry, "The Unravelling of the Cold War Settlement," *Survival: Global Politics and Strategy* 51, no.6 (2009): 58.

enable weaker economies to gain advantages and the asymmetries can gradually even out. The hegemon faces a dilemma about how to respond to the emergence of new centres of power by either allowing hegemony to wither away or abusing the administrative control over the economic system to prevent the rise of rivals. Either way, rising powers will balance the hegemon and the rivalry will replace economic liberalism with neo-mercantilism.

The dichotomy of the Cold War struggle between capitalism and communism incentivised capitalist states to moderate the excesses of free market capitalism to be more ideologically competitive. After the Second World War, the West sought to mitigate what Polanyi referred to as "disembedded liberalism," which is the idea that market-driven capitalism, economic processes, and activities became detached or disembedded from their social and cultural contexts.[183] The West pursued embedded liberalism in which each state could limit the free market to distribute wealth and mitigate social disruption to avoid the social instability that arises from making society a mere appendage to the market. The era from 1945 to the 1970s was defined as "embedded liberalism" since market-oriented economic policies were combined with a social and political framework in which each respective capitalist country aimed to address the potential negative social consequences of unregulated capitalism.

However, the economic stagnation of the 1970s was eventually resolved by neoliberal economic policies spearheaded by President Ronald Reagan and Prime Minister Margaret Thatcher. Restrained capitalism in which market efficiency was limited came to an end, as the political Left could not redistribute wealth and the political Right could not protect traditional communities and values to the same extent. The creation of a flexible market to overcome stagnation entailed rapid deregulation, accepting higher unemployment and economic inequality, weakening the unions, and dismissing the state's societal responsibilities.[184] While unfettered capitalism was a remedy to the stagnation of the 1970s, it developed into a prevailing neoliberal ideology led by scholars such as Milton Friedman and Friedrich Hayek.

183 J. G. Ruggie.

184 G. Davidson and P. Davidson, *Economics for A Civilized Society* (New York: Norton, 1988), 138.

Concurrently, the U.S. made great efforts to expand its primacy globally by establishing a global division of labour while securing a preferable position in global value chains. For example, concerns about Japan's technological and economic rise in the 1980s were resolved with economic measures. The U.S. imposed high tariffs on Japanese semiconductors and a wide variety of goods, banned the Japanese export of several products to the U.S., and required the Japanese to open their semiconductor patents to the U.S. Furthermore, as the security provider of Japan, the U.S. also had strong leverage in the Plaza Accords in the mid-1980s and Japan had to agree to a major realignment of its currency that ended its spectacular economic rise.

The U.S. also removed economic barriers to cement its economic leadership position and sought to establish stronger core-periphery relations via economic liberalism. To a large extent, this imitated the British repeal of the Corn Laws in the 1840s, enabling it to saturate foreign markets with manufactured goods in return for opening its own agriculture to competition. Western economies prospered greatly by increasing their focus on intangible assets such as intellectual property rights and reducing the share of less valuable tangible assets.[185] Simply put, the U.S. would invent the iPhone leaving China to assemble it. U.S. technologies and finance dominated the world, while U.S. manufacturing was outsourced.

The concentration of economic power and the triumph of capitalism in the Cold War fuelled the hubris regarding free market capitalism as the solution to organising society.[186] Yet, the international distribution of labour was not sustainable as China and others began to climb up global value chains with industrial policies like that of the American System, and thus challenged the role of the U.S. as the technological leader. The hegemon has systemic incentives to build trust in a liberal international economic system, yet a declining hegemon will revert to neo-mercantilist policies in defence of its primacy. Most notably, President Trump launched an economic war against China that was also embraced by the Biden administration. However, unlike Japan which was dependent for its security on the U.S., China is an

---

185 L. Baruch, *Intangibles: Management, Measuring and Reporting* (Washington D.C.: Brookings Institution Press, 2001).

186 T. Piketty, *Capital in the Twenty-First Century* (Cambridge: Harvard University Press, 2014.

independent pole of power largely capable of withstanding economic coercion.

Economic liberalism also became less sustainable at the national level. The outsourcing of U.S. manufacturing created domestic economic and social havoc that undermined its political stability. U.S. capital and labour which otherwise would have been tied to manufacturing and ideally assigned to more skilled and profitable professions was instead mostly channelled to low-skilled and low-paid jobs, weakening the middle class and social cohesion. Paul Krugman, a Nobel Prize-winning economist, recognised that economic liberalism was causing problems: "It's hard to avoid the conclusion that growing U.S. trade with Third-World countries reduces the real wages of many and perhaps most workers in this country. And that reality makes the politics of trade very difficult."[187]

The existence of a middle class is imperative for capitalism to function and to preserve political stability. As the middle-class declines, societies become more polarised as rich versus poor, exploiter versus exploited, globalists versus nationalists, and "us" versus "them."

A neoliberal ideology of globalisation emerged that insisted the state should not interfere in markets. Furthermore, the state went from being a guarantor that ensured social stability by upholding responsible regulation, to be seen as an inefficient and technologically stagnant actor. As economic power continued to concentrate since the 1970s, the lower-skilled workers in the West experienced stagnation and even a fall in the real value of their salaries. Concurrently, workers had to accept less job security, more flexibility, higher unemployment, and longer working hours. Neoliberalism failed to address the paradox of globalisation that global markets, national sovereignty, and democracy become contradictory.[188]

Globalisation made the international economy much more efficient, yet the elimination of tariffs and non-tariff barriers resulted predictably in downward pressure on wages, dismantlement of regulations and employee protection laws in order to construct a more flexible and competitive workforce. As economic liberalism and new

187 P. Krugman, "Trouble With Trade," *The New York Times*, 28 December 2007.

188 D. Rodrik, *The Globalization Paradox: Why Global Markets, States, and Democracy Can't Coexist* (Oxford: Oxford University Press, 2012).

technologies reduced the restriction of national borders, the economic interests and political loyalties also departed from the state. The world became more interconnected, yet the social cohesion of the nation-state diminished. In the 1990s, it was predicted that the concentration of capital would give rise to an elite without national loyalties: "This world economy will soon be owned by a cosmopolitan upper class which has no more sense of community with any workers anywhere than the great American capitalists of the year 1900."[189]

The American Empire began to demonstrate similarities to the Roman Empire after its conquest of the Mediterranean region. Similar to how the peasants of the Roman Empire were disenfranchised by the influx of agricultural products from the new regions, so were American manufacturers destroyed by global markets as mutual dependence within the U.S. was severed.[190] Rather than defending the well-being of their own people, both the Romans and the Americans considered the creative destruction to be a necessary sacrifice for advancement. A divide between the beneficiaries and the victims of globalisation subsequently began to grow. Corporations operating globally can undermine the state as they "have little need for national loyalty, view national boundaries as obstacles that thankfully are vanishing, and see national governments as residues from the past whose only useful function is to facilitate the elite's global operations."[191]

The concentration of economic wealth converted the U.S. into a corporate state as large corporations increasingly asserted their influence over the government. A dilemma arises as governments recognise the corporations must be powerful enough to compete in international markets, yet recognising that their excessive power enables corporations to corrupt state power. The influence of the energy industry on the Bush administration is a common case study as leaders from the industry were assigned top political positions. This problem is exacerbated as the tech giants assert increasing influence over the government. The government pushes back in the power struggle with

---

189 R. Rorty, *Achieving Our Country: Leftist Thought in Twentieth-Century America* (Cambridge: Harvard University Press, 1998).

190 E. Todd, *After Empire: The Breakdown of the American Order* (New York: Columbia University Press, 2003).

191 S. P. Huntington, "Dead Souls: The Denationalization of the American Elite," *The National Interest,* 1 March 2004, 8.

powerful corporations as national loyalties are demanded with the growing demand that "What is good for Silicon Valley is good for the U.S." As the government and corporations move towards harmonising interests according to the fascist political economy, democracy is shattered, leaving individuals exposed to the abuses of unconstrained power.

Governments have incentives to make corporations a tool to ensure that political and economic power serves the nation. This was made evident by the Twitter files, which revealed that the Democratic Party cooperated with tech giants to censor its own citizens and the political opposition.[192] The tech giants are also weaponised against foreign adversaries. In an op-ed entitled "Protecting democracy is an arms race: Here's how Facebook can help," Mark Zuckerberg argued that Facebook is determined to confront "bad actors" globally that seek to spread disinformation and interfere in elections. To confront such challenges, Zuckerberg advocated for the "combined forces of the U.S. private and public sectors," identifying these "bad actors" as Russia, Iran and other states that Washington considers its main adversaries.[193] Facebook also made itself a foreign policy tool of the U.S. government by agreeing to cooperate with two sub-organisations of the National Endowment for Democracy (NED) that are renowned for manipulating civil society in other states, the International Republican Institute and the National Democratic Institute.

In a more militarized approach, the co-founder of Google and the former U.S. Deputy Secretary of Defence co-authored an article arguing for the need of "the U.S. military to restore its technological superiority over potential adversaries." The duo suggested that U.S. global hegemony is a condition for peace and stability: "Our military primacy allowed us to shape the global economy—unlocking trillions of dollars for U.S. companies and citizens," with the added value argument that "our hegemony has helped protect democracy worldwide against challenges from authoritarianism."[194]

---

192 J. Clark, "Release of 'Twitter Files' revs GOP's Pursuit of Big Tech, Dem Collusion," *The Washington Times*, 4 December 2022.

193 M. Zuckerberg, "Protecting democracy is an arms race. Here's how Facebook can help," *The Washington Times*, 4 September 2018.

194 E. Schmidt and R.O. Work, "How to Stop the Next World War," *The Atlantic*, 5 December 2022.

The Decline of Political Liberalism

Introduced in the late 18th century with the French Revolution, political liberalism transformed politics by challenging traditional hierarchies of groups and elevating the individual in political and social life. Yet, the slogan of the French Revolution: "Liberty, Equality, Fraternity" was not synonymous with radical individualism, insofar as fraternity refers to the brotherhood and unity of society, in which individuals transcend their differences to work together for a larger community that shares a common fate. It aimed to establish a balance between the individual and the group.

The Enlightenment endeavoured to establish societies based on reason, which exposed the duality of humankind as humanity also is comprised of immutable instincts formed by evolution over tens of thousands of years. One of the strongest instincts of human beings is to organise in groups as a source of security and meaning, this sets limitations on individualism and the efficacy of its capacity to reason. Socrates and Plato warned that the excesses of democracy can liberate the individual from the hierarchical structures and authorities of the group that enable cohesive societies to function. In *The Republic*, Plato argues that society unravels due to excess liberty, and—in response—the people will invite a tyrant to restore order:

> Can liberty have any limit? Certainly not... By degrees the anarchy finds a way into private houses.... The son is on a level with his father, he having no respect or reverence for either of his parents; and this is his freedom.... Citizens chafe impatiently at the least touch of authority.... Liberty overmasters democracy... the excessive increase of anything often causes a reaction in the opposite direction.... And so tyranny naturally arises out of democracy, and the most aggravated form of tyranny and slavery out of the most extreme form of liberty.[195]

The development of the liberal democratic nation-state became a powerful vessel for human freedom and development as it established a

195 Plato, *The Republic* (translated by Benjamin Jowett) (Ontario: Devoted Publishing, 2016), 216.

balance between the individual and the group. The nation-state created a group identity with a common future based on a shared language, culture, history, and values. The stability of the collective provided the foundation for advancing individual rights. However, liberal thinkers such as Thomas Paine have rejected traditions as undemocratic, contending that allowing the past to influence the present as tantamount to giving voting power to the dead. Similarly, John Stuart Mill referred to the "despotism of custom" as a "hindrance to human advancement."

Liberalism eventually began to decouple itself from the nation-state as ethnic identities declined, national cultures were replaced by multiculturalism, and radical secularism did not merely seek a division between state and religion but suppressed the role of Christianity in society. The nation-building process of homogenising the population that made peasants into Frenchmen and immigrants into Americans began to reverse, producing sub-groups with competing tribal identities.[196] Political polarisation fuels the rise of competing political identities as liberals and conservatives fail to find a common middle ground which both sides can serve their orientations.

In less homogenous societies in which the group has less in common, there is also a breakdown in fraternity and social cohesion. In complex societies, there is less social capital as defined by strong connections and relationships among the people. The consequence is fewer reliable friendships, fewer donations to charity, less volunteering, and even diminished democracy as there is less voting.[197] A society that consists merely of individuals occupying the same geographical space without much in common experiences a decline in civil society as a balance to state power.

Even as individuals are liberated from the group, they are also deprived of meaning, insofar as humans are social beings that organise in groups and find meaning in their contribution to the group. Yet, in a liberal society in which citizenship is defined excessively by individual rights instead of responsibilities to the collective, solitude and the loss of meaning become a problem. Individuals who reject their

196 E. J. Hobsbawm, *Globalisation, Democracy and Terrorism* (London: Little Brown, 2007), 93.

197 R. D. Putnam, "E pluribus unum: Diversity and Community in the Twenty-First Century," *Scandinavian Political Studies* 30, no.2 (2007): 153.

connection to the group are solely defined by themselves, and will likely fall victim to narcissism and nihilism.

Democracy itself will struggle to sustain itself in fragmented societies. The fundamental requirement for democracy is national unity.[198] National unity implies that "the vast majority of citizens in a democracy-to-be must have no doubt or mental reservations as to which political community they belong to."[199] The group or society must present a collective identity as the political pluralism within a democracy must be confined within "accepted boundaries" because "cleavage must be tempered by consensus."[200] If society fragments into sub-groups that can deem each other as the "out-group" or "other," then the enablement of a common cause and social conformity entails defeating and destroying the adversary. The U.S. population increasingly defines its "tribe" by competing political identities that define "us" and "them." The liberals believe the conservatives seek to destroy progressiveness, and the conservatives believe that the liberals aim to destroy the traditional nation-state. Both sides claim to represent freedom as an uncompromising principle.

Such indications have emerged in the political discourse of the West as, for example, when British Prime Minister David Cameron accused the opposition leader Jeremy Corbyn of being a threat to national security and pursuing a "Britain-hating ideology" due to his justice-related endeavours that questioned actions of the British state.[201] Similarly in the U.S., the Democrats and Republicans describe each other as a threat to the nation. How can there be a peaceful transfer of power if the opponent is deemed illegitimate and believed to pursue "our" destruction? The predictable result is that many Democrats contested the legitimacy of President Trump's 2016 victory, and many Republicans dispute the election victory of President Biden in 2020. Elections become more vulnerable to utilitarian morality in which the rigging of an election is seen as virtuous by preventing the rise of

198 A. Lijphart, "Consociational Democracy," *World Politics* 21, no. 2 (1969).

199 D. A. Rustow, "Transitions to Democracy: Toward a Dynamic Model," *Comparative Politics* 2, no.3 (1970): 350.

200 L. J. Diamond, "Three Paradoxes of Democracy," *Journal of Democracy* 1, no. 3 (1990): 49.

201 N. Watt, "Cameron accuses Corbyn of 'Britain-hating ideology' in conference speech," *The Guardian*, 7 October 2015.

evil. The erosion of fraternity in the U.S. destroys the required unity for national social cohesion, political stability, and democracy.

Authoritarian Liberalism: Democratic Decline at Home and Aggression Abroad

Democracy and liberalism are often portrayed as two sides of the same coin. This is largely correct during periods of prosperity and globalisation, although democracy and liberalism can be in direct conflict once the socio-economic challenges of globalisation intensify. In the late 19th century, liberalism was challenged by democracy in a similar manner as in our contemporary era.

Globalisation from the 1850s to the 1870s entailed deregulation, concentration of economic power, and mass migration. A growing democratic uprising emerged against the consequences of liberal excesses. Economic liberalism and social liberalism interacted as the ability of factories to reduce salaries for workers was aided by migration, enabling new and cheaper labour to become available. A nationalist uprising ensued as an instrument to restore socio-economic control over national borders and thus combat the disruptive impact of globalisation. The liberal elites pursuing globalisation were thus challenged by a democratic demand for nationalism in the form of increasing economic protectionism and limiting immigration.

Liberal thinkers such as John Stuart Mill often put themselves on the side of liberalism above democracy. Mill was devoted to the progress of liberalism and reason in Victorian England that was, to a large extent, organised by custom. Mill therefore argued that "the most virtuous and best-instructed of the nation will acquire that ascendancy over the opinions and feelings of the rest, by which alone England can emerge from this crisis of transition, and enter once again into a natural state of society."[202]

If freedom of speech is an instrument to counter the "despotism of custom" with superior arguments, is freedom of speech a means to an end or an end in itself? Freedom of speech assists in countering social conformity and advances the goals of reason and individualism in a society based on traditions and customs. Yet, for a utilitarian

202 J. S. Mill, *The Spirit of the Age* (Chicago: Chicago University Press, 1942), 93.

progressive, freedom of speech and democracy could be problematic in a society that desires to be organised more by customs, faith, and traditions. As a liberal thinker devoted to progress, John Stuart Mill cautioned that public opinion rules the world, and that problems therefore derived from "collective mediocrity" and "low state of the human mind." A case could therefore be made for the rise of a liberal aristocracy, in which those committed to individualism and reason would be elevated to progressive dominance. Mill was a utilitarian who believed that morality depends on the outcome: "I regard utility as the ultimate appeal on all ethical questions; but it must be utility in the largest sense, grounded on the permanent interests of man as a progressive being."[203] To some extent, Mill favoured replacing the despotism of custom with the despotism of liberal progress.

The contemporary liberal elites of the West similarly act as if they have a mandate of liberal progress that supersedes the democratic will domestically. Similarly, they view this ideological superiority as entitling them to lead the wider world as opposed to accepting the compromises of multipolarity. The development of the nation-state entailed the construction of social conformity by consigning non-conforming citizens to second-class citizenship. The attempts to replace the nation-state with the liberal state suggest that the in-group "we" is defined primarily by social conformity to liberal principles, and those failing to conform to these principles are therefore punished. Thus, authoritarian liberalism emerged in which the state embraces progressive ideals such as individualism, secularism and multiculturalism, while dissent is not accepted as legitimate as it represents an existential threat to the liberal creed of the group.

Domestic divisions between liberal elites and the people creates a demand for populists, who function as a corrective mechanism to balance the excesses of liberalism. The liberal elites degenerate into an oligarchy and the populist masses seek radical change without necessarily having good solutions. Populists are also vulnerable to xenophobia as ethnicity and other distinctive features of a tribe are traits by which human beings form groups. Some unsavoury populists emerged in the late 19th century in response to liberal globalisation, and the same applies to the populists of the 21st century.

---

203 Ibid.

Populism is a response to authoritarian liberalism. The rise of populism is "an illiberal democratic response to decades of undemocratic liberal policies" in which a neoliberalist consensus among the political elites dictates policies on immigration, economics, and integration without a proper democratic mandate.[204] The populists who challenge the elites come in different nationalist shades—some arguing for the continued superiority of the West while others see the need to adjust to new realities of a post-Western global multipolarity.

The prevalence of liberal ideology depicts opposition to liberal policies as malign and dangerous tribalism that had to be denounced and overcome rather than appeased. An increasingly scornful and polarised relationship developed between the cosmopolitan elites that prospered from globalisation and the working-class which was disadvantaged by globalisation and sought refuge among peers in a community based on traditional values.

Rather than addressing the socio-economic reasons for the divisions, the "petulant, self-righteous, intolerant" liberal elites expressed disdain for the people clinging to traditional national culture: "'Middle America'—a term that has both geographic and social implications—has come to symbolise everything that stands in the way of progress: 'family values,' mindless patriotism, religious fundamentalism, racism, homophobia, retrograde views of women."[205] Huntington noted that the average citizen tends to prioritise a national identity, traditional values and culture, and the preservation of national unity. However, for the globalised elites:

> these concerns are secondary to participating in the global economy, supporting international trade and migration, strengthening international institutions, promoting American values abroad, and encouraging minority identities and cultures at home. The central distinction between the public and elites is not isolationism versus internationalism, but nationalism versus cosmopolitanism.[206]

---

204 C. Mudde, "Europe's Populist Surge: A Long Time in the Making," *Foreign Affairs* 95, no. 6 (2016): 30.

205 C. Lasch, *The Revolt of the Elites and the Betrayal of Democracy* (New York: Norton & Company, 1996), 28–29.

206 S. P. Huntington, "Dead Souls: The Denationalization of the American

The neoliberal consensus that followed the Cold War could not be balanced by conservatism, as conservatives had reinvented themselves as supportive of the unfettered market. The neoliberal consensus implied that "The desolation of settled communities and the ruin of established expectations will not be mourned and may well be welcomed by fundamentalist market liberals."[207] Rorty similarly anticipated that radical economic liberalism would be followed by a pendulum swing to increased political radicalism:

> Members of labor unions, and unorganized and unskilled workers, will sooner or later realize that their government is not even trying to prevent wages from sinking or to prevent jobs from being exported. Around the same time, they will realize that suburban white-collar workers—themselves desperately afraid of being downsized—are not going to let themselves be taxed to provide social benefits for anyone else. At that point, something will crack. The nonsuburban electorate will decide that the system has failed and start looking around for a strongman to vote for—someone willing to assure them that, once he is elected, the smug bureaucrats, tricky lawyers, overpaid bond salesmen, and postmodernist professors will no longer be calling the shots.... Once the strongman takes office, no one can predict what will happen.[208]

Populists' unpredictability and challenge to the status quo result in undemocratic means to counter democracy. In the U.S., the legal system is used to target the political opposition as evidenced by the "Russiagate" years and the unprecedented lawfare waged against Trump in 2023 during pre-election season. In Germany, the political media elites began openly debating whether the populist party, Alternative for Germany (AfD), should be banned once it rose to the second-largest political party in the polls. The predictable consequence

---

Elite," The *National Interest*, 1 March 2004.

207 J. Gray, *Enlightenment's Wake: Politics and Culture at the Close of the Modern Age* (London: Routledge, 1995), 100.

208 R. Rorty, *Achieving Our Country: Leftist Thought in Twentieth-Century America* (Cambridge: Harvard University Press, 1998), 81.

is that liberalism will be a dividing force in the West, while the world will be less likely to look toward the West as a teacher of democracy.

Cultural Decline and Soft Power

The excesses of liberalism can exhaust culture, which is a reference to the customs, values, beliefs, behaviours, symbols, and artefacts that are transferred from one generation to the next and thus function as the collective consciousness of the group. A key criticism by Max Weber of modern capitalism and the rationalisation movement was the disenchantment of the world:

> The fate of our times is characterized by rationalization and intellectualization, and, above all, by the "disenchantment of the world." Precisely the ultimate and most sublime values have retreated from public life either into the transcendental realm of mystic life or into the brotherliness of direct and personal human relations.[209]

A cultural crisis in the West was expected by Weber as the increasing erosion of tradition and spirituality would undermine the moral foundation and social cohesion of society. U.S. soft power has been a huge source of influence that made hegemony more acceptable globally, as American society and culture were emulated around the world. Joseph Nye wrote extensively on American soft power as unrivalled in the history of the world, yet by 2004 he cautioned about the decline of America's soft power largely due to the militaristic U.S. foreign policy.[210] Problems also derive from unfettered liberalism. The immensely popular U.S. pop culture became a key source of attraction to the extent it undermined and weakened folk culture, which is defined by the culture that is passed down through generations and offers an anchor in a common cultural past. Once the pop culture is degraded, and folk culture is absent, society may fracture. A lesson from ancient Rome was that civilisations, much like stars, shine the strongest when

209 M. Weber, *Essays in Sociology* (Milton Park: Routledge, 1948), 155.

210 J. S. Nye, "The decline of America's soft power," in D. Skidmore (ed.), *Paradoxes of Power* (New York: Routledge, 2015).

their decadence has already commenced. An immature obsession with self-indulgence masquerades social decline and fragmentation.

Aleksandr Solzhenitsyn cautioned during a speech at Harvard in 1978 that the capitalist states would likely suffer the same decadence as the communists as both ideologies failed to sufficiently preserve the traditional and spiritual. Solzhenitsyn argued that in the East, the communist party had suffocated their spiritual life but the West was also exhausting itself: "In the West, commercial interests tend to suffocate it. This is the real crisis. The split in the worlds is less terrible than the similarity of the disease plaguing its main sections."[211] George Kennan later suggested that the ideological victory of the Cold War had to be reassessed as the U.S. had transformed itself into a sick society. The excesses of liberalism produced "unrestrained decadence," which had already manifested itself in a "pathological preoccupation with sex and violence, the weird efforts to claim for homosexuality the status of a proud, noble and promising way of life."[212] It is paradoxical that at the alleged height of Western civilisation in terms of advancing its ideals and values, one sees that the excesses of individualism and materialism fragments the culture and social institutions. Society succumbs to emotional solitude, social safety nets collapse, indebtedness destroys communities, people seek refuge in substance abuse, obesity proliferates, all while shopping and shallow entertainment distract from growing nihilism.[213]

Friedrich Nietzsche referred to a common theme in Western philosophy: the death of God. With the decline of Christianity in the 19th century, the absence of other sources of meaning, morality, and order became a cause for concern. Destroying the societal structures without replacing them with new institutions leads to nihilism, anarchy, and collapse.[214] Dostoyevsky questioned the durability of secular morality as law must be a reflection of morality to be sustainable. When the religious foundation of laws disappears, then morality is no longer based on eternal principles and can be altered by merely changing

---

211 A. Solzhenitsyn, "The Exhausted West," *Harvard Magazine*, July-August 1978, 26.

212 G.F. Kennan, *The Kennan Diaries* (New York: Norton & Company, 2014).

213 E. Luttwak, *Turbo Capitalism* (New York: HarperCollins Publishers, 1999), 207–208.

214 F. Nietzsche, *Thus spoke Zarathustra* (London: Penguin Books, 1968), 64.

laws. Unacceptable practices such as torture can merely be renamed "enhanced interrogation techniques."

British philosopher Roger Scruton cautioned that "Europe is rapidly jettisoning its Christian heritage and has found nothing to put in the place of it save the religion of 'human rights.'"[215] Human rights can become a very subjective concept. For example, whether it should be acceptable to marry a partner of the same sex or to have more than one spouse will all depend on subjective narratives of those who are discriminated against.[216] Human rights are not based on anything permanent and can be defined as whatever law suggests. Case in point, abortion used to be deemed an immoral act of killing an unborn child, but has now in some places been socially constructed as support for women's rights to control their bodies as a basic human right. Conversely, recognition of biological differences between genders that justified protected spaces for women can be socially constructed as hate.

During the Ukraine War, the West's unifying principles of human rights and liberal values were demonstrated to have a very weak foundation. Selective outrage over human rights violations and even acceptance of targeting civilians by the political media establishment became commonplace. Humanitarian principles on limiting weapons such as depleted uranium and cluster ammunition that cause great suffering for the civilian population were reframed as legitimate tools for self-defence. Censorship was transformed from an unacceptable authoritarian practice to a necessity to defend the public from disinformation. Even the rules against collective punishment enshrined in the Geneva Convention could be cast aside as the collective West argued that everything Russian was part of "Putin's war machine." Russian and Belarusian individuals were targeted without due process. Germany even criminalised expressions of support for the Russian invasion and began confiscating the cars of ordinary Russian tourists as sanctions, not distinguishing between imports and personal use.[217] Even famous Russian painters, composers, authors, and other artists

---

215 R. Scruton, "The Future of European Civilization: Lessons for America," *The Heritage Foundation*, 8 December 2015.

216 Ibid.

217 Spiegel, *"Deutscher Zoll konfisziert russische Autos"* ["German Customs Confiscate Russian Cars"], *Der Spiegel*, 6 July 2023.

dating back to the 19th were "cancelled" in an apparent effort to purge Russian culture. Hence, the Ukraine War ended the distribution of power and the rules governing the world order of liberal hegemony.

The abandonment of key values that define the collective West was not limited to the Ukraine War, as evident by two other wars that coincided with the Ukraine War. Geopolitical considerations incentivised both the EU and U.S. to remain silent or even provide support during the ethnic cleansing and war crimes of the Armenia-Azerbaijan conflict and Israel-Gaza conflict.

Cultural decadence causes internal fragmentation and incentivises other centres of power to look towards alternative economic, political, and social orders to organise society. Sergey Karaganov, an influential Russian scholar and advisor to both Yeltsin and Putin, argued that the West did not have anything else to teach Russia. Karaganov already insisted in 2016 that even most Europeans "wanted to be part of the Europe of Konrad Adenauer and Charles de Gaulle that valued European Christian heritage, and therefore for the next decades, Europe will not be a model that is attractive to Russia."[218] The sense of cultural decline in the West is undoubtedly shared by other parts of the world. In August 2023, Hungarian Prime Minister Viktor Orban argued that today's Western values meant three things: migration, LGBTQ, and war.

The Manipulation of Global Civil Society

World order is not limited to inter-state relations as it also encompasses the relationship between peoples. The formation of a global civil society suggests that even though the international system is divided into a system of state sovereignty, people can form relations across national borders. Much like how civil society is an important balance to state power, so does global civil society prevent individuals from being reduced to instruments of state power in the power politics between states.

The concept of global civil society is appealing as people across borders can stand together to address common challenges. Challenges ranging from environmental degradation, human rights abuses,

218 Spiegel, "We Are Smarter, Stronger and More Determined," *Spiegel*, 13 July 2016.

pollution, and disease are not limited to borders, thus it is natural for civil society to cooperate across national borders. Global civil society's obvious flaws are the lack of accountability, the ability of some states and regions to dominate the agenda, and the corruption by governments.

Civil society is intended to limit state power, but this creates an incentive for foreign powers to hijack the civil society of other countries to undermine the power of the national government. The liberal argument for creating a less state-centric world order by empowering civil society vis-à-vis governments has been corrupted as the collective West, although primarily the U.S. government, has asserted the right to organise civil society around the world. The assumption is that Washington's foreign policy is driven by altruism and commitment to developing civil society as a component of democracy, as opposed to weaponizing the civil society of other states to the detriment of democracy in the pursuit of power interests.

Civil society is to a large extent organised by non-governmental organisations (NGOs), and the conflicting narratives about their roles demonstrate their contested role in the post-Cold War world order. UN Secretary-General Kofi Annan described NGOs as the consciousness of humanity, while South Africa's President Nelson Mandela denounced NGOs for carrying out foreign interests against the national government. The Western narratives of NGOs frame the rise of international NGOs almost exclusively as a humanitarian and progressive "force for good," although in other parts of the world, they are often experienced as imperial instruments of power to enable foreign powers to rival the authority of the government and even pursue regime change.

Both the U.S. and the Soviet Union used aid as a weapon and interfered in the domestic affairs of other states in a power rivalry that was legitimised by their respective universal values. Washington's strategy for global dominance and the advancement of liberal capitalism was organised by manipulating the civil societies of other states. The U.S. envisioned a greater role for NGOs in the 1980s and asked the other governments of the Organisation for Economic Cooperation and Development (OECD) to pour money into NGOs, which were then used as propagandists.[219]

The U.S. developed pseudo-NGOs that were government-funded and often staffed with people with ties to the intelligence community. The purpose was to shift the responsibility for propaganda and covert operations from the CIA to "non-governmental organisations" such as the National Endowment for Democracy and Freedom House, which operated closely with the U.S. government. By operating them in plain sight, the U.S. would no longer be embarrassed when its intelligence operations were revealed to subvert the civil society of other states.

The most prominent of the U.S. government-funded NGOs is the National Endowment for Democracy (NED), which was created in 1983 as a private organisation. Although, it is funded by the U.S. Congress and was inaugurated by President Ronald Reagan. In his inauguration ceremony speech, Reagan argued: "This program will not be hidden in shadows. It'll stand proudly in the spotlight, and that's where it belongs. We can and should be proud of our message of democracy."[220]

A CIA whistle-blower, Philip Agee, confirmed that NED had been founded as a "propaganda and inducement program" to subvert foreign countries under the guise of advancing liberal democratic values.[221] A cofounder of NED, Allen Weinstein, admitted that "a lot of what we do today was done covertly 25 years ago by the CIA."[222] *Washington Post* reporter David Ignatius acknowledged that NED had become the "sugar daddy of overt operations" as the U.S. could topple governments under the guise of "democracy promotion," support paramilitary operations under the appearance of backing "freedom fighters," and peddle propaganda that would simply be called "information."[223] The relationship between the CIA and NED was outlined

---

219 T. Tvedt, "Development NGOs: Actors in a global civil society or in a new international social system?." *Voluntas: International Journal of Voluntary and Nonprofit Organizations* 13, no. 4 (2002): 368.

220 R. Reagan, "Remarks at a White House Ceremony Inaugurating the National Endowment for Democracy," *The American Presidency Project*, 16 December 1983.

221 J. Stevenson, *A Drop of Treason* (Chicago: The University of Chicago Press, 2021), 241.

222 D. Ignatius, "Innocence Abroad: The New World of Spyless Coups," *Washington Post*, 22 September 1991.

223 Ibid.

in a letter by CIA Director William J. Casey to Edwin Meese, a White House counsellor to President Reagan. Casey advocated that the CIA keep some distance from NED to ensure it would not undermine NED's credibility: "Obviously we here [at the CIA] should not get out front in the development of such an organization, nor do we wish to appear to be a sponsor or advocate."[224]

The NGOs that facilitate global civil society operate with budgets of billions of dollars, and the agenda is set by the financiers who are not solely influenced by altruism. American NGOs were deeply involved in the colour revolutions in Serbia in 2000, Georgia in 2003, Kyrgyzstan in 2005, Ukraine in 2004 and 2014.

Countries across the world have responded to the manipulation of their civil society by expelling the NGOs of the U.S. government or establishing "foreign agent" laws. Countries that have taken action against NED include Russia, China, Egypt, Belarus, Venezuela, Uzbekistan, Nicaragua, Ethiopia, Iran, Cambodia, Hungary and others. India's Foreign Minister Subrahmanyam Jaishankar similarly criticised the harmful efforts by people such as George Soros to manipulate and corrupt India's civil society:

> Soros is an old, rich opinionated person sitting in New York who still thinks that his views should determine how the entire world works. Now if I would only stop at old, rich and opinionated, I would put it away. But he is old, rich, opinionated and dangerous. Because what happens is when such people actually invest resources in shaping narratives. People like him think an election is good if the person they want to see [win], wins and if the election throws up a different outcome then they will say it is a flawed democracy and the beauty is that all this is done under the pretense of advocacy of open society.[225]

---

224 R. Parry, "CIA's Hidden Hand in 'Democracy Groups'," *Consortium News*, 8 January 2015.

225 B. Das, "'Old, Dangerous, Rich': S Jaishankar's not-so-kind description of George Soros, *Business Today*, 18 February 2023.

Military Corruption and Exhaustion: War at the End of Empire

After the Cold War, the U.S. had an opportunity to demilitarise. The expenditures saved could have been used to rebuild infrastructure and the U.S. economy, revive its geoeconomic leadership internationally, and resolve socio-economic problems at home. Furthermore, shrinking the military would also reduce the corrupting impact of the military-industrial complex on the political system. Instead, U.S. efforts to cement hegemony through military superiority exacerbated the problems that were already accumulating.

The curse of excessive power is the loss of focus, priorities, and strategic thinking that is in higher demand when a country has fewer resources. A superpower can afford to take risks and engage in folly as the costs can be absorbed. Yet over time, the costs of military adventurism, forever wars, and nation-building accrue and become unsustainable.

It is difficult to change direction and scale back an empire even when wars fail to deliver their objectives, debts soar, and blowback becomes evident. President Eisenhower's farewell speech in 1961 included a warning that "we must not fail to comprehend [the] grave implications" of constructing a military-industrial complex due to its corrupting influence on politics. Eisenhower had initially used the term military-industrial-congressional complex in his notes but changed the wording to avoid alienating Congress by being too explicit about their susceptibility to corruption.[226]

An industry that has war as its business will become capable of corrupting policymaking if it becomes too powerful. Case in point, the decision to expand NATO, and thus cancelling the post-Cold War settlement of an inclusive pan-European security architecture, was partly influenced by the military-industrial complex. The influential U.S. Committee to Expand NATO was set up by Bruce Jackson. The *New York Post* reported on the conflict of interest: "At night Bruce L. Jackson is president of the U.S. Committee to expand NATO, giving intimate dinners for Senators and foreign officials. By day, he is director of strategic planning for Lockheed Martin Corporation, the

226 A. Roland, *Delta of Power: The Military-Industrial Complex* (Baltimore: John Hopkins University Press, 2021).

world's biggest weapons maker."[227] In another report by the *New York Times*, it was revealed that "American arms manufacturers, who stand to gain billions of dollars in sales of weapons, communication systems and other military equipment if the Senate approves NATO expansion, have made enormous investments in lobbyists and campaign contributions to promote their cause in Washington."[228]

A country permanently at war will create complex bureaucracies where the power resides, which are sustained by politicians, technocrats, journalists, and academics who are linked directly to the bureaucracy. Besides directly lobbying politicians, the military-industrial complex has also manipulated the creation of knowledge and dissemination of information by financing and the think tanks that write the policy reports for politicians; it has an overwhelming influence in the media by providing "expert opinions." The think tanks even function as a waiting room for politicians before returning to government in a revolving door system. The top positions in the Obama administration were filled with the staff of the think tank CNAS, which contributed greatly to reversing Obama's election pledge of ending the Iraq War.[229] Thus, the military-industrial complex influences the creation of policy papers to influence policymakers that are on their payroll and also mobilise public support in the media for the decisions.

In the ultimate expression of unfettered capitalism, policy is for sale to the highest bidder. Matthew Rojansky, the director of the Wilson Center think tank, the Kennan Institute, expresses his concern that his industry has become corrupted by a business model in which political influence and access are for sale. Think tanks funded by the arms industry no longer bother to pretend to be objective as they "have become advocacy groups, or even lobbyists, by another name," because "political parties want loyal propagandists, not niggling, equivocating academic hangers-on. And potential donors want veteran sharpshooters to fire their policy bullets into exactly the right target at precisely the right moment."[230] When war is the business model that sustains the

227 J. Gerth and T. Weiner, "Arms Makers See Bonanza In Selling NATO Expansion," *The New York Times*, 29 June 1997.

228 K. Seelye, "Arms Contractors spend to promote an expanded NATO," *The New York Times*, 30 March 1998.

229 G. Packer, "Obama's Iraq Problem," *The New Yorker*, 30 June 2008.

230 M. Rojansky and J. Shapiro, "Why Everyone Hates Think Tanks," *Foreign Policy*, 28 May 2021.

bureaucracy, the militaristic society will continuously look for new monsters to slay. The U.S. thus does not act as a rational state as the influence of weapons manufacturers can outcompete national interests as an influence on policymakers.

When the relative decline of the hegemon becomes terminal, the militarism can become unhinged. The rise and fall of great powers are commonly associated with wars, and great powers in decline are often tempted to use their military power to reverse the decline. For example, Austria-Hungary was willing to go to war, triggering the First World War even though it would lose its Emperor because war was the last desperate opportunity to reverse its decline.[231] The U.S. similarly becomes increasingly prepared to start a war with both Russia and China as nuclear-armed great powers in order to hold on to its dominant position in the international system.

Irrational Foreign Policy: Russiagate

The Ukraine War cannot be properly understood without assessing Washington's irrationality as domestic in-fighting influenced its foreign policy. A rational foreign policy is defined by maximising security, which demands that the state acts as a unitary actor that pursues policies that serve the interests of the collective nation. In contrast, states that allow national in-fighting to influence their foreign policy are defined as irrational actors. Russiagate is the most blatant example of the U.S. allowing its domestic squabbles to influence foreign policy. It is reasonable to argue that the Russiagate hoax even set the conditions for the dangerous policy towards Ukraine and the subsequent proxy war.

In June 2016, Wikileaks published emails that revealed the Clinton campaign had colluded with the Democratic National Committee (DNC) to undermine Senator Bernie Sanders and thus make Clinton the winner of the primary.[232] The Clinton campaign responded by accusing Russia of "hacking" the servers to elect Trump, thus shifting the focus of collusion. Declassified notes reveal that CIA Director John Brennan briefed then-President Barack Obama on 26 July 2016,

---

231 K. N. Waltz, "The New World Order," *Millennium* 22, no. 2 (1993): 187.

232 M. Sainato, "Rigged Debates: Wikileaks Emails Confirm Media in Clinton's Pocket," *Observer*, 14 October 2016.

about Clinton's efforts to fabricate the Russia-Trump conspiracy theory. Brennan's notes from his meeting with Obama specifically stated that Clinton used the false allegations as "a means of distracting the public from her use of a private email server" and "to vilify Donald Trump by stirring up a scandal claiming interference by the Russian security service."[233] The day after losing the presidential election to Trump, Clinton's team met and decided to spread the narrative of an election stolen by Trump and his handlers in the Kremlin.[234]

The Steele dossier was presented as at the initial evidence that allowed the media and the U.S. government to accuse Trump of being an agent of Russia. It was later revealed that both the FBI and the Justice Department knew that Steele was working for the Clinton campaign.[235] The allegation of Russia hacking the servers was fabricated, and the allegations of the secret server linking Trump with the Russian Alfa-Bank were based on the false statement by Michael Sussman, also working for the Clinton campaign.[236] The involvement of the politicians, intelligence community and the media in the Russiagate hoax was eventually criticised by the *New York Post*: "The tragic fact is that once-prestigious press organizations, including *CNN* as well as *MSNBC*, the *New York Times* and the *Washington Post*, weren't fooled by the collusion hoax. They were an essential part of it."[237]

The consequence of Russiagate was that Trump's efforts to make peace with Russia were denounced as evidence of collusion and treason.[238] Opposition to Trump was expressed with outrageous statements that Russia had attacked the U.S. with comparisons to the September 11 attacks and Pearl Harbour.[239] Stories about Russia

---

233 R. Scarborough, "Hillary Clinton behind plan to tie Trump to Russia, CIA warned FBI's Comey, Strzok," *The Washington Times*, 7 October 2020.

234 J. Allen and A. Parnes, *Shattered: Inside Hillary Clinton's Doomed Campaign* (New York: Crown Publishing Group, 2017).

235 A. McCarthy, "Steele's Shoddy Dossier," *National Review*, 6 June 2019.

236 G. Greenwald, "The Indictment of Hillary Clinton's Lawyer is an Indictment of the Russiagate Wing of the U.S. Media," *Glenn Greenwald* (Substack blog), 19 September 2021.

237 L. Smith, "Adam Schiff lied about the Trump investigation – and the media let him," *New York Post*, 8 May 2020.

238 R. Sakwa, *The Lost Peace: How the West Failed to Prevent a Second Cold War* (Cornwall: Yale University Press, 2023).

239 A. Macleod, "The Utility of the RussiaGate Conspiracy," *FAIR*, 27 July 2018.

attacking America's democracy continued to fill the headlines for years, which produced animosity and sanctions.

The Russiagate allegations also influenced the 2020 presidential elections. The Biden laptop scandal during the presidential election resulted in America's domestic in-fighting resulting in increased tensions with the world's largest nuclear power. The intelligence community intervened in the election as more than 50 former intelligence officials signed a letter, published in *Politico*, supporting the narrative that the Biden laptop scandal was a Russian disinformation campaign and did not prove the crime of the Biden family. One year later, in September 2021, *Politico* acknowledged the authenticity of the Hunter Biden emails and that Russia was not involved in any way.[240]

Meanwhile, the fabricated story of Russia paying the Taliban to kill American soldiers became a talking point against Trump. While some advocated for sanctions, Senator Ben Sasse argued that the U.S. military should put Russian military intelligence officers "in body bags."[241] Kamala Harris—the Democrat's Vice-Presidential candidate at the time—also referred to the Russian bounties in her debate with Vice President Mike Pence, as she was positioning the Biden-Harris administration as one that would hold Russia accountable for its attack on the U.S. During the impeachment trial of President Donald Trump, the Chair of the House Intelligence Committee and leading figure in the Russiagate affair, Adam Schiff, explained the need to arm Ukraine: "The United States aids Ukraine and her people so that we can fight Russia over there and we don't have to fight Russia here."[242]

Conclusion

The excesses of liberalism have undermined international law, diplomacy, economic liberalism, political liberalism, soft power, global civil society, the military, and the rationality of U.S. foreign policy. By committing itself to liberal hegemony and unfettered

240 R. Lizza, R. Bade, T. Palmeri, and E. Daniels, "Politico Playbook: Double trouble for Biden," *Politico*, 21 September 2021.

241 A. Bolton, "GOP senator: Congress must find out what Trump knew of Russian bounties, and when," *The Hill*, 29 June 2020.

242 U.S. Senate, "Proceedings of the United States Senate in the Impeachment Trial of Donald John Trump: Volume II: Trial Proceedings," *U.S. Government Publishing Office*, 31 January 2020, 804–805.

liberalism as the uniform solution to organise society, the West risks the decline of civilisation itself. The destruction of the West is not the consequence of an external shock or threat but self-inflicted injury by dismantling the key civilisational pillars required for success.

The implications can hardly be overstated as the foundation for the West's collective identity and the world order has been based on the endurance of ever-more liberalism. The consequence is the fracturing of Western societies and much of the world distancing itself from the ideology that was seemingly victorious after the Cold War. The ideological commitment to unconstrained liberalism implies that the West will have great difficulties with course corrections and irrational policies should thus be expected. Furthermore, the opposition in the West that seeks course correction will likely be vulnerable to being represented by unsavoury nationalists as the pendulum swings to the other extreme.

6.

NATO Expansion and the Collapse of the Pan-European Order

THE DECISION to pursue a world order based on the collective hegemony of the West after the Cold War had a profound impact on the European security architecture. There was an understanding that NATO expansion would cancel the agreements for an inclusive pan-European security architecture, that Europe would be redivided, that Russia would be alienated, and that conflicts would be revived. A remarkably large number of political leaders recognised these consequences and warned against reigniting the Cold War by expanding NATO. The decision was nonetheless made to expand NATO as Russia was weak and conflicts could be managed under the collective hegemony of the West. An expanded NATO would become an insurance policy against future conflicts with Russia, which would predictably be caused by NATO expansion. This contradiction that set the West on a collision course with Russia was to underpin the new world order.

This chapter explores the agreements to develop an inclusive pan-European security architecture with Russia according to the Westphalian principles of sovereignty equality, indivisible security, and a Europe without dividing lines. It addresses how, concurrently, NATO expansion rejected the Westphalian balance of power, pursued sovereign inequality, enhanced its security at the expense of Russian security, and redivided the continent with a permanent peacetime military alliance. NATO became an instrument to cement U.S. hegemony in Europe and perpetuate Russian weakness via a new strategy of containment that included undermining Russia's nuclear retaliatory capabilities. Russia, seeing these developments as an existential threat, sought to discourage Western unilateralism and promoted multilateral alternatives in accordance with Westphalian principles.

A Common European Home versus Europe Whole and Free

After the division of Europe following the Second World War, the capitalist bloc and the communist bloc sought to strengthen the common world order without undermining their respective regional orders. The main breakthrough came with the Helsinki Accords in 1975, which outlined a common framework for European security. The agreement bolstered key Westphalian principles of order such as sovereign equality, indivisible security, refraining from the threat or use of force, non-intervention in internal affairs, and territorial integrity. Yet, the agreement also included principles of justice such as equal rights and self-determination of peoples, respect for human rights and fundamental freedoms such as freedom of thought, conscience, and religion. Principles of human security to elevate justice were thus included in the agreement of state-centric principles of order.

The subsequent enhancement of trust inspired Gorbachev to initiate extensive domestic reforms and to launch his proposal to develop a "Common European Home," which envisioned demilitarising foreign affairs by dismantling both the Warsaw Pact and NATO. The confrontational military blocs would be replaced by an overarching common European institution to harmonise and unite the capitalist and communist blocs.

The U.S. countered Gorbachev's "Common European Home" with the concept of a "Europe Whole and Free" in 1989. The U.S. was similarly dismissive of Mitterrand's European confederation project as it was feared that Europe would unify outside U.S.-centric institutions. The U.S. proposal for a "Europe Whole and Free" insisted on the universalism of liberal democracy as the foundation for a common Europe. Translated into power politics, the U.S. sought to expand the trans-Atlantic system to the entirety Europe under the leadership of the U.S. as the defender of capitalism and liberal democracy.[243] While Gorbachev desired a common Europe house with many rooms housing

243 R. Sakwa, *The Lost Peace*.

the different ideologies, the U.S. insisted on one room. Nonetheless, the efforts to end the zero-sum division of Europe eventually resulted in Moscow allowing the falling of the Berlin Wall and then, at the Malta Summit in 1989, the U.S. and the Soviet Union declared the end of the Cold War.

An inclusive pan-European security architecture was seemingly moving forward. The Charter of Paris for a New Europe in 1990, based on the Helsinki Accords, outlined a new post-Cold War security architecture. The Charter upheld key principles such as sovereign equality and indivisible security in a Europe with no dividing lines. The Charter also expanded the concept of security beyond traditional military concerns to include broader aspects of human rights, democracy, economic cooperation, and environmental sustainability. Strategic ambiguity appeared to conceal conflicts between state-centric order and human-centric justice. Case in point, the Charter proclaimed:

> With the ending of the division of Europe, we will strive for a new quality in our security relations while fully respecting each other's freedom of choice in that respect. Security is indivisible and the security of every participating State is inseparably linked to that of all the others.

The principle of indivisible security and the right to freely choose security arrangements can be considered contradictory. On the topic of expanding NATO, it could and was argued that every state has the freedom to make its own choice to join it. That said, undeniably, expansion would redivide the continent and undermine the principle of indivisible security. However, there was no rule to suggest that NATO would be compelled to offer membership to any state. To preserve the principles of the Charter of Paris for a New Europe, NATO would have to remain a status quo power and not pursue expansionism. In contrast, by preserving the military bloc and declaring an "open-door policy," NATO created a dilemma between Europe without dividing lines and the freedom to join any group of states.

As NATO became dominant in Europe and monopolised on security, the real choice of European states was to either join NATO and have security or remain outside without equal security. The right to choose security arrangements was indeed only a right to choose

NATO, as the U.S. was openly hostile to any security arrangements that were not organised around the U.S. Moscow's proposal since 2004 to create a "Single Economic Space" between Russia, Belarus, Ukraine and Kazakhstan was widely denounced in the West as an expression of "imperial ambitions" that had to be resisted.[244] All other Russian-led integration efforts were similarly challenged by the West. When China and Solomon Islands announced a security agreement in 2022, the U.S. responded that it was a source of "significant concerns" and the U.S. would "respond accordingly." As Solomon Islands is thousands of kilometres away from the U.S. mainland, it can be assumed that the U.S. would under no circumstances accept any Chinese or Russian troops in North or Central America. The "freedom of choice" argument is therefore very dishonest as it is promoted simply because there are no credible alternatives to NATO in Europe.

The project for an inclusive pan-European security architecture advanced further in 1994 with the establishment of the Organisation for Security and Cooperation in Europe (OSCE). The OSCE translated the principles of the Helsinki Accords and the Charter of Paris for a New Europe into an actual security organisation. The founding document of the OSCE was similarly based on the key principles of sovereign equality, indivisible security, and a Europe without dividing lines.

Yet, the OSCE remained largely impotent as the U.S. feared it would challenge its hegemonic rule.[245] As Charles de Gaulle famously argued, NATO was an instrument for U.S. primacy from across the Atlantic. The U.S. desire for hegemony in Europe did not dissipate after the Cold War, instead, it was amplified. Former U.S. national security advisor Brzezinski advocated greater aspirations for NATO expansion as "Europe is America's essential geopolitical bridgehead in Eurasia... NATO entrenched American political influence and military power on the Eurasian mainland."[246] Parallel to the agreements of

---

244 N. Gvosdev, "Parting With Illusions: Developing a Realistic Approach to Relations with Russia," *CATO Institute*, 29 February 2008.

245 M. E. Sarotte, "In victory, magnanimity: U.S. foreign policy, 1989–1991, and the legacy of prefabricated multilateralism," *International Politics* 48, no. 4/5 (2011).

246 Z. Brzezinski, "A Geostrategy for Eurasia," *Foreign Affairs* 76, no. 5 (1997): 53.

a pan-European security architecture, the U.S. began to pursue NATO expansion under the slogan of "Europe Whole and Free."

The failure to end bloc politics by including Russia in an inclusive Europe also meant that the West failed to reform itself. The unified and collective West emerged as a fundamentally militaristic region after the Second World War and could have transformed itself after the Cold War. Furthermore, the assumption of superiority resulted in the failure of diplomacy as the West believed it did not have much to learn from the result of the world.

Incrementalism or salami tactics is an attractive strategy for an expansionist power. As the name suggests, salami tactics involve cutting off thin slices gradually. Expansionism creates a reaction from the country that has its security diminished as a consequence, and even allies become apprehensive. But no one action is so outrageous that it justifies a major response, while over time the full expansionist objective is achieved. The U.S. used such tactics to mitigate Russian opposition and to alleviate concerns among European allies. These salami tactics enabled Washington to dismiss and ridicule complaints and to depict any responses from Russia as disproportionate or even as unprovoked aggression.

Redividing Europe to Advance U.S. Hegemony

NATO expansion entailed redividing Europe and incrementally reviving the Cold War. In January 1994, President Clinton recognised that NATO expansion could redivide the continent. So Clinton advocated developing the inclusive Partnership for Peace instead of expanding NATO as the U.S. could not afford to "draw a new line between East and West that could create a self-fulfilling prophecy of future confrontation."[247] Nonetheless, the Partnership for Peace initiative did not become an alternative to NATO expansion, rather it became a stepping-stone to NATO membership by facilitating the reconfiguration of their armed forces in line with NATO standards. Deception by Washington was deliberate, as evidenced by the Clinton administration saying one thing to the Russians and something completely different behind closed doors. U.S. Ambassador Chas Freeman,

247 B. Clinton, "Remarks to Multinational Audience of Future Leaders of Europe," *U.S. Diplomatic Mission to Germany*, 9 January 1994.

a veteran diplomat who was involved in constructing a NATO-centric Europe after the Cold War, argued:

> Clinton was talking out of both sides of his mouth. He was telling the Russians that we were in no rush to add members to NATO, and that our preferred path was the Partnership for Peace. The same time he was hinting to the ethnic diasporas of Russophobic countries in Eastern Europe… we were going to get these countries into NATO as fast as possible.[248]

At the end of 1994, Yeltsin wrote a letter of concern to Clinton about NATO expansion: "Adoption of an expedited timetable plans to start negotiations with the candidates already in the middle of the next year will be interpreted and not only in Russia as the beginning of a new split of Europe."[249] Thomas Pickering, the U.S. ambassador to Moscow, cautioned in 1993 that "the one constant in what we have heard from all Russian interlocutors has been extreme sensitivity about the role of NATO."[250]

Across the Clinton administration, there was a recognition that NATO expansion would alienate Russia, yet many believed the post-Cold War peace could be sustained as Russia was weak and could not do anything about its grievances. William Perry, the U.S. Defence Secretary between 1994 and 1997, argued that "in the early years [after the Cold War] I have to say that the United States deserves much of the blame" for the deteriorating relations with Russia.[251] According to Perry, expanding NATO was a provocation that predictably undermined the peace with Russia. Perry also argued that Russia was "beginning to get used to the idea that NATO could be a friend rather than an enemy… but they were very uncomfortable about having NATO right up on their border." Perry also recognised that NATO expansion would alienate Moscow, although as Vice-President Al Gore argued:

---

248 A. Maté, "'U.S. fighting Russia 'to the last Ukrainian': Veteran U.S. diplomat,'" *The Grayzone*, 24 March 2022.

249 National Security Archive, "NATO Expansion: What Yeltsin Heard," *George Washington University*, 16 March 2018.

250 M. E. Sarotte, *Not One Inch: America, Russia, and the Making of Post-Cold War Stalemate* (New Haven: Yale University Press, 2021), 167.

251 J. Borger, "Russian hostility 'partly caused by West'," claims former U.S. defence head," *The Guardian*, 9 March 2016.

"we could manage the problems this would create with Russia." Perry describes Washington's derisive attitude towards a weakened Russia:

> It wasn't that we listened to their argument and said [we] don't agree with that argument… Basically the people I was arguing with when I tried to put the Russian point…. the response that I got was really: "Who cares what they think? They're a third-rate power." And of course that point of view got across to the Russians as well. That was when we started sliding down that path.[252]

Advocates of NATO expansionism recognised it was provocative and perceived as a threat, yet the assumption was that Russia would eventually have to get used to the new realities. U.S. Secretary of State Madeleine Albright recognised in her memoir that "Yeltsin and his countrymen were strongly opposed to enlargement, seeing it as a strategy for exploiting their vulnerability and moving Europe's dividing line to the east, leaving them isolated."[253] U.S. Deputy Secretary of State Strobe Talbott also confirmed that "Many Russians see NATO as a vestige of the cold war, inherently directed against their country. They point out that they have disbanded the Warsaw Pact, their military alliance, and ask why the West should not do the same."[254] Yet, the sentiment among the NATO expansionists in Washington remained that Russia would eventually have to adjust to the new realities on the ground.

Nonetheless, there were large parts of the political and military elites who openly opposed NATO becoming an expansionist military alliance. In 1995, 20 former U.S. officials wrote an open letter opposing NATO expansion as it risked "convincing most Russians that the United States and the West are attempting to isolate, encircle, and subordinate them, rather than integrating them into a new European system of collective security."[255] In 1997, 50 prominent U.S. foreign

---

252 Ibid.

253 M. K. Albright, *Madam Secretary* (New York: Miramax Books, 2004), 320.

254 S. Talbott, "Why NATO Should Grow," *The New York Review*, 10 August 1995.

255 R. T. Davis, "Should NATO Grow? A Dissent," *The New York Review*, 21 September 1995.

policy experts, which included former senators, diplomats, military officers, and academics sent a letter to President Clinton, warning that NATO expansion "is a policy error of historic proportions."[256] The group, which included former U.S. Secretary of Defence Robert McNamara and the famous anti-Soviet hawk Richard Pipes, further cautioned against redividing Europe: "NATO expansion will draw a new line of division between the 'ins' and the 'outs,' foster instability, and ultimately diminish the sense of security of those countries which are not included."[257]

None other than political giant George Kennan, the architect of the U.S. containment policy against the Soviet Union, warned in 1997 that "expanding NATO would be the most fateful error of American policy in the entire post-cold-war era" as it would undermine Russian security. Kennan lambasted the inability of Washington to overcome its Cold War mentality: "Why, with all the hopeful possibilities engendered by the end of the cold war, should East-West relations become centered on the question of who would be allied with whom and, by implication, against whom."[258]

William Burns, a former U.S. Ambassador to Russia, who later became the director of the CIA, wrote in his memoirs: "Hostility to early NATO expansion is almost universally felt across the domestic political spectrum here." Burns cautioned that the decision to expand NATO was "premature at best, and needlessly provocative at worst." Burns writes, "a gathering storm of 'stab in the back' theories slowly swirled, leaving a mark on Russia's relations with the West that would linger for decades."[259]

The West attempted to mitigate Russia's apprehensions by establishing the NATO-Russia Founding Act of 1997, which guaranteed there would be no "permanent stationing of substantial combat forces" in the former Warsaw Pact states. This served as a temporary measure to reduce opposition, and there is evidence to suggest that Washington did not intend to honour its obligations. Russia had been

---

256 ACA, "Opposition to NATO Expansion," *Arms Control Association*, 26 June 1997.

257 Ibid.

258 G. F. Kennan, "A Fateful Error," *The New York Times*, 5 February 1997.

259 W. J. Burns, *The Back Channel: A Memoir of American Diplomacy and the Case for Its Renewal* (New York: Random House, 2019), 108–109.

left with few options and the only deal on the table did not include any firm security guarantees that NATO would uphold its side of the deal. When briefed on the negotiations for the NATO-Russia Founding Act, President Clinton reportedly responded: "So let me get this straight," this deal is merely an assurance "that we're not going to put our military stuff into their former allies who are now going to be our allies, unless we happen to wake up one morning and decide to change our mind."[260] Fast-forward a few years and there were no more pretences about honouring the Founding Act as military bases and missiles were placed in Poland and Romania, and the U.S. had its eyes set on Ukraine.

A Neo-Containment Strategy

Jack Matlock, the U.S. Ambassador to the Soviet Union from 1987 to 1991 who contributed to negotiating an end to the Cold War, warned that false narratives emerged in Washington to facilitate global primacy. Matlock noted that the public was told that the purpose of NATO was to eliminate the dividing lines in Europe, however, these divisions were already gone. Matlock cautioned that "expanding the military organization that had maintained a defensive line in the middle of the continent was a good way to revive the division."[261] Instead of fulfilling the commitment to establish an inclusive European security architecture, Matlock argued that Washington repeated the mistake made at Versailles in 1919 by excluding Russia and establishing a security order that would perpetuate the weakness of Russia.

Irrespective of its rhetoric about expanding the zone of peace and stability, NATO also prepared for a possible conflict with Russia. Defenders of Clinton's decision to expand the military bloc continuously referred to an expanded NATO as a "hedge" or "insurance policy" against a possible conflict with Russia in the future.[262] As Secretary of State Madeleine Albright explained in April 1997: "On

---

260 M. E. Sarotte, *Not One Inch*, 267.

261 J. F. Matlock, *Superpower Illusions: How Myths and False Ideologies Led America Astray—and How to Return to Reality* (New Haven: Yale University Press, 2010), 172.

262 U.S. Senate, "The Debate on NATO Enlargement: Hearings Before the Committee on Foreign Relations (7 October–5 November)," *U.S. Government Printing Office*, 1998.

the off-chance that in fact Russia doesn't work out the way that we are hoping it will… NATO is there."[263] What Yeltsin heard was that his alleged partners in Washington had taken out an insurance policy to ensure victory over Russia if relations would deteriorate. In January 1994, prior to deciding to expand NATO, Secretary of State Warren Christopher and Clinton's top Russia adviser Strobe Talbott argued that NATO expansion would facilitate the containment of Russia.[264] The justification of NATO's post-Cold War existence was therefore to respond to the security threats that had been created by its expansion.

Former U.S. Secretary of State James Baker warned that the purported need for an insurance policy could become a self-fulfilling prophecy. Baker noted that proponents of NATO expansionism desired a favourable position in case Russia would, in the future, regard its own expansion as the best response to threats, yet NATO expansion would then realise this threat and encourage Russia to assert control over its neighbourhood.[265] Criticising the revival of containing Russia, Baker stated the obvious: "The best way to find an enemy is to look for one, and I worry that that is what we are doing when we try to isolate Russia."[266]

In order to avoid provoking a negative response from Russia or appearing aggressive, the pro-expansion group within the National Security Council advocated in 1994 that the "'insurance policy'/'strategic hedge' rationale (i.e., neocontainment of Russia) will be kept in the background only, rarely articulated."[267] NATO's internal cohesion also became dependent on strategic ambiguity about its position vis-à-vis Russia as some Western European states were uncomfortable with declaring Russia a threat, while on the other hand some Eastern European states would lose confidence in the U.S. and NATO if Russia were to be dismissed as a threat. The Eastern European states had historical reasons for their fear and animosity towards Russia, although

263 T. G. Carpenter and B. Conry, *NATO Enlargement: Illusions and Reality*. Cato Institute, 1998, p.205.

264 S. Kieninger, S., "Helmut Kohl and NATO Enlargement: The Search for the Post-Cold War Order," *American-German Institute*, 7 July 2020.

265 J. A: Baker, "Russia in NATO?," *Washington Quarterly* 25, no.1 (2002): 93–103.

266 Ibid., 100.

267 M. E. Sarotte, "How to Enlarge NATO: The Debate inside the Clinton Administration, 1993–95," *International Security* 44, no. 1 (2019): 32.

using NATO as an instrument against a possible future threat nonetheless would aggravate the security dilemma by undermining Russian security. Subsequently, NATO's relation with Russia became defined by the dishonest "deterrence-cooperation dichotomy" as NATO aimed to deter and contain Russia, while simultaneously reassuring Russia that it is not deemed a threat to avoid an unfavourable reaction.

Nonetheless, the U.S. would need to preserve some tensions with Russia in order to promote the view that it was an external threat and thereby preserve alliance cohesion and limit economic connectivity with Russia. U.S. influence in Europe largely relies on Europe's security dependence, and excessive trust and peace in Europe would reduce that influence. Furthermore, the military-industrial complex was a key promoter of NATO expansion as it would create more revenue. The arms industry subsequently became the dominant financier of think tanks and lobbying groups to shape U.S. foreign policy.[268] George Kennan argued at the end of the Cold War that the U.S. economic system had become too dependent on a military adversary:

> Were the Soviet Union to sink tomorrow under the waters of the ocean, the American military-industrial complex would have to go on, substantially unchanged until some other adversary could be invented. Anything else would be an unacceptable shock to the American economy.[269]

Predicting a New Cold War

Key American political leaders recognised that conflict, and even war, could be the likely consequence of NATO expansionism. In an interview with the *New York Times*, George Kennan outlined the folly and predicted the consequences of expansion:

> I think it is the beginning of a new cold war… There was no reason for this whatsoever. No one was threatening anybody else. This expansion would make the Founding Fathers of this country turn over in their graves…. Of course there is going to be a bad reaction from Russia, and then [the NATO

268 G. Diesen, *The Think Tank Racket* (Atlanta: Clarity Press, 2023).
269 N. Cousins, *The Pathology of Power* (New York: Norton, 1987), iv.

expanders] will say that we always told you that is how the Russians are—but this is just wrong.[270]

Ambassador Jack Matlock similarly warned in 1997 at a Senate Foreign Relations Committee that NATO expansion was misguided and "may well go down in history as the most profound strategic blunder made since the end of the Cold War." Matlock explained that "it could well encourage a chain of events that could produce the most serious security threat to this nation since the Soviet Union collapsed."[271] With similarly strong language, Pat Buchanan, a former presidential candidate and advisor to Nixon, argued that the growing resentment in Russia was the fault of Washington: "full blame must rest squarely with the haughty U.S. elite that has done its best to humiliate Russia. Why are we doing this?."[272] Buchanan predicted that Russia would one day recover and respond to this threat, which would place the U.S. in an all-or-nothing dilemma: "risk confrontation with a nuclear-armed Russia determined to recreate its old sphere of influence, or renege on solemn commitments and see NATO collapse."[273]

The contemptuous attitude towards a weakened Russia was also recalled by U.S. Deputy Secretary of State, Strobe Talbott, who referred to a conversation with President Clinton in 1996 in which the U.S. president outlined what cooperation with Russia entailed: "We keep telling ol' Boris, 'O.K., now, here's what you've got to do next—here's some more shit for your face.'"[274] The willingness to alienate a weakened Russia perplexed foreign policy experts such as Thomas Friedman:

---

270 T. L. Friedman, "Foreign Affairs; Now a Word From X.," *The New York Times*, 2 May 1998.

271 U.S. Senate, "The Debate on NATO Enlargement: Hearings Before the Committee on Foreign Relations (7 October–5 November)," *U.S. Government Printing Office*, 1998, 236.

272 P. J. Buchanan, *A Republic, Not an Empire: Reclaiming America's Destiny* (Washington D.C.: Regnery Publishing, 1999), 25.

273 Ibid.

274 S. Talbott, *The Russia Hand: A Memoir of Presidential Diplomacy* (New York: Random House, 2007), 201.

> The mystery was why the U.S.—which throughout the Cold War dreamed that Russia might one day have a democratic revolution and a leader who, however haltingly, would try to make Russia into a democracy and join the West—would choose to quickly push NATO into Russia's face when it was weak.[275]

The ability to alienate and humiliate Russia while at the same time having Russia adjust to new realities was premised on the assumption that the worst deal offered by the West would still be the only option for Russia. The idea that the West could continue expanding as Russia had no other partners was also reiterated by Zbigniew Brzezinski, who suggested the West was "Russia's only choice—even if tactical—thus provided the West with a strategic opportunity. It created the opportunity for the progressive geopolitical expansion of the Western community deeper and deeper into Eurasia."[276] In a speech at the Atlantic Council in 1997, then-Senator Joe Biden predicted that NATO membership for the Baltic States would cause a "vigorous and hostile" response from Russia. However, Biden suggested that Russia's alienation did not matter as they did not have anywhere else to go. Biden mocked Moscow's warnings that Russia would be compelled to look towards China in response to NATO expansion and joked that if the partnership with China failed to deliver then Russia could alternatively form a partnership with Iran.[277]

NATO expansion created dramatic changes to the military balance in Europe and arms control began to collapse under the hegemonic project. NATO expansionism placed increasing strains on the Conventional Armed Forces in Europe (CFE), which was further exacerbated by NATO's missile defence. A leaked U.S. cable in March 2008 noted that Moscow had warned that "CFE would not survive NATO enlargement."[278] The Anti-Ballistic Missile (AMB) Treaty of

---

275 T. L. Friedman, 2022. "This Is Putin's War. But America and NATO Aren't Innocent Bystanders," *The New York Times*, 21 February 2022.

276 Z. Brzezinski, *The Choice: Global Domination or Global Leadership* (New York: Basic Books, 2009), 102.

277 G. Kaonga, "Video of Joe Biden Warning of Russian Hostility if NATO Expands Resurfaces," *Newsweek*, 8 March 2022.

278 "NATO: February 28th HLTF and NRC (ACE) Meetings," *Wikileaks*, 7 March 2008.

1972, the Intermediate-Range Nuclear Forces (INF) Treaty, and the Open Skies Treaty all sequentially collapsed partly due to the rejection of a security architecture based on mutual constraints.

Dismantling Russia's Nuclear Deterrence: NATO's Missile Defence

Missile defence represented a departure from a world order based on mutual deterrence to one of global primacy. Russia's nuclear deterrent is an important obstruction to U.S. hegemony and missile defence is designed to gradually undermine that Russian deterrent. A strategic missile defence system cannot be considered to be defensive vis-à-vis Russia as it could not possibly intercept all Russian nuclear missiles in a Russian first strike. Instead, missile defence has an offensive function as it is designed to intercept Russia's second strike, which are the retaliatory capabilities that would survive a U.S. first strike. Strategic missile defence thus converts nuclear weapons from a defensive deterrent to an offensive nuclear weapons system. The Anti-Ballistic Missile Treaty (ABM-Treaty) was signed with the Soviet Union in 1972 with the explicit understanding that strategic missile defence systems would upset the strategic balance.

The acquisition of a strategic missile defence system does not suggest that the U.S. has the intention to destroy Russia in a nuclear first-strike attack. Rather, the mutual understanding that the U.S. *could* destroy Russia in a first strike gives the U.S. escalation dominance, the ability to escalate tensions until the opponent is compelled to capitulate.[279] It sends a signal to Moscow that Washington could launch a decapitating nuclear first strike on Russia, enabling the U.S. to escalate and to take an uncompromising stance in any conflict with Russia, knowing that Russia would eventually need to capitulate or back down.

One month after the collapse of the Soviet Union, President Bush asked Congress in his State of the Union Address to revive the development of strategic missile defence: "I urge you again to pass the Strategic Defense Initiative, SDI."[280] A leaked draft of the Pentagon's

279 G. Snyder, *Deterrence and Defense: Toward a Theory of National Security* (Princeton: Princeton University Press, 1961).

280 G. Bush, "Address Before a Joint Session of the Congress on the State of the Union," *The American Presidency Project*, 28 January 1992.

Defense Planning Guidance (DPG) outlined a strategy to perpetuate U.S. global hegemony by "precluding the emergence of any potential future global competitor." The document outlined that Russia remains "the only power in the world with the capability of destroying the United States" and until Russian nuclear forces become harmless, the U.S. will continue to live with a threat. The DPG then called for the "early introduction" of a strategic missile defence system.[281]

In 2001, the U.S. announced it would unilaterally withdraw from the 1972 AMB Treaty, in order to develop strategic missile defence. The capabilities and intentions indicated a transition to a hegemonic posture. A paper by RAND Corporation on "Future Roles of U.S. Nuclear Forces" similarly recognised a departure from deterrence to counterforce capabilities in which nuclear weapons transition from defensive to offensive weapons: "What the planned force appears best suited to provide beyond the needs of traditional deterrence is a *preemptive counterforce capability against Russia and China.* Otherwise, the numbers and the operating procedures simply do not add up."[282] Counterforce is an offensive nuclear strategy that entails destroying the adversaries' weapons before they can be launched and thereby minimising their ability to retaliate with a second strike. Such concerns were confirmed by the Pentagon's Nuclear Employment Strategy of 2013 which outlined the objective of enhancing "counterforce capabilities."[283]

Lieber and Press concluded in a controversial technical study in 2006 that the U.S. "stands on the verge of attaining nuclear primacy," and "It will probably soon be possible for the United States to destroy the long-range nuclear arsenals of Russia or China with a first strike."[284] These findings were supported in a technical study by the Federation of American Scientists which concluded that the missile

---

281 U.S. Department of Defense, draft *1994-99 Defense Planning Guidance* (DPG), Washington, D.C., 18 February 1992.

282 *Future Roles of U.S. Nuclear Forces: Implications for U.S. Strategy* (Santa Monica: RAND Corporation, 2003), 92.

283 H. M. Kristensen, "Falling Short of Prague: Obama's Nuclear Weapons Employment Policy," *Arms Control Association*, September 2013.

284 K. A. Lieber, and D. G. Press, "The Rise of U.S. Nuclear Primacy," *Foreign Affairs* 85, no. 2 (2006), 43.

defence system can easily be reconfigured to target Russian retaliatory capabilities.[285]

As NATO was the dominant security system in Europe, Washington could methodically use the demand for "alliance solidarity" to mute criticism from allies. When President Clinton attempted to advance missile defence plans, he met strong opposition from France, Germany, Spain, Italy, Netherlands, Canada and Belgium.[286] French President Chirac sent a letter to Clinton warning missile defence would be "detrimental to international stability."[287] Even former U.S. Under Secretary of State for Policy Walter Slocombe urged greater understanding for Russian security concerns as missile defence "will inevitably proceed to technologies and scales of deployment that could conceivably put Russian retaliatory capability at risk."[288]

However, pressure campaigns focusing on support for NATO were successful. Leaked cables revealed how the U.S. pressured Norway to abandon its opposition to missile defence, making it an issue of NATO solidarity as Norway would have a "hard time defending its position if the issue shifts to one of alliance solidarity."[289] Eventually, all the NATO allies fell in line and began to dismiss Russian security concerns about the strategic balance as Russian paranoia and a zero-sum mentality. As a European diplomat argued: "the Russians are right on the substance of missile defence, but they have behaved so badly that they have lost the argument. We cannot be seen as giving them a veto on these types of issues."[290]

Washington's missile defence plans also used incrementalism/ salami tactics to overcome opposition. Former U.S. Secretary of

---

285 Y. Butt and T. Postol, "Upsetting the Reset: The Technical Basis of Russian Concern Over NATO Missile Defence," *Federation of American Scientists*, FAS Special Report No. 1, September 2011.

286 S. Rynning, "Reluctant Allies? Europe and Missile Defense," in H. Bertel and S.Rynning (eds.), *Missile Defence: International, Regional and National Implications* (Routledge, 2006), 118.

287 B. Graham, *Hit to Kill: The New Battle Over Shielding America from Missile Attack* (New York: Public Affairs Store, 2003), 157.

288 W. B. Slocombe, "Stability Effects of Limited Missile Defenses: The Case for the Affirmative," *Pugwash Occasional Papers* 3, no. 1 (2002).

289 U.S. Embassy, Oslo, "Norway Standing Alone Against Missile Defense, OSLO 000072," *Wikileaks,* 12 February 2008.

290 M. Leonard and N. Popescu, "A Power Audit of EU-Russia Relations," *European Council on Foreign Relations* 9 (2009), 16.

Defence Donald Rumsfeld argued in 2003 in favour of a "spiral development" policy in which incremental steps would be taken to develop missile defence. Rumsfeld argued:

> Instead of taking a decade or more to develop someone's vision of a "perfect" shield, we have instead decided to develop and put in place a rudimentary system by 2004—one which should make us somewhat safer than we are now—and then build on that foundation with increasingly effective capabilities as the technologies mature. We intend to apply this "spiral development" approach to a number of systems.[291]

Washington could thereby easily ridicule and dismiss Russian security concerns. Case in point, in 2007, U.S. Secretary of State Condoleezza Rice mocked Moscow's concerns about the U.S. placing 10 interceptive missiles in Eastern Europe as *"purely ludicrous, and everybody knows it."*[292] Within a few years, the capabilities had increased drastically, and the planned interceptive missiles had risen to several hundred. NATO also pretended to accommodate Russia by extending an invitation to cooperate on missile defence, which was intended to reassure Russia that it was not the target. Robert Gates, a former Secretary of Defense and a former Director of the CIA, admitted in his memoirs that the U.S. was "just kicking the can down the road on missile defence, playing for time. The Russians recognized that they were being presented with a *fait accompli*, and that our offers of cooperation were more like take it or leave it."[293]

NATO expansion further enabled the U.S. to achieve first-strike capabilities and thus escalation dominance that would require Russia to capitulate in any conflict. Both Romania and Poland were assigned important roles by hosting the strategic missile defence system close to Russian borders. The missile launchers at these sites can also be

---

291 D. Rumsfeld, "U.S. Department of Defense Prepared Statement for the Senate Appropriations Defense Subcommittee: 2004 Defense Budget Request," Washington, D.C., 14 May 2003.

292 "Idea of U.S. threat to Russia is 'ludicrous'—Rice," *Reuters,* 26 April 2007.

293 R. Gates, *Duty: Memoirs of a Secretary at War* (New York: Knopf Publishing, 2014), 162.

exchanged with a variety of offensive missiles such as the Tomahawks. The U.S. then withdrew unilaterally from the INF Treaty in 2019, which had previously restricted medium-range missiles from ranges between 500 and 5,500 kilometres.

These developments created fear in Moscow that the next stage of NATO's expansionist missile defence system would be to place missiles in Ukraine. A key topic of discussion in January and February 2022, prior to Russia's invasion of Ukraine, was Moscow's demands that the U.S. not place missiles in Ukraine as the U.S. had done in Poland and Romania.

A Betrayed Russia Readjusts to New Policies under Putin

NATO expansionism became the principal security concern for Russia. When it became evident that the pan-European security architecture would be abandoned in favour of expanding NATO, Yeltsin asked Clinton: "Why do you want to do this? We need a new structure for Pan-European security, not old ones." Yeltsin cautioned against a "new encirclement" of Russia: "I see nothing but humiliation for Russia if you proceed. How do you think it looks to us if one bloc continues to exist while the Warsaw Pact has been abolished?" Yeltsin continued in vain to insist that the OSCE as an inclusive security organisation had to be "the principal mechanism to build new security order in Europe. NATO is a factor, too, of course, but NATO should evolve into a political organisation."[294]

Yeltsin cautioned against the hegemonic ambitions of Washington: "History demonstrates that it is a dangerous illusion to suppose that the destinies of continents and of the world community in general can somehow be managed from one single capital."[295] Gorbachev also argued that NATO expansionism betrayed the Helsinki Accords, the Charter of Paris for a New Europe, and the OSCE as agreements for pan-European security:

---

294 National Security Archive, "NATO Expansion: What Yeltsin Heard," George Washington University, 16 March 2018.

295 E. Sciolino, "Yeltsin Says NATO is Trying to Split the Continent Again," *The New York Times*, 6 December 1994.

> NATO's eastward expansion has destroyed the European security architecture as it was defined in the Helsinki Final Act in 1975. The eastern expansion was a 180-degree reversal, a departure from the decision of the Paris Charter in 1990 taken together by all the European states to put the Cold War behind us for good. Russian proposals, like the one by former President Dmitri Medvedev that we should sit down together to work on a new security architecture, were arrogantly ignored by the West. We are now seeing the results.[296]

Much focus was devoted to the original sin and betrayal, as Gorbachev was offered numerous verbal assurances that NATO would not take advantage of Moscow's weakness and expand. Reassurances that NATO would not become an expansionist military alliance were imperative to obtain Soviet support for Germany's reunification. NATO has consistently rejected these assurances, although declassified documents provide irrefutable evidence that promises were made to not expand NATO by James Baker, George Bush, Hans-Dietrich Genscher, Helmut Kohl, Robert Gates, Francois Mitterrand, Margaret Thatcher, Douglas Hurd, John Major, and Manfred Wörner.[297] In February 1990, U.S. Secretary of State James Baker provided his renowned promise that NATO would not move "one inch" to the east:

> Would you prefer to see a unified Germany outside of NATO, independent and with no U.S. forces or would you prefer a unified Germany to be tied to NATO, with assurances that NATO's jurisdiction would not shift one inch eastward from its present position?[298]

In a meeting with Shevardnadze, Baker provided similar assurances, stating "there would, of course, have to be iron-clad guarantees

---

296 M. Schepp and B. Sandberg, "Gorbachev Interview: 'I Am Truly and Deeply Concerned'," *Spiegel*, 16 January 2015.

297 National Security Archive, 'NATO Expansion: What Gorbachev Heard," George Washington University, 12 December 2017.

298 M. E. Sarotte, *Not One Inch*, 55.

that NATO's jurisdiction or forces would not move eastward."[299] West German officials seeking Moscow's support for reunification similarly sought to reassure Moscow that NATO would not expand. The West German foreign minister, Hans-Dietrich Genscher, made this explicit in several speeches: "Whatever happens in the Warsaw Pact, an extension of NATO's territory to the east, that is, nearer to the borders of the Soviet Union, will not happen."[300] NATO Secretary-General Manfred Wörner, similarly assured Moscow on 17 May 1990 that "The very fact that we are ready not to deploy NATO troops beyond the territory of the Federal Republic gives the Soviet Union firm security guarantees."[301] These documented promises continue to be dismissed by the West as "myths and misperceptions."[302] Former CIA Director Robert Gates criticised "pressing ahead with expansion of NATO eastward, when Gorbachev and others were led to believe that wouldn't happen."[303]

NATO expansion destroyed the foundations of Yeltsin's pro-Western political platform. Yeltsin's presidency had largely been built on the assumption that Gorbachev's "Common European Home" was more feasible by abandoning the Soviet system and committing Moscow to liberal democracy and free market capitalism. Russia even began to ignore its partnerships in the east, from Central Asia to China, as these relationships were believed to hold Russia back on its path to the West. However, excessive dependence solely on the West deprived Russia of its bargaining power, which placed Moscow in a position where it had to accept unilateral concession without even being included in the European security architecture.

When NATO invaded Yugoslavia without a UN mandate in 1999, the message to Russia was clear: NATO represents European security and can supersede international law—and Russia has no veto over NATO. Kissinger warned that NATO's transformation from a defensive alliance to an offensive alliance contradicted repeated

299 A. Brown, *The Human Factor: Gorbachev, Reagan, and Thatcher, and the End of the Cold War* (Oxford, Oxford University Press, 2020), 325.

300 M. E. Sarotte, *Not One Inch,* 52.

301 NATO, "Address by Secretary General, Manfred Wörner to the Bremer Tabaks Collegium," 17 May 1990.

302 "Myths and Misconceptions in the Debate on Russia," Chatham House, 13 May 2021.

303 National Security Archive, "NATO Expansion: What Gorbachev Heard."

assurances by the U.S. and Europe that Russia did not have anything to fear from NATO expansion.[304] Nonetheless, Russia feared NATO's illegal war would set a precedent, thus if NATO expanded further towards Russian borders it would "create a base to intervene in Russia itself."[305] NATO's illegal invasion of Yugoslavia followed the usual salami tactics. After the invasion, NATO pursued legal cover and implicit Russian consent by obtaining a UN mandate in June 1999 for the occupation of Kosovo under the specific condition of upholding Yugoslavia's territorial integrity. The occupation was instead used to change realities on the ground, and in 2008 the majority of NATO member states, in violation of international law, recognised the independence of Kosovo.

Yeltsin stepped down on 31 December 1999 and handed the presidency over to his prime minister, Vladimir Putin. The role of Putin was not to reverse the pro-Western policies but to redefine them. Putin's revised Western-centric foreign policy aimed to negotiate integration *with* the West as equals, rather than *into* the West as an applicant aspiring to meet conditionality.[306] This required Russia to abandon its unilateral concessions and instead negotiate from a position of strength. Putin recognised that NATO expansionism, the cancellation of the pan-European security architecture, and Russia's marginalisation in Europe were the result of weakness. Putin argued:

> We have done everything wrong.... From the beginning, we failed to overcome Europe's division. Twenty-five years ago, the Berlin Wall fell, but invisible walls were moved to the East of Europe. This has led to mutual misunderstandings and assignments of guilt. They are the cause of all crises ever since.[307]

---

304 P. Dibb, "NATO's 'expansionist policy' fuels fear," *Financial Review*, 17 June 1999.

305 M. Kramer, "Putin Is Only Part of the Russian Picture," *The Washington Post*, 23 January 2000.

306 D. Trenin, "Ukraine and the New Divide," *Russia in Global Affairs*, 22 August 2014.

307 N. Bertrand, "PUTIN: The deterioration of Russia's relationship with the West is the result of many 'mistakes'," *Business Insider*, 11 January 2016.

At the Munich Security Conference in February 2007, Putin gave his famous speech that summarised Russia's concerns about the unipolar world based on "one centre of authority, one centre of force, one centre of decision-making." Putin warned that in the unipolar system "the United States, has overstepped its national borders in every way." Although, the system was also a threat to the U.S. as unipolarity "is pernicious not only for all those within this system, but also for the sovereign itself because it destroys itself from within." At the heart of Russia's concerns was NATO expansionism as the dominant policy manifestation of unipolarity. Putin argued that "NATO has put its frontline forces on our borders," and warned that this was an immense provocation:

> And we have the right to ask: against whom is this expansion intended? And what happened to the assurances our western partners made after the dissolution of the Warsaw Pact? Where are those declarations today? No one even remembers them. But I will allow myself to remind this audience what was said. I would like to quote the speech of NATO General Secretary Mr Woerner in Brussels on 17 May 1990. He said at the time that: "the fact that we are ready not to place a NATO army outside of German territory gives the Soviet Union a firm security guarantee." Where are these guarantees?[308]

Russia's policies increasingly sought to balance Western unilateralism and offer multilateral alternatives. Russia committed itself to withdrawing its peacekeepers from both Moldova and Georgia at the 1999 OSCE Istanbul Summit, which was devoted to elevating collective security in Europe. However, it became evident that NATO would take the dominant role rather than the OSCE and NATO would merely replace Russian peacekeepers. Thus, Russia began to walk back these commitments and frozen conflicts became an instrument to obstruct NATO's continued march to the east. The Russian concerns about NATO attempting to replace the OSCE were seemingly well-founded. In 2003, the Dutch Chairman of the OSCE suggested that

308 V. Putin, "Speech and the Following Discussion at the Munich Conference on Security Policy," *President of Russia,* 10 February 2007.

the Russian peacekeeping forces in Moldova should be replaced with an OSCE Peace Consolidation Force, which would then "outsource" the peacekeeping to the EU.[309] The same Chairman of the OSCE, Jaap de Hoop Scheffer, then became the Secretary General of NATO the following year.

Moscow continued to propose multilateral formats to construct an inclusive Greater Europe. Both Yeltsin and Putin had floated the idea of joining NATO if it would be the dominant security institution in Europe, although this was met with a cold shoulder in the West.[310] Even Gorbachev had suggested to Baker that the Soviet Union could join NATO: "After all, you say that NATO is not directed against us, that it is just a security structure that is adapting to the new reality. So we will propose to join NATO."[311] After the terrorist attacks on September 11 2001, Putin was the first foreign leader to call Bush. Russia saw an opportunity to position itself as a strategic partner of the U.S. in the war on terror by offering its sympathy and support. The support included providing important intelligence and logistic networks for the invasion and occupation of Afghanistan. Yet, the U.S. shortly thereafter began to support colour revolutions in Georgia and Ukraine to install pro-West/anti-Russian governments.

In 2005, Russia and the EU were—seemingly—able to partly mitigate renewed bloc politics with the Common Spaces Agreement. The agreement committed both sides to harmonise their integration efforts towards their shared neighbourhood to prevent new dividing lines: "They agree to actively promote [regional cooperation and integration] in a mutually beneficial manner, through close result-oriented EU-Russia collaboration and dialogue, thereby contributing effectively to creating a greater Europe without dividing lines and based on common values."[312] However, shortly thereafter, the EU launched the Eastern Partnership that invited all its eastern neighbours except Russia. The Eastern Partnership aimed to integrate the pan-European

---

309 J. Löwenhardt, "The OSCE, Moldova and Russian diplomacy in 2003," *Journal of Communist Studies and Transition Politics* 20, no.4 (2004), 107.

310 C. A. Kupchan, "NATO's Final Frontier: Why Russia Should Join the Atlantic Alliance," *Foreign Affairs* 89, no. 3 (2010), 112.

311 S. Savranskaya and T. Blanton, *Gorbachev and Bush: The Last Superpower Summits* (Budapest: CEU Press, 2020), 159.

312 European Council, "15th EU-Russia Summit," *European Council*, 10 May 2005, 32.

space towards an EU-centric approach to energy security and infrastructure, which to some extent entailed decoupling from Russia.

In 2008, Moscow proposed constructing a new pan-European security architecture. It was opposed by Western states as it was feared it would weaken the primacy of NATO.[313] In 2010, Moscow proposed an EU-Russia Free Trade Zone to facilitate a Greater Europe from Lisbon to Vladivostok, which would provide mutual economic benefits and contribute to mitigating the zero-sum format of the European security architecture. However, all suggestions for a Helsinki-II agreement were ignored or criticised as a sinister ploy to divide the West.

Russia's effort to promote cooperation in multilateral formats coexisted with efforts to deter NATO unilateralism. Incrementalism or salami tactics could be countered by drawing red lines. The purpose of drawing red lines is to communicate vital security interests and severe consequences for breaching them, with a view to preventing the opponent from making a hazardous miscalculation. Deterrence rests on the three Cs: capability, credibility, and communication. Russia has built the capabilities to deter, demonstrated credibility in terms of its preparedness to use those capabilities, and aimed to communicate how it would react if NATO overstepped these red lines. However, the communication strategy is hampered by the security dilemma: the failure to give strict and sufficient warnings can embolden NATO to test Russian red lines, while excessive warnings of a fierce response will be interpreted as aggressive and thus incite NATO to counter the Russian threat. This reflects a wider dilemma in terms of how to respond to NATO expansion as a benign response will be interpreted by the West as consent and willingness to adjust to the new realities, while opposing NATO expansion will be construed as Russia rejecting democracy and becoming an enemy. Either way, NATO and its military infrastructure continue rolling towards Russian borders.

When Russia seized Crimea in the 2014 referendum, President Putin referred to the failure of the West to respect Russia's red lines and NATO's tendency to pretend to seek a peaceful resolution while presenting Russia with *fait accompli*. In Putin's words:

---

313 G. Diesen and S. Wood, "Russia's proposal for a new security system: confirming diverse perspectives," *Australian Journal of International Affairs* 66, no. 4 (2012): 450–67.

> They cheated us again and again, made decisions behind our back, presenting us with completed facts. That's the way it was with the expansion of NATO, in the east, with the deployment of military infrastructure at our borders. They always told us the same thing: "Well, this doesn't involve you."[314]

Conclusion

The expansionism of NATO was an important component of the new world order based on hegemony and liberal values. While NATO had been a source of stability during the Cold War as a defensive status-quo actor, post-Cold War NATO transformed itself into a revisionist actor by expanding and launching illegal wars of aggression. The ideological expectation of a pacifying effect of the inter-democratic community was confronted with the realities of power politics. Preserving and expanding the Cold War security architecture contributed to reviving the zero-sum logic that liberal hegemony endeavoured to transcend. Trust and arms agreements collapsed over 30 years due to the failure to reform the European security system. Irrespective of its intentions, NATO expansion destroyed the pan-European security architecture and revived the Cold War in Europe as widely predicted. As recognised by George Kennan and others, the decision to expand NATO was a momentous mistake. Russia's domestic and foreign policy, guided by the overarching objective of emulating and integrating with the West, had to be replaced with a strategy of balancing Western unilateralism.

The failure to reach a mutually acceptable post-Cold War order in Europe has wider implications for the world order. Russia was alienated from the West at a time when new centres of power emerged in the world and Moscow has systemic incentives to support efforts to create a post-Western world order. When Russia abandoned its ambitions for a Greater Europe, it was replaced by a Greater Eurasia. Translated into specific policies, Russia began to modernise a powerful army that faced the West, while its economic connectivity was gradually reoriented to the East. The universal ideals of liberal democracies in a

314 "Quotation of the Day for Wednesday, March 19, 2014," *The New York Times*, 19 March 2014.

divided Europe were increasingly rejected as they provided legitimacy for sovereign inequality and a rules-based international order that cemented Western exceptionalism.

7.

Ukraine as a Pawn in a Divided Europe: 1991–2014

THE FUTURE of the Western-centric world order largely depends on its ability to create a Europe without Russia. Positioning Ukraine within the orbit of the West is imperative to ensure that Russia can no longer be a European power and to limit Moscow's position in the post-Soviet space. Russia's history since the collapse of Kievan Rus has largely been a struggle to connect with reliable maritime transportation corridors as a requirement to fully participate in the international economy and to project military power. Evicting Russia from its Black Sea Fleet in Sevastopol and converting the Black Sea into a NATO lake would be a detrimental blow to Russia's standing as a great power.

In *The Grand Chessboard*, an influential book by former national security advisor Zbigniew Brzezinski about establishing a unipolar world order, the significance of Ukraine can hardly be overstated. Brzezinski argues that "Without Ukraine, Russia ceases to be a Eurasian empire," although "if Moscow regains control over Ukraine, with its 52 million people and major resources as well as its access to the Black Sea, Russia automatically again regains the wherewithal to become a powerful imperial state, spanning Europe and Asia."[315]

This chapter explores Ukraine as a divided state in a divided Europe. The domestic divisions within Ukraine have subsequently been exacerbated by NATO and Russia, which have backed competing political groups to position Ukraine within their respective

315 Brzezinski, Z.,. *The Grand Chessboard: American Primacy and its Geopolitical Imperatives* (New York: Basic Books, 1997), 46.

orbits. Heretofore, Russia was content with Ukraine remaining a neutral country as a bridge between Europe and Russia, as this harmonised with its aspirations of constructing a Greater Europe. In contrast, the West has insisted that Ukraine make a civilisational choice.

A Divided Ukraine

National identities are closely linked to the foundational myth of the original people, and the historical narrative of shared suffering and victories that defines "us" versus the "other."[316] Ukraine has been a divided state due to competing foundational myths and a lack of shared ideals, myths, traditions, symbols, and common historical memory that clearly defines "us" and "them."

The Russians, Ukrainians and Belarusians link their cultural ancestry to Kievan Rus as the foundation of their respective national identities. Kievan Rus was the first Eastern Slavic state that originated at the end of the ninth century with its capital in Kiev. The fragmentation of Kievan Rus in the mid-thirteenth century created three new centres of power that all aspired to be the political and cultural successor of Kievan Rus: Vladimir-Suzdal, Novgorod and Galicia-Volhynia. The Vladimir-Suzdal Principality eventually evolved into the Grand Duchy of Moscow, which accrued political and cultural power under Mongol occupation. The cultural and religious influence of Moscow further strengthened as it took over the seat of the Orthodox Church. This became even more meaningful after the fall of Constantinople. Moscow cemented its leadership by defeating and expelling the Mongols and then filled the power vacuum by bringing the various regions under a Moscow-led state. Thereafter, Russia and Ukraine continued to live for centuries under the same state.

Ukraine's close ties to Russia over the centuries have been a double-edged sword that created two competing identities and perspectives on relations with Russia. In eastern Ukraine, the shared history with Russia created a "fraternal bond" between Ukrainians and Russians to the extent that some even contest the purpose of having

316 S. Hall, "The question of cultural identity," in S. Hall, D. Held, D. Hubert, and K. Thompson (eds.), *Modernity: An Introduction to Modern Societies* (Wiley-Blackwell, 1996).

two separate states for one nation. However, in western Ukraine, the shared history with Russia is commonly seen as reflecting an imperial past that continues to dilute and undermine Ukrainian sovereignty and its distinctive Ukrainian identity. Aleksandr Solzhenitsyn rightly recognised that "It is useless to tell Ukrainians that we all descended, by birth and spiritually, from Kiev, and it is just as useless to expect Russians to recognise the fact that people beyond the Dnieper River are different."[317]

Broadly speaking, this history created two national identities in Ukraine that are, to a large extent, in direct opposition. The Eastern Slavic and the Ethno-cultural Ukrainian identities are constructed in opposition to each other in terms of defining "us" as the in-group and "them" as the out-group. The Eastern Slavic identity considers Ukrainians and Russians to be indigenous peoples of Ukraine, which results in the advocacy for a bi-ethnic, bicultural, and bilingual Ukraine. Here, the main opposition and threat to nation-building as defined under the Eastern Slavic identity is Ethnic-cultural nationalists who have created an artificial division between the two groups. In contrast, the Ethno-cultural Ukrainian identity considers Ukrainians to compromise a single native people and titular population, and nation-building therefore entails assimilating and uniting the population into one ethnic identity, one culture and one language.[318] The "other," or out-group, that is believed to be the principal threat to nation-building is therefore the Eastern Slavs who are believed to perpetuate the imperial legacy.

Only approximately 20 percent of the Ukrainian population are ethnic Russians, although the surveys from before 2014 revealed that the majority of Ukrainians subscribed to the Eastern Slavic identity.[319] Language unavoidably becomes a key aspect of nation-building. While the Ethno-cultural Ukrainians often consider it unacceptable that more than 80 percent of Ukrainians used Russian as the language

---

317 A. Solzhenitsyn, *"Ugodilo zernishko, promezh dvuh zhernovov"* ["The Grain Fallen Between two Millstones"], *Noviy Mir,* November 1998.

318 S. Shulman, "The contours of civic and ethnic national identification in Ukraine," *Europe-Asia Studies* 56, no. 1 (2004).

319 Ibid., 10.

of convenience, the Eastern Slavic Ukrainians reject being demoted to a national minority without equal language rights.[320]

The 1991 Declaration of Independence of Ukraine provides a narrative for distinctiveness and sovereignty by stipulating that Kievan Rus was the origin of a "thousand-year tradition of state-building in Ukraine," as opposed to merely being a secessionist part of Russia. The Ethno-cultural Ukrainians aim to monopolise the history of Kievan Rus as it is believed to be vital to sustain sovereignty. They fear that recognising Moscow as the successor state may delegitimise the distinctive history and identity of Ukraine, with an imperial historiography that assumes that bringing Ukraine and Belarus back under the control of the "big brother" is in fact restoring normality.[321] The shared origin of Kievan Rus can thus naturalise imperialism and even frame nation-building as suspending Ukrainian sovereignty.

Given this, the Ethno-cultural Ukrainians have a strong incentive to embrace a narrative of Russians being the successors of the Mongols' Golden Horde. The ethno-cultural Ukrainians are susceptible to the belief in a xenophobic portrayal of Russians as an uncivilised and barbaric Asiatic horde that is alien to both Ukraine and Europe.[322] The need to monopolise the history of Kievan Rus fuels an extremism that regards the relationship between Eastern Slavic Ukrainians and the Russian Federation as antagonistic. For the West, the Ethno-cultural Ukrainian group can be seen as an illiberal partner given its efforts to de-Russify Ukraine and thus create a Europe without Russia.

The Russian Empire and the Soviet Union

The contested narrative of Kievan Rus has produced conflicting interpretations of the history that followed. Did the alignment of Galicia-Volhynia with Poland and Lithuania represent a continuation of Kievan Rus, or was it Polish–Lithuanian expansionism that divided the peoples of Kievan Rus? Was the Treaty of Pereyaslav in 1654 between the Cossacks and the Tsar a Russian annexation of

320 Ibid.

321 T. Kuzio, "Historiography and national identity among the Eastern Slavs: towards a new framework," *National Identities* 3, no. 2 (2001): 115.

322 A. Lieven, *Russia and Ukraine: A Fraternal Rivalry* (Washington, D.C.: United States Institute of Peace Press, 1999), 13.

Ukraine, or was it a reunification of the fraternal peoples of Russia and Ukraine? Did the following three centuries of living in the same state constitute imperialism that Russified Ukraine, or did it become a common history of one people living together as one nation?

During the Second World War, Hitler established a partnership with Stepan Bandera and the fascist Organisation of Ukrainian Nationalists (OUN). Should Bandera and OUN be condemned as fascists who committed genocide against Jews, Poles and Russians, or were they freedom fighters? In Western Ukraine, there are groups who commemorate and mourn the 9th of May as a continuation of Russian domination, while in Eastern Ukraine the 9th of May is celebrated as the Soviet Union's victory day over the Nazis. Should Soviet history be celebrated for its achievements or condemned as Russian occupation? Post-Soviet Ukraine struggled to answer these questions as they were so divisive.

The dilemma arose insofar as a common historical narrative is imperative for nation-building, yet strategic ambiguity was necessary to prevent divisions and civil war. Case in point, the history of the Great Famine of 1932–1933, or Holodomor, resulted in millions of deaths. The famine killed Ukrainians, Russians, and other peoples of the Soviet Union, although the overwhelming majority of victims were Ukrainians. A pervasive narrative among the Ethno-cultural Ukrainians is that a deliberate Russian genocide of Ukrainians took place as part of a wider campaign to erase the Ukrainian nation. It has been suggested that Holodomor was instigated as part of a larger plot to destroy the Ukrainian intelligentsia, the Ukrainian Orthodox Autocephalous Church, Ukrainian culture, and the Ukrainian language.[323] For the Eastern Slavic Ukrainians, the narrative is unacceptable as it delegitimises them and their culture, religion, language and national identity, and saddles them with a legacy of genocide. The narrative of genocide manifests itself in societal and political hierarchy. It divides society into victims and perpetrators, which enables the former to use this historical construct to extract political concession in perpetuity as reparations and amends can never come to an

323 R. Lemkin, "Soviet genocide in the Ukraine," in L. Y. Luciuk (ed.), *Holodomor: Reflections on the Great Famine of 1932–1933 in Soviet Ukraine* (Kingston, The Kashtan Press, 2008), 164.

end.[324] In 1993, Posen cautioned that nationalist narratives depicting the Holodomor as a genocide could spark a civil war in Ukraine and possibly a war with Russia:

> If Ukraine begins to blame the famine on Russians, this could be quite dangerous politically. If, instead, the famine continues to be blamed on a Communist Party headed by a renegade Georgian psychopath, then this experience will cause less trouble.[325]

However, the delegitimization of the Soviet Union by the Ethno-cultural Ukrainians can, ironically, also delegitimise the borders of Ukraine and open the doors for secessionism and Russian annexations. The Soviet Union created the contemporary borders of Ukraine by adding vast regions of the Russian Empire to the administrative domain of Ukraine. The eastern and southern regions of Ukraine from Kharkov to Odessa were part of the Russian Empire. Crimea was added to Ukraine even later as Khrushchev altered the administrative borders of Crimea to transfer the peninsula from the Russian Republic to the Ukrainian Republic of the Soviet Union in 1954 to celebrate the 300th anniversary of the Treaty of Pereyaslav that reunited the Russian and Ukrainian peoples. When Russia annexed Crimea in 2014, Putin brought up the history of Ukraine to justify the reunification with Crimea but also to deliver a warning about the wider region that was transferred to Ukraine:

> After the revolution, the Bolsheviks, for a number of reasons—may God judge them—added large sections of the historical South of Russia to the Republic of Ukraine. This was done with no consideration for the ethnic makeup of the population, and today these areas form the southeast of Ukraine. Then, in 1954, a decision was made to transfer the Crimean region to Ukraine, along with Sevastopol, despite the fact that it was a city of union subordination. This was

---

324 E. Herman and D. Peterson, *The Politics of Genocide* (New York: University Press, 2010).

325 B. R. Posen, "The Security Dilemma and Ethnic Conflict," *Survival* 35, no. 1 (1993): 39.

the personal initiative of the Communist Party head Nikita Khrushchev.[326]

While Ukraine has been a deeply divided country, the political leadership has found some common ground in terms of preserving state sovereignty and territorial borders. Towards this end, the challenge for Ukraine was to develop a distinctive national identity from Russia but avoid the proclivity for an anti-Russian identity. Similarly, Ukraine had to diversify its economic connectivity to avoid excessive economic dependence on either the West or Russia as this would make it untenable to manage the internal divisions in Ukraine.

Ukraine as Pawn in Great Power Politics

The ability of Ukraine to manage its internal divisions has been undermined by foreign powers exploiting the internal divisions in Ukraine. In the second half of the 19th century, Dostoyevsky argued that the English divide-and-rule policy to preserve a balance of power on the continent relied on promoting ethnic hatred to contain Russia: "England needs the Eastern Slavs to hate us with all the strength of the hatred she herself bears towards us."[327]

When Germany defeated Russia in the First World War, Germany depicted the Brest-Litovsk Treaty of March 1918 as a German liberation of Eastern European territories from Russia. Although, liberation meant transferring control over these territories to Germany. The Brest-Litovsk Treaty was the first instance where an independent Ukrainian state emerged, although the Bolshevik revolution resulted in the reabsorption of Ukraine under Moscow's sovereignty into the Soviet Union.

After recovering from its defeat, Germany began to renew its efforts in the 1930s to assert influence over Eastern Europe. Nazi Germany, to a great extent, legitimised its expansion under the banner of freedom by yet again positioning itself as the champion of

326 V. Putin, "Address by President of the Russian Federation," *President of Russia*, 18 March 2014.

327 F. Dostoevsky, *A Writer's Diary, Volume 2: 1877–1881* (Illinois: Northwestern University Press, 1997), 898.

Ukrainian independence.[328] Nazi Germany cultivated allies in Ukraine by appealing to the ethno-cultural nationalists in Ukraine with the promise of freedom and independence. A German radio station in Vienna began to broadcast fascist messages into Ukraine in 1938 to instigate racial hatred and anti-Russian nationalism. Hitler then formed a common cause and a partnership with Ukrainian fascists such as Stepan Bandera as the leader of the Organisation of Ukrainian Nationalists (OUN) after 1933.[329]

After the Second World War, the U.S. immediately began to develop relations with anti-communist groups and anti-Russian groups. With the disappearance of Nazi Germany as the dominant threat, the Soviet Union became the next power to be contained and defeated. Supporting fascist groups was a means to this end. At the beginning of the war in 1941, future President Harry Truman, then a Senator, had outlined an American pragmatism that would also define his presidency: "If we see that Germany is winning the war, we ought to help Russia; and if Russia is winning, we ought to help Germany, and in that way let them kill as many as possible."[330] The British similarly developed "Operation Unthinkable" in 1945, a military plan devised by Prime Minister Winston Churchill that outlined a surprise attack on the Soviet Union on 22 May 1945, shortly after Nazi Germany had been defeated. The plan envisioned the UK and U.S. along with re-armed German forces penetrating deep into the Soviet Union and occupying strategic territory in a repeat of what Nazi Germany had attempted in 1942.[331]

Washington considered Ukrainian Ethno-nationalists and fascists to be useful partners due to their uncompromising anti-Russian and anti-communist views. Declassified U.S. archives and Soviet secret police files confirm that the U.S. began to develop cooperation with Bandera and the OUN immediately after the defeat of Nazi

---

328 I. Kamenetsky, *Hitler's Occupation of Ukraine (1941–1944)* (Wisconsin: The Marquette University Press, 1956), 9.

329 R. Bellant, *Old Nazis, the New Right, and the Republican Party* (Boston: South End Press, 1991).

330 A. Whitman, "Harry S. Truman: Decisive President," *The New York Times*, 27 December 1972.

331 U.K. Government, "Operation Unthinkable: Report by the Joint Planning Staff," Catalogue ref: CAB 120/691 (Kew, Richmond: The National Archives, 1945).

Germany.[332] Such CIA operations were consistent with other U.S. clandestine "stay-behind operations" after the Second World War. Under "Operation Gladio," which lasted until 1990, NATO in conjunction with the CIA conducted false-flag terrorist attacks against its own populations that were blamed on the Red Brigades.[333] In 1990, the European Parliament demanded the end to CIA and NATO terrorism within Western Europe, and called for dismantling the Gladio organisation:

> whereas for over 40 years this organization has eluded all democratic controls and has been run by the secret services of the states concerned in collaboration with NATO… whereas in certain Member States military secret services (or uncontrolled branches thereof) were involved in serious cases of terrorism and crime as evidenced by various judicial inquiries.[334]

Supporting ethnic nationalism in the Soviet Union and Yugoslavia was instrumental in undermining the supranational authority of the communist states and thus weakening key adversaries.[335] Hitler's chief of the Wehrmacht's military intelligence on the eastern front, Reinhard Gehlen, was thereafter hired by the CIA (OSS) to run American Intelligence in Europe. Gehlen brought the immense Nazi spy network into the American fold. The Gehlen Organisation established close cooperation with Ukrainian nationalists and fascists for intelligence gathering, undermining social cohesion, and for propaganda purposes through Radio Free Europe. Notably, Hitler's Chief of Staff, Adolf Heusinger, became the Chairman of the NATO Military Committee in 1961–1964.

---

332 J. Burds, "The Early Cold War in Soviet West Ukraine, 1944–1948," *The Carl Beck Papers in Russian & East European Studies*, no. 1505 (2001): 12.

333 D. Ganser, *NATO's Secret Armies: Operation Gladio and Terrorism in Western Europe* (New York: Routledge, 2005).

334 EurLex, "Journal of the European Community 1990. Minutes of proceedings of the sitting of Thursday 22 November 1990," *European Union EurLex official website*, no. C 324/186.

335 G. W. Lapidus, *Ethnonationalism and Political Stability in the USSR*, National Council for Soviet and East European Research, Council Contract Number 627–3 (1984).

A Divided Ukraine in a Divided Post-Cold War Europe

After the Cold War, the fate of Ukraine largely depended on the will and ability to mitigate its internal divisions with a collective pan-European security architecture. In a divided Europe, the opposing sides would predictably pull Ukraine in opposite directions and thus exacerbate the international divisions. The decision of the West to pursue a unipolar world order, and thus collective hegemony in Europe, resulted in "European integration" becoming a zero-sum geopolitical project in which the states between the West and Russia would have to make a civilisational choice. Redividing Europe would unavoidably result in the great powers fighting proxy conflicts within the deeply divided societies in Moldova, Georgia and Ukraine.

The West's effort to construct a Europe without Russia resulted in a natural alliance with Ethno-cultural Ukrainians, while Russian efforts to preserve its influence in Ukraine resulted in alignment with the Eastern Slavic Ukrainians. Henry Kissinger cautioned that the internal divisions in Ukraine should not be aggravated by zero-sum geopolitics:

> Far too often the Ukrainian issue is posed as a showdown: whether Ukraine joins the East or the West. But if Ukraine is to survive and thrive, it must not be either side's outpost against the other—it should function as a bridge between them… The west is largely Catholic; the east largely Russian Orthodox. The west speaks Ukrainian; the east speaks mostly Russian. Any attempt by one wing of Ukraine to dominate the other—as has been the pattern—would lead eventually to civil war or break up. To treat Ukraine as part of an East-West confrontation would scuttle for decades any prospect to bring Russia and the West—especially Russia and Europe—into a cooperative international system.[336]

The legacy of the Brest-Litovsk Treaty was revived as the West aimed to "liberate" Ukraine from Russian influence by having Kiev

336 H. Kissinger, "How the Ukraine crisis ends," *The Washington Post*, 5 March 2014.

align itself with NATO and the EU. Ideology tends to mute the West's security dilemma sensibility as zero-sum bloc politics is interpreted as confirming the "European perspective," pursuing the "European choice," or embracing "shared values." In terms of power politics, liberation meant that Western institutions would expand and replace Russian influence.

The ideological argument for pursuing European integration through NATO and the EU proposed that exclusive inter-democratic security institutions could develop a more sustainable peace.[337] Yet, developing a democratic Europe without Russia is problematic as these two objectives are contradictory. The West supported or remained silent concerning de-Russification policies in the former Soviet republics as a component of "European integration." The EU and NATO indirectly supported the denial of basic citizenship rights such as voting to Russian speakers in Estonia and Latvia.[338] Their version of nation-building that entails de-Russifying Ukrainian society by eliminating the Russian language and culture aligns with the West's larger effort to establish a Europe without Russia. The former Soviet Republics aspiring for closer cooperation with the West signalled their return to Europe by denouncing their shared history with Russia as Russian imperialism and commemorating "Soviet Occupation Day" and establishing museums of "Soviet occupation." In Moldova, the de-Russification policies discriminating against Russian and pro-Russian minorities contributed to the early 1990s conflict with and de facto secession of Transnistria. The liberal hegemonic world order thus exacerbates rather than resolves these conflicts, as conflict resolution is not consistent with the objective of constructing a Europe without Russia.

The narrative of the integration process of former Warsaw Pact countries has artificially been applied to Ukraine. Countries like Poland are profoundly hostile to Moscow for good reason as the Cold

---

337 G. Diesen, G., *EU and NATO relations with Russia: After the Collapse of the Soviet Union* (London: Routledge, 2015).

338 Recognition of Russian speakers as citizens of Estonia and Latvia was not a condition for closing the OSCE mission or obtaining EU membership; EU referendums were accepted without the participation of "non-citizens"; and the European Parliament grants Latvia and Estonia voting power for citizens that are not recognised; the EU has not mitigated the situation by for example recognising Russian as an official language.

War alliance was experienced as an occupation and an era of limited sovereignty. Poland and other Central and Eastern European countries were therefore in a rush to join the EU and NATO. There was no desire for a "Common European Home"—rather they wanted further distance from Moscow by being on the other side of new dividing lines. The desire to join an exclusive Europe organised by NATO and the EU provided Washington and Brussels with the power to demand democratic reforms as a condition for membership.

However, Ukraine is not Poland. Ukraine was not looking for a saviour to liberate it from the imperial clutches of Moscow. Between 1991 and 2014, the majority of Ukrainians had very favourable views of Russia and negative views of NATO. Socialising Ukraine towards NATO incentivised the instigating of conflicts between Russia and Ukraine. As precedent, when Bismarck provoked or a least exploited the French attack in 1870, the German states unified as war tends to consolidate the definition of "us" and "them."

Yet, Washington still struggled to bring Ukraine into its orbit by expanding NATO due to Ukrainians' reluctance and the Western Europeans' apprehensions about instigating a civil war and provoking a Russian invasion. In the 1990s, President Kuchma framed Ukraine's policy towards the West as aspiring for a common "return to Europe with Russia."[339] The policy rejected the civilisational choice between East and West. Strengthening ties with Europe would enable Ukraine to diversify its partnerships to avoid excessive dependence on Russia which could undermine state sovereignty. Furthermore, the common return with Russia also prevented the development of new dividing lines between Ukraine and Russia that could trigger a civil war and a conflict with Russia. Correspondingly, a Russian return to Europe with Ukraine was consistent with Russia's objective of constructing a Greater Europe based on Gorbachev's "Common European Home."

---

339 T. Kuzio, "Neither East nor West: Ukraine's security policy under Kuchma," *Problems of Post-Communism* 52, no. 5 (2005): 65.

The Orange Revolution of 2004

The Western support for Ukraine's Orange Revolution in 2004 resulted in the installation of Yushchenko as president, who represented the hostile anti-Russian sentiments of Ethno-cultural nationalists in Western Ukraine. Popular demands for democratic reforms and tackling corruption were hijacked by international NGOs that were largely funded by the U.S. government. Thereafter, the protests took on a strong anti-Russian dimension and linked the regime change to advocacy for NATO and EU membership.[340]

The U.S. developed a template for revolutions across the post-Soviet space and branded them as "democratic revolutions."[341] Leading these regime change operations were NED, Freedom House, USAID and other government-funded NGOs that were staffed by people linked to U.S. intelligence. Case in point, James Woolsey, a former CIA Director and former head of Freedom House, explained that Freedom House contributed to "help bring about a movement toward democracy in Ukraine" during the Orange Revolution.[342]

The *Guardian* recognised that the U.S. was behind the chaos in Ukraine and referred to the Orange Revolution in 2004 as "an American creation, a sophisticated and brilliantly conceived exercise in western branding and mass marketing" for the purpose of "winning other people's elections."[343] Another article by the *Guardian* labelled the Orange Revolution as a "postmodern coup d'état" and a "CIA-sponsored third world uprising of cold war days, adapted to post-Soviet conditions."[344] Although, the EU also had a role in interfering in Ukraine's domestic affairs to ensure a pro-West/anti-Russian government would take power. As Yushchenko became president, he

340 D. Lane, "The Orange Revolution: 'People's Revolution' or Revolutionary Coup?," *The British Journal of Politics and International Relations* 10, no. 4 (2008).

341 G. Sussman, *Branding Democracy: U.S. Regime Change in Post-Soviet Eastern Europe* (New York: Peter Lang, 2010).

342 J. Woolsey, "World: James Woolsey, Former CIA Director, Speaks To RFE/RL At Forum 2000," *RFE/RE*, 10 October 2005.

343 I. Traynor, "U.S. campaign behind the turmoil in Kiev," *The Guardian*, 26 November 2004.

344 J. Steele, "Ukraine's postmodern coup d'état," *The Guardian*, 26 November 2004.

named the European Parliament the "godparents" of the new Ukraine due to its strong support of the Orange Revolution.[345]

After 2004, Ukraine began to drift towards conflict with Russia as the government diligently pursued NATO membership against the will of the vast majority of Ukrainians. In 2005 the French presidential advisor, Maurice Gourdault-Montagne, recognised that Ukraine had become the main risk for a possible war in Europe. According to Gourdault-Montagne, pushing NATO expansion to Ukraine was creating serious security concerns in Moscow.[346]

Bringing Ukraine into the Western orbit would endow Washington with influence over pipelines that carried 80 percent of gas transiting from Russia to Europe and diminish Russia's presence in the Black Sea by ending its lease of Sevastopol. The disruption to the energy connectivity between Europe and Russia became a key source of conflict. Russia began to pressure and punish the new authorities in Kiev by ending subsidies of energy supplies and forcing Ukraine to pay market prices. When Kiev responded by siphoning gas transited from Russia to Europe, the Russians cut supplies. The myth of the Russian "energy weapon" was thus born.

The April 2008 Promise of NATO Membership

The U.S. pursued NATO expansion, seeking to institutionalise and cement Ukraine's position within the Western orbit before Yushchenko could be voted out of office. At the NATO Bucharest Summit in April 2008, the military alliance promised future membership to both Georgia and Ukraine. The NATO Summit Declaration affirmed that "We agreed today that these countries [Ukraine and Georgia] will become members of NATO."[347] The U.S. was eager to offer Ukraine a Membership Action Plan (MAP) as the first step to entry. Germany and France led the opposition against this step as it

345 V. Yushchenko, "Viktor Yushchenko: Ukraine's future is in the EU—Address by President of Ukraine to the European Parliament," EP05-022EN, European Parliament, 23 February 2005.

346 "Eur A/S Fried's September 1 meetings with senior MFA and Presidency officials on improving relations with Europe," *Wikileaks*, 9 September 2005.

347 NATO, "Bucharest Summit Declaration, Issued by the Heads of State and Government participating in the meeting of the North Atlantic Council in Bucharest," NATO, 3 April 2008.

was deemed to be too provocative. As a compromise, NATO offered future membership without any specific path.

The opposition to NATO within Ukrainian society was immense, yet Washington still had a friendly Ukrainian government in power in 2008. A Gallup poll in May 2008 exposed the fact that 43 percent of Ukrainians considered NATO a threat to Ukraine and merely 15 percent associated NATO with protection.[348] A 2008 Gallup poll prior to the NATO Summit had revealed that Ukrainians favoured ties with Russia rather than with the U.S. Forty-six percent of Ukrainians answered it was more important to have close relations with Russia, while only 10 percent of Ukrainians supported close relations with the U.S. over Russia.[349] Most of all, Ukrainians did not want to make a civilisational choice.

In late March 2008, one week before the NATO Summit in Bucharest where Ukraine was promised future membership, Tony Blair explained his thoughts about how to manage relations with Russia in a meeting with American political leaders. A leaked American cable revealed the following views about how to manage Russia:

> "The problem with managing Putin and Russia," said Blair, "is that we have to deal with them when it comes to Iran." The rest of the strategy, he said, should be to make Russia a "little desperate" with our activities in areas bordering on what Russia considers its sphere of interest and along its actual borders. Russia had to be shown firmness and sown with seeds of confusion.[350]

The U.S. and European leadership recognised that pulling Ukraine into NATO would likely spark a civil war and lead to a war with Russia. In February 2008, prior to the April 2008 Bucharest NATO summit, the then U.S. ambassador to Moscow, William Burns, who later became the director of the CIA, warned in a memo that

---

348 J. Ray and N. Esipova, "Ukrainians Likely Support Move Away From NATO," *Gallup*, 2 April 2010.

349 C. English, "Ukrainians See More Value in Ties With Russia Than U.S.," *Gallup*, 15 February 2008.

350 Telegraph, "Tony Blair and John McCain talk about Israel/Palestine and Russia handling," *The Telegraph*, 27 March 2008.

threatening NATO expansion could provoke a Russian military intervention:

> Not only does Russia perceive encirclement, and efforts to undermine Russia's influence in the region, but it also fears unpredictable and uncontrolled consequences which would seriously affect Russian security interests... Russia is particularly worried that the strong divisions in Ukraine over NATO membership, with much of the ethnic-Russian community against membership, could lead to a major split, involving violence or at worst, civil war. In that eventuality, Russia would have to decide whether to intervene; a decision Russia does not want to have to face.[351]

Burns also warned that pulling Ukraine into NATO was considered a threat by the entire Russian political spectrum, and that threatening NATO expansion would be met with a fierce response from Moscow:

> Ukrainian entry into NATO is the brightest of all redlines for the Russian elite (not just Putin). In more than two and a half years of conversations with key Russian players, from knuckle draggers in the dark recesses of the Kremlin to Putin's sharpest liberal critics I have yet to find anyone who views Ukraine in NATO as anything other than a direct challenge to Russian interests. NATO would be seen as throwing down the strategic gauntlet. Today's Russia will respond. Russian-Ukrainian relations will go into a deep freeze. It will create fertile soil for Russian meddling in Crimea and Eastern Ukraine.[352]

The former British ambassador to Russia, Roderic Lyne, shared the concerns of his American counterpart:

---

351 W. J. Burns, "Nyet means nyet: Russia's NATO Enlargement Redlines," *Wikileaks*, 1 February 2008.

352 W. J. Burns, *The Back Channel: A Memoir of American Diplomacy and the Case for Its Renewal* (New York: Random House, 2019), 233.

> And then we arrive to the 2008 Bucharest summit of NATO, which was a massive mistake on the Western side trying to push Georgia and Ukraine into NATO. It was stupid on every level at that time. If you want to start a war with Russia, that's the best way of doing it. Moreover, any poll in Ukraine showed that two thirds of the Ukrainian public did not want NATO membership.[353]

Jaap de Hoop Scheffer, NATO's Secretary General in 2008, recognised that NATO should have respected Russia's red lines and should therefore not have pledged membership to Ukraine and Georgia in 2008. Scheffer recalled how Germany and France resisted offering membership. President Bush's Secretary of State Condoleezza Rice and his Secretary of Defence Robert Gates were also not enthusiastic about the idea. Nonetheless, Bush was the Commander in Chief and the U.S. pushed through NATO's promise of future membership which angered Russia immensely. In retrospect, De Hoop Scheffer admitted that Putin became more aggressive in response to the proposed NATO expansion.[354] Years later, former U.S. Secretary of Defence and CIA Director Robert Gates, recalled the mistake of the Bucharest Summit in his memoirs:

> When Russia was weak in the 1990s and beyond, we did not take Russian interests seriously. We did a poor job of seeing the world from their point of view, and of managing the relationship for the long term.... The relationship with Russia had been badly mismanaged after Bush 41 left office in 1993. Getting Gorbachev to acquiesce to a unified Germany as a member of NATO had been a huge accomplishment. But moving so quickly after the collapse of the Soviet Union to incorporate so many of its formerly subjugated

353 R. Lyne, "The UC Interview Series: Sir Roderic Lyne by Nikita Gryazin," *Oxford University Consortium*, 18 December 2020.

354 G. J. Dennekamp, "De Hoop Scheffer: Poetin werd radicaler door NAVO" [De Hoop Scheffer: Putin became more radical because of NATO], *NOS*, 7 January 2018.

> states into NATO was a mistake.... Trying to bring Georgia and Ukraine into NATO was truly overreaching.[355]

Fiona Hill, a former official at the U.S. National Security Council and a leading anti-Russian hawk in Washington, recognised that Moscow had put Europe and the world on notice in 2007 when Putin made it clear in Munich that further NATO expansion would not be tolerated. Hill was a national intelligence officer in 2008 and recalls that she warned Bush that "Putin would view steps to bring Ukraine and Georgia closer to NATO as a provocative move that would likely provoke pre-emptive Russian military action. But ultimately, our warnings weren't heeded."[356]

Germany had been reluctant to push NATO expansion for similar reasons. A Wikileaks cable from June 2008 revealed the German government's motivations for opposing a Membership Action Plan (MAP) for Ukraine. The Germans presented three key reasons: "1) overall low public support for NATO membership, 2) a deep divide between the eastern and western parts of the country on this question, and 3) a weak government with a small majority in the Rada." The Germans subsequently believed that pushing NATO expansionism too quickly could "break up the country."[357]

German Chancellor, Angela Merkel, explained that she had opposed offering Ukraine the MAP as it would have been interpreted by Moscow as "a declaration of war."[358] However, Merkel's solution was not to try to cement Ukraine's neutrality. In 2022, she rather argued that Ukraine was weak in 2008 and would have been overrun by Russia, thus the incremental militarisation of Ukraine was required.[359] However, offering future membership and pursuing a strategy of gradually making Ukraine a de facto member of NATO

---

355 R. M. Gates, *Duty: Memoirs of a Secretary at War* (New York: Knopf Doubleday Publishing Group, 2014).

356 F. Hill, "Putin Has the U.S. Right Where He Wants It," *The New York Times*, 24 January 2022.

357 "Germany/Russia: Chancellery views on MAP for Ukraine and Georgia," *Wikileaks*, 6 June 2008.

358 A. Walsh, "Angela Merkel opens up on Ukraine, Putin and her legacy," *Deutsche Welle*, 7 June 2022.

359 A. Osang, "You're Done with Power Politics," *Spiegel*, 1 December 2022.

painted a target on Ukraine as Russia would face an existential threat unless it responded to NATO's plans for Ukraine.

One of the key interests for Russia to defend was evidently its Black Sea Fleet located in Sevastopol, Crimea. Former Russian Prime Minister Primakov informed U.S. Ambassador Burns that the threat of NATO offering a MAP to Ukraine was creating an earthquake in Russia. Primakov told Burns that he was scheduled to appear in a TV debate that would question whether Russia should reconsider Crimea's status as Ukrainian territory. Pointing to such dangerous developments, Primakov warned Burns that "this is the kind of discussion that MAP produces."[360]

The importance of a neutral or pro-Russian Ukraine to Russian security can hardly be overstated and it was common knowledge to Western leaders. John Scarlett, the Former British Chief of the Secret Intelligence Service (MI6), wrote that Putin may pray for mountains in Ukraine as a buffer against the West:

> Vladimir Putin says he is a religious man, a great supporter of the Russian Orthodox Church. If so, he may well go to bed each night, say his prayers, and ask God: "Why didn't you put some mountains in Ukraine?" If God had built mountains in Ukraine, then the great expanse of flatland that is the North European Plain would not be such encouraging territory from which to attack Russia repeatedly. As it is, Putin has no choice: he must at least attempt to control the flatlands to the west.[361]

The Return to Neutrality in 2010 followed by the Maidan Coup in 2014

Yushchenko's policies were deeply unpopular as Ukrainians rejected the attempts to join NATO and the mere economic downturn from moving away from Russia. Ukraine's greatest economic growth had occurred before 2004 as most of Ukraine's exports went to Russia and the CIS countries. Yushchenko was punished once the

---

360 "Russia-Ukraine: NATO and Holodomor," *Wikileaks*, 3 April 2008.

361 J. Scarlett, "Introduction," in T. Marshall, *Prisoners of Geography: Ten Maps that Explain Everything about the World* (London: Elliott & Thompson, 2016), 1.

Ukrainians could vote. At the end of Yushchenko's term, *Newsweek* labelled Yushchenko the world's most unpopular leader with a 2.7 percent approval rating.[362] The Russia-friendly Viktor Yanukovich subsequently won the presidential election in 2010, which the OSCE confirmed was a free and fair election.[363]

In June 2010, President Yanukovich approved a bill that cemented Ukraine's neutrality and thus prevented the country from joining NATO. This could be considered a return to neutrality and was consistent with Ukraine's constitution of 1 July 1990, which stipulated that Ukraine has the "intention of becoming a permanently neutral state that does not participate in military blocs." Furthermore, Yanukovich also signed an agreement with Russia in April 2010 to extend the lease for Russia's Black Sea Fleet for another 25 years as the lease was due to expire in 2017.

In 2011, even NATO admitted that it had lost significant influence in "post-Orange" Ukraine as both the government and the people opposed NATO accession: "The greatest challenge for Ukrainian-NATO relations lies in the perception of NATO among the Ukrainian people. NATO membership is not widely supported in the country, with some polls suggesting that popular support of it is less than 20%."[364] The solution would be to support a coup in February 2014, with a view to enabling NATO to permanently sever Ukraine from Russia.

The government of Yanukovich aimed to further strengthen Ukraine's economic position. The strategy of Yanukovich was to play off the EU and Russia against each other to get the optimal position wherein Ukraine could keep its access to the Russian market, yet also open greater access to the EU market. By diversifying its economic dependencies, Ukraine would also have enhanced its political autonomy. But the EU had no intentions of allowing Ukraine to maintain its economic and political connectivity with Russia. During negotiations,

---

362 O. Matthews, "Viktor Yushchenko's Star Has Fallen," *Newsweek*, 13 March 2009.

363 P. P. Pan, "International observers say the Ukrainian election was free and fair," *OSCE*, 9 February 2010.

364 NATO, "'Post-Orange Ukraine': Internal dynamics and foreign policy priorities," *NATO Parliamentary Assembly* (October 2011): 11.

the EU offered limited economic opportunities to Ukraine, yet outlined political conditionalities that could undermine relations with Russia.

The EU initiated pressure on Ukraine to abandon its neutral status, offering the Deep and Comprehensive Free Trade Area (DCFTA) to Ukraine and other former Soviet Republics in November 2013 which effectively was an ultimatum to choose either the West or Russia. The proposed agreement itself violated the earlier Common Spaces Agreement between the EU and Russia that had committed both sides to harmonise integration initiatives towards the shared neighbourhood. Once Ukraine failed to choose the West, the U.S. played the leading role in toppling the government and installing a government of its choosing.

The political media establishment framed the EU's Association Agreement as a mere trade agreement preoccupied with topics such as student exchanges, as opposed to being a zero-sum geopolitical project. The agreement pursued the objective of exclusive influence in Ukraine by reorganising and shifting its economy and security from Russia to the West. It would have committed Ukraine to "gradual convergence in the area of foreign and security policy, including the Common Security and Defence Policy."[365] The agreement would disrupt Ukraine-Russian security cooperation and was likely intended as a stepping-stone to NATO membership. The objective was to pull Ukraine into the Western sphere of influence, and the EU subsequently rejected any multilateral alternatives.

Ukrainians were deeply divided on the civilisational choice between the West and Russia as Ukrainians in the West favoured the EU, while Ukrainians in the East and South preferred the Russian-led Eurasian Customs Union.[366] Ukraine and Russia proposed to replace the zero-sum Association Agreement with a trilateral EU-Ukraine-Russia agreement that would allow Ukraine to function as a bridge rather than as a Western bastion against Russia. EU Commission President Barroso rejected the idea as unacceptable: "When we make a bilateral deal, we don't need a trilateral agreement," and compared multilateralism that accommodates Russian influence with

365 European Union, "EU-Ukraine Association Agreement—the complete texts," European External Action Service, 2013.

366 "Poll: Ukrainian public split over EU, Customs Union options," *Kyiv Post*, 26 November 2013.

imperialism by asserting: "the times for limited sovereignty are over in Europe."[367] EU officials and representatives referred to the Association Agreement with Ukraine as a "civilizational choice" between the West and Russia.[368]

The EU-Ukrainian agreement was not compatible with the Russian-led Eurasian Economic Union. Without Ukraine, the Eurasian Economic Union would have been a decidedly Asian project that left Russia without much influence in Europe. Sowing divisions between Russia and Ukraine was therefore critical for the construction of a Europe without Russia. U.S. Secretary of State Hillary Clinton had announced the previous year that Washington was determined to undermine the development of the Eurasian Economic Union: "We are trying to figure out effective ways to slow down or prevent it."[369] A few months prior to the coup in February 2014, Carl Gershman, the president of the National Endowment for Democracy, argued that "Ukraine is the biggest prize" as it could also be a bridgehead to destabilise Russia: "Putin may find himself on the losing end not just in the near abroad but within Russia itself."[370]

Russia countered the EU with a combination of economic pressure and the offer of a large loan to Ukraine. The EU's ultimatum to Ukraine backfired as Kiev decided to reject the Association Agreement and instead chose Russia as its most important neighbour.[371] The EU and the U.S. responded by challenging the legitimacy of the government and rallying the Ukrainian public against the "Yanukovich regime." Donald Tusk, the Polish Prime Minister who would later become the President of the European Council, called for the EU to channel three million Euros to "the development of citizens' movements" to oppose President Yanukovich.[372] The European MP and former prime minis-

---

367 A. Marszal, "EU will not accept Russian veto, says Barroso," *The Telegraph*, 29 November 2013.

368 J. Sherr, "Ukraine and Europe: Final Decision?" *Russia and Eurasia*, Chatham House Programme Paper 2013/05 (July 2013): 2–3.

369 C. Clover, "Clinton vows to thwart new Soviet Union," *Financial Times*, 7 December 2012.

370 C. Gerschman, "Former Soviet states stand up to Russia. Will the U.S.?," *Washington Post*, 26 September 2013.

371 N. N, Petro, "How the E.U. Pushed Ukraine East," *The New York Times*, 3 December 2013.

372 A. Rettman, "EU chairman blames Yanukovych for 'destabilising' Ukraine," *EU Observer*, 27 January 2014.

ter of Belgium, Guy Verhofstadt stood on a stage on Maidan Square and outlined how the EU would support the protesters against their government:

> Today the European Union finally decided to put a decisive step and to start with sanctions against the regime in Ukraine… What we are gonna do is that every week a new delegation of the European Union and the European parties and the European parliament shall come on this place until you have won your fight.[373]

Yet, it was the U.S. that became the decisive force in the coup. Victoria Nuland, U.S. Assistant Secretary of State for European and Eurasian affairs, revealed in December 2013 as the riots in Kiev were ongoing, that the U.S. had invested more than $5 billion since 1991 to assist Ukraine in achieving "the future it deserves."[374] The U.S. officially claimed it was working with all sides to reach a peaceful solution, although a leaked phone call between Victoria Nuland and Geoffrey Pyatt, the U.S. Ambassador to Ukraine exposed how the U.S. was planning the coup and hand-picking the successor government. The phone call, leaked two weeks before the coup, discussed making Arseny Yatsenyuk the Prime Minister and other details of the makeup of the future post-coup government. Nuland also outlined how the UN could be used to legitimise the process and "glue this thing together."[375] Carpenter referred to the U.S. meddling as "breathtaking" as Nuland and Pyatt were caught deciding who should be in the new Ukrainian government and who should be kept out, at a time when Yanukovich was still the lawful president of Ukraine.[376]

All the violence on the Maidan was attributed to the government despite the overt presence of far-right groups with fascist symbols.

---

373 Glenn Diesen, "MEP Guy Verhofstadt on Maidan, promising EU support and sanctions 'until you have won your fight'," 20 February 2014, video posted 23 October 2023, 4:37, https://www.youtube.com/watch?v=rmAU5QRK4i8&t=1s .

374 J. J. Mearsheimer, "Why the Ukraine crisis is the West's fault: The liberal delusions that provoked Putin," *Foreign Affairs* 93, no. 5 (2014): 80.

375 "Ukraine crisis: Transcript of leaked Nuland-Pyatt call," *BBC*, 7 February 2014.

376 T. G. Carpenter, "America's Ukraine Hypocrisy," CATO Institute, 6 August 2017.

The West immediately used the killing of protesters on the Maidan by snipers to mount more pressure on the Ukrainian government and demand that Yanukovich step down. However, the majority of wounded protesters testified that they were shot from buildings controlled by the opposition, corroborating evidence of the direction of the shots. The trial that followed also revealed that several protesters were shot even before the special Berkut police unit was deployed.[377]

Shortly after the killings, the EU was seemingly aware that there was evidence pointing toward the Maidan opposition. A leaked phone call between the EU foreign affairs chief Catherine Ashton and Estonian foreign minister Urmas Paet exposed that the EU leadership knew or suspected that the new post-coup leadership in Kiev had ordered the shooting as a provocation. Paet stated that "there is a stronger and stronger understanding that behind snipers it was not Yanukovych, it was somebody from the new coalition."[378] Killing people from both sides was seemingly an initiative to deliberately escalate tensions and make a political settlement more difficult to achieve.

Kiev ultimately agreed to an EU-brokered compromise for a national unity government on 21 February 2014, with European powers signing on as guarantors of the agreement. However, the Western-backed opposition toppled Yanukovich shortly thereafter. Instead of honouring the agreement as guarantors, the Europeans sent their top officials to Kiev to boost the legitimacy of those who seized power in the coup.[379] Less than a day after the coup, Washington formally recognised them as the new authorities in Kiev.

The West made great efforts to brand the coup as a legitimate "democratic revolution," although it became a difficult narrative to sell. Yanukovich had been elected in what the OSCE had recognised to be a free and fair election, and there was no evidence that Yanukovich would not have stepped down if he had lost in the next election. The Maidan protests did not enjoy democratic majority support from the Ukrainians and even fewer supported a coup.[380] British Foreign

377 I. Katchanovski, "The far right, the Euromaidan, and the Maidan massacre in Ukraine," *Journal of Labor and Society* 23, no.1 (2020).

378 E. MacAskill, "Ukraine crisis: Bugged call reveals conspiracy theory about Kiev snipers," *The Guardian*, 5 March 2014.

379 R. Sakwa, *Frontline Ukraine: Crisis in the Borderlands* (London: I.B. Tauris, 2014).

380 "Ukraine's revolution and the far right," *BBC*, 7 March 2014.

Minister William Hague deceived the public by claiming that the toppling of President Yanukovich had been done in compliance with the constitution, contrary to the clear rules in the Ukrainian constitution that specified procedures for removing the head of state.[381] The allegations of Yanukovich being corrupt were undoubtedly correct, but then so were his predecessors and successors.

The U.S. role in toppling Yanukovich was referred to as "the most overt coup d'état in history" by George Friedman.[382] Washington had infiltrated Ukrainian civil society with government-funded NGOs with ties to intelligence agencies. A *New York Times* report also challenged the narrative of a democratic revolution: "In 2014 the United States backed an uprising—in its final stages a violent uprising—against the legitimately elected Ukrainian government of Viktor Yanukovych, which was pro-Russian.[383]

Conclusion

The world order of liberal hegemony had its heyday in the 1990s as countries such as Poland sought to join NATO and the EU while the West could set conditionalities requiring adherence to liberal democratic values. However, Ukraine was not Poland; the fabricated narrative of Ukraine attempting since 1991 to escape Russia's imperial influence by joining NATO conceals the reality of a deeply divided state that favoured close relations with Russia and was profoundly critical of NATO.

Liberal hegemony introduced a paradoxical world order for Ukraine as Western hegemony and liberal democratic values were in direct competition. The West was willing to subvert Ukraine's democracy and constitution by toppling the government. Liberal hegemony also could not deliver order as supporting the Ethno-cultural Ukrainians to place Ukraine in the West's orbit would risk triggering a civil war and a possible Russian intervention. The destabilisation of

381 D. Morrison, "How William Hague Deceived the House of Commons on Ukraine," *Huffington Post*, 10 March 2014.

382 G. Friedman, "Interesi RF I SSHA v otnoshenii Ukraini nesovmestimi drug's drugom" [The interests of the Russian Federation and the United States in relation to Ukraine are incompatible with each other], *Kommersant*, 19 December 2014.

383 C. Caldwell, "The War in Ukraine May Be Impossible to Stop. And the U.S. Deserves Much of the Blame," *The New York Times*, 31 May 2022.

Ukraine was nonetheless pursued under the mantra of "helping" and "standing with" Ukraine.

During the first Cold War, the dividing lines in Europe were clearly delineated and the status quo had been largely respected, thus the competition for influence and proxy wars occurred in the third world. In the emerging second Cold War, the West and Russia were competing over where the new dividing lines in Europe would be drawn. In the new Cold War, Ukraine was destined to become the main frontline as a NATO-aligned Ukraine would cement the collective hegemony of the West, while a neutral or Russian-leaning Ukraine would enable Russia to maintain a role in Europe.

8.

The Ukrainian Civil War 2014–2022

FOLLOWING THE Western-backed coup in February 2014, the conflict over Ukraine gradually escalated out of control. Efforts to de-escalate or resolve the conflict with the Minsk-2 peace agreement were systematically sabotaged by the U.S. and its allies. While the Orange Revolution of 2004 eventually failed when Yushchenko was voted out, the U.S. and the new authorities in Kiev sought to make the Maidan Revolution permanent. The conflict with Russia was deliberately escalated; the Russian language, culture and the Russian Orthodox Church were marginalised, the political opposition was purged, and U.S. support for the far-right ensured that any democratic efforts to make peace with Russia and restore relations could be obstructed.

This chapter first explores why Russia took the hazardous decision to seize Crimea and support Donbas, which devastated relations with Ukraine and escalated the conflict. Second, the West's sabotage of the Minsk-2 peace agreement is addressed, as well as the U.S.'s efforts to assert its influence over Ukraine. The far right became a powerful instrument to transform Ukraine and perpetuate a proxy conflict with the explicit objective of bleeding Russia. Last, the U.S. and other NATO countries prepared Ukraine for war in an intensifying escalation along the Russian borders, while at the same time rejecting any compromise that could have prevented the war.

Russia Seizes Crimea

The Western-backed coup was seen by Moscow as an existential threat to Russia, and a threat to its compatriots in Eastern and Southern

Ukraine. The central role of the far right and fascist groups in toppling Yanukovich had endowed them with excessive political influence after the coup. This was also recognised in the Western media, for example, the BBC reported that after the coup, Kiev's city council was covered with large neo-Nazi banners, the American confederate flag, and portraits of the fascist ally of Hitler, Stepan Bandera.[384] The first decree by the new Parliament was a call to repeal Russian as a regional language. It seemed likely that language laws would be followed with the suppression of Russian culture and the Orthodox Church.

NATO's incursion into Ukraine was especially dangerous as Crimea had been the home of the Russian Black Sea Fleet since 1783 and is imperative for Russian security. The risk of Russia losing the naval base and even the possibility of NATO taking it over was a red line that Russia could not allow NATO to cross. As CIA Director William Burns had cautioned against and predicted in 2008, U.S. efforts to pull Ukraine into NATO were likely to trigger a civil war in which Russia would likely, but reluctantly, intervene.[385]

Throughout history, a world order organised under the collective hegemony of maritime power has relied on controlling key maritime corridors. The historical weakness of Russia as the largest country by area on the planet has always been the lack of safe and reliable access to maritime corridors to connect it with the wider world. The Black Sea is an indispensable corridor that connects Russia with Europe, the Middle East, and Africa. Russia has fought numerous wars with Turkey, Britain, France and Germany since the 17th century to establish and preserve the Black Sea maritime corridor. Restricting Russian access to the sea has therefore always been a key component of any policy seeking the containment of Russia in Europe. Spykman, a very influential American scholar on the containment of Russia, wrote in 1942: "For two hundred years, since the time of Peter the Great, Russia has attempted to break through the encircling ring of border states and the reach the ocean. Geography and sea power have persistently thwarted her."[386]

---

384 "Ukraine's Revolution and the Far Right," *BBC*, 7 March 2014.

385 W. Burns, "Nyet means nyet: Russia's NATO Enlargement Redlines," *Wikileaks*, 1 February 2008.

386 N. J. Spykman, *America's Strategy in World Politics: the United States and the Balance of Power* (New Brunswick: Transaction Publishers, 1942), 182.

Crimea is pivotal to advancing Western hegemony and diminishing the position of Russia as a strategic rival. When Britain and France went to war against Russia in the Crimean War in 1853, European diplomats had been explicit that the objective had been to push Russia back into Asia and exclude it from European affairs.[387] This intended geopolitical consequence is not less relevant in the 21st century as NATO expansion to Ukraine could convert the Black Sea into a NATO lake.

NATO's aspirations to control maritime corridors require limiting Russia's reliable access to three waterways on its western borders: the Black Sea, the Baltic Sea, and the high north. NATO's Deputy Secretary-General acknowledged in July 2022 that the war in Ukraine is mostly about control over the Black Sea.[388] With the expansion of NATO into Finland and Sweden, former NATO Secretary-General Anders Fogh Rasmussen optimistically announced that now NATO could also block Russia's access to the Baltic Sea: "After the accession of Finland and Sweden to NATO, the Baltic Sea will now be a NATO sea... if we wish, we can block all entry and exit to Russia through St. Petersburg."[389] Furthermore, in 2021 the U.S. reached an agreement for the use of four military bases on Norwegian soil, which will be imperative to intercept Russia's Northern Fleet. Hence, if the Black Sea were indeed converted into a NATO lake, all three waters in Russia's western regions would increasingly fall under U.S. dominance. The strengthening of NATO vis-à-vis Russia would subsequently set off a geopolitical earthquake.

Russia foresaw that the coup in Ukraine would be followed by NATO's further march eastward, and thus sought to reunify Crimea with Russia. The security dilemma for Russia was that it could either seize control over Crimea and alienate the Ukrainians, or respect Ukrainian sovereign territory but then risk the new government in Kiev and NATO pressuring Russia out of the peninsula. By retaking

---

387 J. W. Kipp and W. B. Lincoln, "Autocracy and Reform Bureaucratic Absolutism and Political Modernization in Nineteenth-Century Russia," *Russian History* 6, no. 1 (1979): 4.

388 "Ukraine war to be 'decided on the battlefield,' NATO official says," *Euronews*, 12 July 2022.

389 "Putin's plan includes Baltics, says former NATO chief," *Lrt*, 19 July 2022.

Crimea, Russia escalated the conflict drastically, which motivated an aggressive response from the new authorities in Kiev.

Nonetheless, retaking Crimea was viewed as a limited and obtainable objective. Crimea's population was overwhelmingly supportive of joining Russia, Crimea had its own parliament as an autonomous legislative body that provided the process with some sense of legality, and in any event the peninsula had been transferred to Ukraine under somewhat dubious circumstances by Khrushchev in 1954. As a peninsula, it established a clear geographical delineation. If Russia had annexed other parts of eastern Ukraine, then the main problem would have been to decide where to stop, leaving Russia to face more opposition from the public the further west it might have gone.

The referendum in Crimea meant that "Washington's planned seizure of Russia's historic, legitimate warm-water naval base in Crimea failed."[390] In his speech following the annexation of Crimea, Putin explained Russia's decision as a reaction to aggressive containment policies:

> We have every reason to assume that the infamous policy of containment, led in the 18th, 19th and 20th centuries, continues today… there is a limit to everything. And with Ukraine, our Western partners have crossed the line… Russia found itself in a position it could not retreat from. If you compress the spring all the way to its limit, it will snap back hard…. Are we ready to consistently defend our national interests, or will we forever give in, retreat to who knows where?.[391]

Washington's reference to the sacred principle of territorial integrity in accordance with international law was unconvincing as the West's rules-based international order had introduced the right to self-determination as a competing principle to territorial integrity. It was therefore problematic to make a convincing legal case for why the secession of Crimea was different from the secession of Kosovo.

---

390 J. Pilger, "In Ukraine, the U.S. is dragging us towards war with Russia," *The Guardian*, 13 May 2014.

391 V. Putin, "Address by President of the Russian Federation," *President of Russia*, 18 March 2014.

President Obama attempted to dismiss the comparison as he argued: "Kosovo only left Serbia after a referendum was organized not outside the boundaries of international law, but in careful cooperation with the United Nations and with Kosovo's neighbors."[392] However, everything in the process Obama described was a complete lie as there never even was a referendum in Kosovo.

In consequence, Washington had to rely on the democracy argument by insisting that the referendum in Crimea was illegitimate as it was "held at the barrel of a gun."[393] However, as *Forbes* magazine reported, all polling demonstrates that ethnic Russians, Ukrainians, and Tatars in Crimea were all overwhelmingly supportive of seceding from Ukraine and reuniting with Russia.[394] The lack of loyalty to Ukraine was also evident as following the referendum in Crimea, approximately 75 percent of Ukraine's naval personnel defected to Russia or quit the Ukrainian navy.[395] Stephen Walt argued that Russia's seizure of Crimea should have been predicted as a likely response to the Western-backed coup in Ukraine:

> The Obama administration was clearly taken by surprise when Russia decided to seize Crimea by force. The real question, however, is why Obama and his advisors thought the United States and the European Union could help engineer the ouster of a democratically elected and pro-Russian leader in Ukraine and expect Vladimir Putin to go along with it.[396]

Russia's reaction to the Western-backed coup in Ukraine had several implications for international law. Besides violating the UN Charter by retaking Crimea without permission from the state authority, Moscow was also in breach of the Budapest Memorandum. On 5

---

392 D. Morrison, "Obama Lied About a Referendum in Kosovo," *Huffington Post*, 31 March 2014.

393 U.S. Embassy in Ukraine, "Anniversary of the So-Called 'Annexation' of Crimea by the Russian Federation," 19 March 2015.

394 K. Rapoza, "One Year After Russia Annexed Crimea, Locals Prefer Moscow To Kiev," *Forbes*, 20 March 2015.

395 S. Greer and M. Shtekel, "Ukraine's Navy: A Tale Of Betrayal, Loyalty, And Revival," *RFE/RL*, 27 April 2020.

396 S. Walt, "No Contest," *Foreign Policy*, 4 March 2014.

December 1994, the U.S., UK, and Russia had met in the Hungarian capital and pledged security guarantees in three separate agreements with Ukraine, Belarus, and Kazakhstan. These three countries agreed to relinquish their nuclear weapons in return for security guarantees. The Budapest Memorandum outlined security guarantees that included among other provisions the commitment to "respect the independence and sovereignty and the existing borders of Ukraine," and "to refrain from economic coercion designed to subordinate to their own interest the exercise by Ukraine of the rights inherent in its sovereignty and thus to secure advantages of any kind."

In accordance with the rules-based international order, NATO countries refer to liberal democratic norms to exempt themselves from constraints imposed by international law. While Russia breached the Budapest Memorandum, the NATO states first violated the commitment to refrain from economic coercion to advance their own interests and security advantages. However, NATO countries claim that their use of economic coercion and violation of Ukrainian sovereignty was in support of democracy and human rights as opposed to advancing their own interests. Thus, under the guise of altruism, NATO freed itself from the security guarantees of the Budapest Memorandum.

When the U.S. imposed sanctions on Belarus in 2013, Washington explicitly stated that the Budapest Memorandum was not legally binding and that U.S. actions were exempted as they aimed to protect human rights:

> Although the Memorandum is not legally binding, we take these political commitments seriously and do not believe any U.S. sanctions, whether imposed because of human rights or non-proliferation concerns, are inconsistent with our commitments to Belarus under the Memorandum or undermine them. Rather, sanctions are aimed at securing the human rights of Belarusians and combating the proliferation of weapons of mass destruction and other illicit activities, not at gaining any advantage for the United States.[397]

---

397 U.S. Embassy in Belarus, "Belarus: Budapest Memorandum," *U.S. Embassy in Minsk*, 12 April 2013.

The Western-backed coup in 2014 had been an even more blatant violation of Ukrainian sovereignty. The West interfered in the domestic affairs of Ukraine, imposed economic sanctions, and finally toppled the Ukrainian president. The Budapest Memorandum was put aside as the West claimed to have supported a "democratic revolution." International law imposes rules and mutual constraints in which the various sides have their foreign policy flexibility limited but in return gain reciprocity and thus predictability. Once the West relieved itself from mutual constraints in the Budapest Memorandum, then Russia also abandoned it. However, by taking back Crimea, Moscow contributed to escalating tensions and thereby provoked a tougher response by Kiev in Donbas.

Russia's Support for Donbas

When people in Donbas also revolted against what they deemed to be an illegitimate regime that had taken power in a coup, the new government in Kiev used military force to suppress the protests. The *Guardian* reported on the arbitrary rules of the West as the protesters who seized government buildings and toppled the democratically elected president were hailed as freedom fighters, while the West then condemned the protesters who rejected the legitimacy of the unelected government that had seized power on the streets.[398]

There was a tendency in the West to deny the people of Donbas agency by referring to them as "Russians" or "secessionists." Denying agency to Donbas was important for narrative control. No longer was the Donbas militia a people protecting their own land, basic language and cultural rights against a government that took power in an unconstitutional coup and had rescinded them, rather they were soldiers of a hostile foreign power. However, as two analysts from the Pentagon-linked RAND Corporation acknowledged, even by Kiev's own estimates, "the vast majority of rebel forces consisted of locals—not soldiers of the regular Russian military."[399]

---

398 S. Milne, "It's not Russia that's pushed Ukraine to the brink of war," *The Guardian*, 30 April 2014.

399 S. Charap and S. Boston, "The West's Weapons Won't Make Any Difference to Ukraine," *Foreign Policy*, 21 January 2022.

Instability spread across southern and eastern Ukraine. On 2 May 2014, pro-Maidan and anti-Maidan protesters clashed in Odessa, which resulted in the anti-Maidan protesters seeking refuge in the Trade Union House. The pro-Maidan protesters set the building on fire and dozens of people were burned alive. Videos from the scene demonstrate that pro-Maidan protesters were shooting at people attempting to escape the fire through the windows, and many of those who jumped from the windows were clubbed to death on the pavement.[400] The Ukrainian government delayed the investigation, and the West largely left the event out of the Ukraine narrative.

The inability of the coup government's fragile army to counter Donbas rebels resulted in the use of far-right militias from Western Ukraine. One of the Nazi battalions took the name Azov Battalion after seizing control over Mariupol on the coast of the Sea of Azov, it would later grow to become the Azov Regiment. The NATO-backed government in Kiev launched an "anti-terrorist operation" in April 2014 against the rebels in Donbas who were rejecting the legitimacy of the coup, and the fighting resulted in the death of 14,000 Ukrainians. Fearing a civil war in Donbas, Putin warned Donbas in May 2014 not to pursue a referendum for independence from Ukraine. Instead, Putin insisted that the rising tensions since the coup could be resolved with constitutional changes that provided greater autonomy to the region. Federalisation could be a solution to ensure the preservation of the regional language, culture, and faith, although federalism can also be a double-edged sword by becoming a stepping-stone to secession.

From Washington's perspective, a federal solution to Ukraine was deeply problematic as autonomous rights for Donbas would cement the region's close relationship with Russia and could prevent NATO expansion. Washington had previously sabotaged a similar agreement in 2003 to resolve the dispute between Moldova and Transnistria as it would have prevented NATO's further expansion. Russia negotiated a reunification agreement between Moldova and Transnistria in 2003 that would have required a united Moldova to remain neutral, which would have been consistent with its constitution of 1994 that proclaimed: "The Republic of Moldova proclaims its permanent neutrality."

---

400 R. Sakwa, *Frontline Ukraine: Crisis in the Borderlands* (London: I.B. Tauris, 2014).

The agreement was a compromise wherein Transnistria had to abandon its demands for equal representation as Moldova in the ensuing federal structure; although, in that structure Transnistria was granted sufficient power to block decisions that jeopardised "vital interests" like neutrality. The U.S. and the EU were able to sabotage the agreement at the last moment by pressuring Moldovan President Vladimir Voronin to withdraw from the agreement the day before signing. Both the U.S. and the EU had, in no uncertain terms, told Voronin that they would not support the agreement and the message was simply: "don't do it."[401] Voronin acknowledged that the agreement was "a response to a true compromise between the sides," but recognised that Moldova could not afford to go against the wishes of the U.S. and the EU.[402] A leaked U.S. cable confirmed that Voronin had promised the West that he would not sign any peace agreements without the consent of the West: "He has no intention of signing any bilateral Kozak-II type understanding with the Russians as he believes any Transnistrian settlement must have broad international support."[403] The implicit understanding is that the EU and the U.S. will not support a political solution that preserves close ties with Russia and obstructs Moldova's absorption into NATO.

An agreement to resolve Ukraine's post-coup conflict in 2014 was imperative to end the struggle between the new authorities in Kiev and Donbas, as well as address the disruption to relations between NATO and Russia. As the tensions between NATO and Russia over Ukraine intensified, there were warnings about the need for the West to resolve the crisis through compromise. Professor Stephen Cohen cautioned in 2014 that "Russia will not back off. This is existential.... Putin will compromise at these negotiations, but he will not back off if confronted militarily."[404] Henry Kissinger similarly criticised the discourse about Ukraine as being all about confrontation: "Public discussion on Ukraine is all about confrontation. But do we know

401 J. Löwenhardt, "The OSCE, Moldova and Russian diplomacy in 2003," *Journal of Communist Studies and Transition Politics* 20, no. 4 (2004): 109.

402 M. Vahl and M. Emerson, "Moldova and the Transnistrian conflict," JEMIE, no.1 (2004): 16.

403 "A Tour d'horizon with President Voronin," *Wikileaks*, 18 July 2008.

404 S. Cohen, "'We Are Not Beginning a New Cold War, We are Well into It': Stephen Cohen on Russia-Ukraine Crisis," *Democracy Now*, 17 April 2014.

where we are going?"[405] John Pilger predicted that the West was instigating a civil war in Ukraine that would evolve into a proxy war against Russia:

> NATO's military encirclement has accelerated, along with U.S.-orchestrated attacks on ethnic Russians in Ukraine. If Putin can be provoked into coming to their aid, his pre-ordained "pariah" role will justify a NATO-run guerrilla war that is likely to spill into Russia itself.[406]

However, the problems in Crimea and Donbas were not resolved. Since 2014, the civilian population in Donbas did not receive humanitarian assistance from Ukraine or the West. Pensions and economic support for families were no longer paid and their banking system was blocked. In 2014, Ukraine also built a concrete dam in the Kherson region that blocked 85 percent of the water supply to Crimea, which persisted until 2022 when Russia invaded and restored Crimea's access to water.

The Minsk Agreement: A Peace Agreement or Buying Time for War?

The fighting between Kiev and Donbas was intended to be resolved with the Minsk Protocol reached in September 2014, but the ceasefire broke down. Kiev suffered great losses in the ensuing fighting and found itself encircled in Debaltseve, at which point Berlin and Paris intervened with a peace initiative. The Minsk-2 agreement was subsequently reached in February 2015 and was signed by Kiev, Donbas, Germany, France, and Russia. The Minsk-2 agreement was devoted solely to resolving the domestic conflict between Kiev and Donbas; Russia was not mentioned in the peace agreement. Thus, the agreement should have been supplemented by a NATO-Russia agreement to address the re-division of Europe as the source of the conflict.

The Minsk-2 agreement stipulated that heavy weapons must be pulled back, and that Kiev would have to engage Donbas

405 H. Kissinger, "How the Ukraine crisis ends."
406 J. Pilger, "In Ukraine, the U.S. is dragging us towards war with Russia."

diplomatically to pass the constitutional reforms required to grant the region autonomy:

> On the first day after the pullout a dialogue is to start on modalities of conducting local elections in accordance with the Ukrainian legislation and the Law of Ukraine.... Without delays, but no later than 30 days from the date of signing of this document, a resolution has to be approved by the Verkhovna Rada of Ukraine, indicating the territory which falls under the special regime in accordance with the law "On temporary Order of Local Self-Governance in Particular Districts of Donetsk and Luhansk Oblasts," based in the line set up by the Minsk Memorandum as of 19 September 2014.

Autonomy for Donbas was intended to safeguard its cultural and language rights, and likely also could grant Donbas the ability to prevent future NATO accession. This first step of the peace agreement was never taken as the Ukrainian authorities did not establish a dialogue with Donbas and the Ukrainian parliament rejected the bill on elections in Donbas. The U.S. signed on to the Minsk-2 agreement and the UN voted on it as a resolution to make it a legal treaty. But thereafter, Washington demonstrated no intention of pressuring Kiev to implement it: "Washington has been understandably reluctant to do this in the past; Minsk represents Russia's terms, imposed using armed aggression. Pushing the victim—a good friend of the United States—to do the aggressor's bidding is contrary to U.S. principles."[407] The Western powers kept reiterating that the Minsk-2 agreement was the only path to peace, while simultaneously undermining it.

The U.S. began to sabotage the Minsk Agreement while arming and training the Ukrainian army to change the balance of military power on the ground, thus ensuring Kiev would not have to deliver on its commitments under the Minsk-2 agreement. Some top U.S. officials had very publicly opposed the Minsk-2 peace initiative by Germany and France. At the Munich Security Conference in February 2015, the U.S. delegation purportedly accused German Chancellor Merkel

407 S. Charap, "The U.S. Approach to Ukraine's Border War Isn't Working. Here's What Biden Should Do Instead," *Politico*, 19 November 2021.

of appeasement. U.S. General Philip Breedlove and Victoria Nuland described Angela Merkel as "defeatist," while U.S. Senator John McCain referred to the German-French peace initiative in Minsk as "Moscow Bullshit" that was compared to the appeasement of Hitler.[408]

Between 2015 and 2022, the Russians, Europeans, Americans, and Ukrainians continuously repeated that the Minsk Agreement was the only format for peace. Nonetheless, by concurrently sabotaging the Minsk Agreement, the NATO countries set Ukraine on a path to war. It initially appeared that only the U.S. and UK were undermining the peace agreement, and that Germany and France were simply too weak to push through the deal they had negotiated. However, both the Europeans and the Americans sought to undermine the Minsk Agreement by redefining its terms and thus renegotiating it. The European Parliament declared that Russia has a "particular responsibility for the implementation of the Minsk Agreement,"[409] even though Russia was not identified as one of the conflicting parties and is not even mentioned in the text. While the regional conflict between NATO and Russia had triggered the civil war, the Minsk Agreement had been strictly limited to resolving the domestic dispute between Kiev and Donbas.

After Russia invaded Ukraine in 2022, both Germany and France revealed that they had no intentions to implement the Minsk-2 agreement. Merkel argued that the Minsk Agreement she had negotiated was not necessarily an effort to establish a durable peace—rather Merkel argued in an interview with both *Bild* and *Spiegel* that the Minsk Agreement enabled her to buy time for Ukraine to build itself into a powerful and well-fortified country.[410] Merkel argued this worked as "[Ukraine] used this time to get stronger, as you can see today."[411] The notion that the war began with an unprovoked Russian invasion in 2022 is challenged by none other than NATO Secretary General Jens Stoltenberg, who in February 2023 confirmed:

---

408 J. Huggler, "Ukraine crisis: U.S. officials compare peace efforts to appeasing Hitler," *The Telegraph*, 8 February 2015.

409 European Parliament, "Ukraine: The Minsk agreements five years on," *European Parliament*, March 2020.

410 A. Osang, "You're Done with Power Politics," *Spiegel*, 1 December 2022.

411 T. Hildrebrandt and G. di Lorenzo, *"'Hatten Sie gedacht, ich komme mit Pferdeschwanz?'"* ["'Did you think I was coming with a ponytail?'"], *Zeit*, 7 December 2022.

> the war didn't start in February last year. The war started in 2014. And since 2014, NATO Allies have provided support to Ukraine, with training, with equipment, so the Ukrainian Armed Forces were much stronger in 2022, than they were in 2020, and 2014. And of course, that made a huge difference when President Putin decided to attack Ukraine.[412]

When her French counterpart, former president François Hollande, was asked about Merkel's statement that the Minsk-2 peace agreement was merely intended to buy time, he confirmed: "Yes, Angela Merkel is right on this point" and added that the conflict with Russia would be resolved on the battlefield: "There will only be a way out of the conflict when Russia fails on the ground."[413] However, it is possible that Merkel and Hollande were merely protecting their legacy during a time of fierce resentment towards Russia.

Yet, the rhetoric from the German and French leaders was strikingly similar to that of Ukraine. In February 2023, President Zelensky admitted that he never had the intention of implementing the Minsk agreement: "But as for Minsk as a whole, I told Emmanuel Macron and Angela Merkel: We cannot implement it like this." The plan, according to Zelensky as well, was merely to delay, remarking bizarrely: "Procrastination is perfectly fine in diplomacy. You never know when a decision-maker dies and everything suddenly becomes easier."[414] Former Ukrainian president Petro Poroshenko also confirmed that Kiev, under his administration, had no intention of implementing the Minsk Agreement. Poroshenko argued: "We had achieved everything we wanted" from the peace agreement as "Our goal was to, first, stop the threat, or at least to delay the war—to secure eight years to restore economic growth and create powerful armed forces."[415]

---

412 J. Stoltenberg, "Doorstep statement by NATO Secretary General Jens Stoltenberg ahead of the meetings of NATO Defence Ministers in Brussels," *NATO*, 14 February 2023.

413 T. Prouvost, "Hollande: 'There will only be a way out of the conflict when Russia fails on the ground'," *The Kyiv Independent*, 28 December 2022.

414 *"Putin ist ein Drache, der fressen muss"* ["Putin is a dragon that has to eat"], *Der Spiegel*, 9 February 2023.

415 T. Snider, "Putin and Zelensky finally agree. Here's why that's a bad thing," *Responsible Statecraft*, 5 December 2022.

That the world order had failed in its primary mission to keep order was further underlined by the deception of the Minsk Agreement having been adopted as a resolution at the UN. Retired German General Harald Kujat, the former head of the German Bundeswehr and former chairman of the NATO Military Committee, warned in 2023 that sabotaging the Minsk Agreement meant that the West was guilty of

> a breach of international law, that is clear. The damage is immense. You have to imagine the situation today. The people who wanted to wage war from the beginning and still want to do so have taken the view that you cannot negotiate with Putin. No matter what, he does not comply with agreements. But now it turns out that we are the ones who do not comply with international agreements.[416]

Despite undermining the Minsk-2 peace agreement for seven years, NATO took no responsibility for the subsequent outbreak of war. Jack Matlock, the former U.S. Ambassador to the Soviet Union, argued in October 2022: "The war might have been prevented—probably would have been prevented—if Ukraine had been willing to abide by the Minsk Agreement, recognize the Donbas as an autonomous entity within Ukraine, avoid NATO military advisors, and pledge not to enter NATO."[417] The efforts by NATO to undermine the Minsk Agreement also undermines the trust required for future peace agreements.

U.S. Penetration of Ukraine

A key weakness of the Western-backed Orange Revolution in 2004 was that the installed pro-West/anti-Russian government could be reversed in the following election due to the close socio-economic ties to Russia and the strong opposition to NATO among the Ukrainian public. After Maidan, Washington began to insert itself more directly into the governance of Ukraine.

---

416 Emma, "Russland will verhandeln!" [Russia wants to negotiate!], *Emma,* 4 March 2023.

417 J. F. Matlock, "Why the U.S. must press for a ceasefire in Ukraine," *Responsible Statecraft*, 17 October 2022.

Several Americans took key positions in the Ukrainian government after 2014. In 2014, Natalie Jaresko took the position of Finance Minister of Ukraine and received Ukrainian citizenship on the same day as she took the job. Jaresko was a former U.S. State Department official and former Economic Section Chief of the U.S. Embassy in Ukraine. Thus, she switched from representing U.S. interests in Ukraine to representing those of Ukraine. Aivaras Abromavičius, a Lithuanian citizen educated in the U.S., became the Minister of Economic Development and Trade of Ukraine. In 2015, David Sakvarelidze, an American state prosecutor in New York became the Deputy Prosecutor General of Ukraine and acquired Ukrainian citizenship the same year. Also in 2015, Kiev appointed Georgia's ex-president Mikheil Saakashvili as the governor of Odessa. Throughout the 1990s and 2000s, similar developments had occurred in the Baltic States as Estonia, Latvia, and Lithuania all had presidents who had been North American citizens.

Washington also had great influence and, to a large extent, could seemingly dictate other government appointments. The general prosecutor of Ukraine, Viktor Shokin, complained that since 2014, "the most shocking thing is that all the [government] appointments were made in agreement with the United States." Washington's behaviour, according to Shokin, indicated that they "believed that Ukraine was their fiefdom."[418]

General Prosecutor Shokin's career ended once he opened a corruption case against the Ukrainian energy company Burisma, as the new administrators who were recruited in May and June 2014 were believed to be involved in corruption. One of them was Joe Biden's son, Hunter Biden. Three months after the coup in February 2014, Hunter Biden and a close family friend of U.S. Secretary of State, John Kerry, became board members of Burisma.[419] Hunter Biden had no experience or competencies in the gas industry or Ukraine.

Then-Vice President Joe Biden intervened in the investigation by having General Prosecutor Shokin fired by threatening to withhold a $1 billion U.S. loan guarantee. Biden had insisted that the decision was not related to Burisma or his son, insisting that he had "never spoken to my

---

418 M. M. Abrahms, "Does Ukraine Have Kompromat on Joe Biden?," *Newsweek*, 8 August 2023.

419 P. Sonne and J. Grimaldi, "Biden's Son, Kerry Family Friend Join Ukrainian Gas Producer's Board," *The Wall Street Journal*, 13 May 2014.

son about his overseas business dealing."[420] However, Hunter Biden's business partner in Burisma, Devon Archer, confirmed in July 2023 that Joe Biden was deeply involved in Hunter Biden's business.[421] The sacking of the Ukrainian general prosecutor in March 2016 was also not likely due to his corruption or incompetence. On 11 June 2015, Victoria Nuland had written a letter to Prosecutor General Shokin praising his fight against corruption, which explicitly stated: "We have been impressed with the ambitious reform and anti-corruption agenda of your government" and "I encourage you to continue to work closely with the U.S. Embassy in Kyiv."[422] In 2017, the NATO think tank Atlantic Council and Burisma signed a cooperative agreement, with a focus on "energy security."

After Russia invaded in February 2022, the U.S. further strengthened its grip over Ukraine. In 2023, an American transgender who argued that Russians are not human beings became the new spokesperson for Ukraine's Territorial Defence Forces. As Ukraine's situation became more precarious and dependence on the West increased, Kiev largely outsourced the post-war reconstruction process to BlackRock and J.P. Morgan to manage the Ukraine Development Fund. With the Washington Consensus being imposed on Ukraine with privatisation and deregulation, Western agricultural giants have bought millions of hectares of Ukrainian farmland.

The Ukrainian intelligence agencies and army were also penetrated by the Americans to convert Ukraine into a proxy targeting Russia. The *Washington Post* report: "Since 2015, the CIA has spent tens of millions of dollars to transform Ukraine's Soviet-formed services into potent allies against Moscow."[423] A former U.S. intelligence official explained that the military intelligence service of the Ukrainian government, GUR, was identified as "a smaller and more nimble organization where we could have more impact... GUR was our little baby." The CIA subsequently transformed the GUR as "we

---

420 E. J. Morris and G. Fonrouge, "Smoking-gun email reveals how Hunter Biden introduced Ukrainian businessman to VP dad," *New York Post*, 14 October 2020.

421 U.S. Government, "Comer Statement on Devon Archer's Testimony," *Committee On Oversight and Accountability*, 31 July 2023.

422 M. M. Abrahms, "Does Ukraine Have Kompromat on Joe Biden?"

423 G. Miller and I. Khurshudyan, "Ukrainian spies with deep ties to CIA wage shadow war against Russia," *The Washington Post*, 23 October 2023.

had to kind of rebuilt it from scratch." The new military intelligence services, constructed by the U.S., was later used to conduct terrorist attacks inside Russia such as the killing of Daria Dugina.[424]

Purging the Opposition

While the majority of Ukrainians favoured close ties to Russia before 2014, all such ties were purged as possible instruments of a Russian hybrid war. With U.S. support, the new government in Kiev decoupled from Russia and suppressed large parts of its own population by purging the political opposition, independent media, the Orthodox Church, and all manifestations of Russian language and culture.

The most Russian-friendly political parties included the Party of Regions and the Communist Party. The former was the largest political party in Ukraine from 2007 until the coup in 2014; thereafter both were purged with accusations of treason and largely disappeared from the political map. When popular support for Zelensky began to collapse as a result of betraying his election platform, the opposition came under even stronger pressure. In 2021, the authorities in Kiev arrested the main opposition leader Viktor Medvedchuk, an elected member of the Ukrainian parliament and the leader of its biggest opposition party. In 2023, Kiev even stripped Medvedchuk of his Ukrainian citizenship.

Independent media was also purged under the nationalist slogan "One Nation, One Language, One People." In February 2021, the Ukrainian president shut down three Ukrainian TV channels without any legal support. In August 2021, the government also began to block online media that remained the last vestige of independent media. This censorship was met with either silence or a standing ovation in the West. In 2021, the former U.S. ambassador to Moscow Michael McFaul even celebrated Kiev's crackdown on opposition politicians and media: "His decision to ban pro-Russia television networks, and to charge their owner and Putin ally Viktor Medvedchuk with treason, was a daring act that needs U.S. support."[425] *Foreign Policy* similarly celebrated censorship with the headline: "Ukraine's President Finally Flexes His Muscles: Volodymyr Zelensky is taking on his country's

424 Ibid.

425 M. McFaul, "The U.S. and Ukraine need to reboot their relationship. Here's how they can do it," *The New York Times*, 23 August 2021.

pro-Russian media machine. But can he emerge victorious?"[426] After Russia invaded, even more draconian restrictions were imposed on opposition parties and TV news was nationalised.

Language, culture, and religion were also purged since 2014. The first act of the post-coup Ukrainian parliament in 2014 was to vote in favour of abolishing the language rights of minorities, which removed Russian as the second language in the south and the east of Ukraine. Other minority languages were also scaled, such as Hungarian. Denying the agency of Russian-speaking Ukrainians and banning the Russian language in books, movies and other works was all consistent with the U.S. approach to Ukrainian nation-building, which entailed severing all ties with Russia, democracy notwithstanding.

The U.S. further fuelled the anti-Russian nationalist narrative as the U.S. Senate passed a resolution in 2018 that defined the Holodomor famine as "deliberate" and as a "genocide" directed against the Ukrainians.[427] In a display of solidarity with the Ethno-cultural nationalists, Western states also embraced minor initiatives such as changing the English spelling of the Ukrainian capital from Kiev to Kyiv to resemble the Ukrainian spelling instead of the Russian. The NATO think tank, Atlantic Council, argued in favour of a cultural purge to deprive Russia of soft power:

> Thanks to centuries of political domination and systematic russification, modern Russia still enjoys enormous cultural influence over independent Ukraine…. The Ukrainian authorities have also embraced a number of protectionist policies in order to restrict Russia's soft power penetration inside Ukraine. In 2014, Ukraine banned a range of Russian TV channels, TV series, and books…. Three years later, Ukraine went further and blocked a number of Russian social media platforms. Many of Russia's leading pop stars and celebrities are also no longer welcome in Ukraine.[428]

---

426 D. Peleschuk, "Ukraine's President Finally Flexes His Muscles," *Foreign Policy*, 12 February 2021.

427 U.S. Senate, "Resolution 435, Calendar No. 608," U.S. Senate, 14 March 2018.

428 M. Pesenti, "Ukraine's cultural revival is a matter of national security," *Atlantic Council*, 19 January 2021.

In January 2019, the Ukrainian Orthodox Church was severed from the Russian Orthodox Church in a major religious schism. In 2022, Kiev began purging the Orthodox Church and arresting priests. Ukraine also ordered a historically Russian-aligned wing of the Orthodox Church to leave a monastery complex in Kiev in a further religious crackdown.

Constructing an ultra-nationalist Ukraine

After Maidan, the far-right role in Ukraine grew immensely in terms of shaping the national identity and taking political power. The new government in Kiev initially attempted to resist its influence, yet both Poroshenko and Zelensky had to eventually align themselves with the far right. Subsequently, streets were renamed after the Nazi collaborator Stepan Bandera, while Kiev began "whitewashing Nazi collaborators on a statewide level."[429]

Across the Western media, there was a recognition that Ukraine had a problem with the rise of Nazis and the far right. Svoboda had previously been denounced by the EU as a "racist, anti-Semitic and xenophobic" political party.[430] Yet, during the Maidan uprising, U.S. senator John McCain had pledged his solidarity to the revolution as he stood next to the leader of Svoboda, Oleh Tyahnybok, who had previously taken a firm stand against "the Moscow-Jewish mafia ruling Ukraine" and "the Moskali, Germans, Kikes [Jews] and other scum who wanted to take away our Ukrainian state."[431] The Right Sector similarly used the red and black flags of the OUN. Azov blatantly used two combined symbols from Nazi Germany as their official emblem, the wolfsangel in front of the black sun. As reported in *Foreign Policy* in March 2014, shortly after the coup: "The uncomfortable truth is that a sizeable portion of Kiev's current government—and the protesters who brought it to power—are, indeed, fascists."[432]

---

429 L. Golinkin, "Secretary Blinken Faces a Big Test in Ukraine, Where Nazis and Their Sympathizers Are Glorified," *The Nation*, 6 May 2021.

430 European Parliament, *Resolution on the situation in Ukraine,* 13 December 2012.

431 B. Whelan, "Far-right group at heart of Ukraine protests meet U.S. senator," *Channel4 News*, 16 December 2013.

432 A. Foxall and O. Kessler, "Yes, There Are Bad Guys in the Ukrainian Government," *Foreign Policy*, 18 March 2014.

The name of the paramilitary group C14 refers to the 14 words coined by the American white supremacist David Lane: "We must secure the existence of our people and a future for white children."[433] On 5 February 2022, less than three weeks before the Russian invasion, the leader of C14, Yevhan Karas argued that the nationalists had been the decisive force at Maidan. According to Karas, even though the nationalists were a minority at Maidan in terms of the percentage of protesters, they represented the majority in terms of efficiency and influence: "if not for the nationalists that whole thing would have turned into a gay parade." Karas also told his audience that the West did not give weapons to help Ukrainians but did so because "we have started a war" that was fulfilling the goals of the West. The nationalists were supported by the West due to their resilience: "because we have fun, we have fun killing and we have fun fighting."[434]

The far right is a powerful ally of both Kiev and NATO. They are motivated to fight, often well-trained, and ideologically inclined to reject any compromise with Russia. During the Cold War, the U.S. had cultivated relations with Ukrainian fascists as they were deemed to be reliable anti-communists and anti-Russian. After Maidan, the far right fiercely rejected the Minsk Agreement and opposed any concessions to Donbas or Moscow. For Washington, the far right represented a powerful veto power against any electoral result that would result in reconciliation with Moscow.

In Washington, there was division about how to manage Ukraine due to a recognition that the far right was unpredictable and could be difficult to control. President Obama had been apprehensive about openly sending arms to Ukraine as he recognised it could "[end] up in the hands of thugs" and the conflict would spiral out of control.[435] Senior Pentagon official Derek Chollet acknowledged there was a power struggle within Washington as at one point "just about every senior official was for doing something that the president opposed."[436]

---

433 N. N. Petro, *The Tragedy of Ukraine* (Boston: De Gruyter, 2023), 113.

434 A. Rubenstein and M. Blumenthal, "How Ukraine's Jewish president Zelensky made peace with neo-Nazi paramilitaries on front lines of war with Russia," *The Grayzone*, 4 March 2022.

435 P. Baker, "Obama Said to Resist Growing Pressure From All Sides to Arm Ukraine," *The New York Times*, 10 March 2015.

436 D. Chollet, *The Long Game: How Obama Defied Washington and Redefined America's Role in the World* (PublicAffairs, 2016).

Nonetheless, the U.S. began its weapon sales and training of Ukrainian soldiers in 2014, and the CIA launched a covert program in 2015 to train Ukrainian paramilitaries "to kill Russians."[437] While the CIA program was established under Obama, it intensified under Trump. U.S. Brigadier General Joseph E. Hilbert later implied that Russia had made a mistake by not launching its invasion sooner: "the worst thing the Russians did was give us eight years to prepare."[438]

The uprising in Donbas after the coup further strengthened the far right. The Ukrainian army was in poor condition in 2014 and many soldiers defected when they were asked to turn their guns on fellow Ukrainians in Donbas. As Russia took back Crimea and supported the uprising in Donbas, the Azov Regiment and other fascist groups further grew in influence as they were important instruments in the fight against Donbas. The Azov Regiment became formally integrated into Ukrainian National Guard in November 2014, which meant that the official uniform of soldiers in the Ukrainian armed forces included Nazi insignia.[439]

In 2015, the U.S. Congress recognised the Azov Battalion as a Nazi organization and subsequently banned U.S. military assistance to the group.[440] However, one year later, in 2016, the U.S. Congress removed the ban on funding Nazis in Ukraine.[441] The fascists had proven to be excellent soldiers, they had acquired much political influence, and they could function as a veto against any government in Kiev that would seek reconciliation with Donbas and Russia.

Over the next three years, the U.S. Congress passed spending bills that included a ban on financing the Azov Battalion as this was recognised to as a neo-Nazi group, although every year the provision about not financing Azov was removed. Only in 2018 was the provision kept and Democratic congressman Ro Khanna proudly stated

---

437 Z. Dorfman, "CIA-trained Ukrainian paramilitaries may take central role if Russia invades," *Yahoo News*, 13 January 2022.

438 G. Norman, "Top U.S. military official relays 'worst thing' Russia did before invading Ukraine," *Fox News*, 4 May 2022.

439 T. Lister, "The Nexus Between Right-Wing Extremists in the United States and Ukraine," *Combating Terrorism Center at West Point* 13, no. 4 (2020): 35.

440 R. Parry, "U.S. House Admits Nazi Role in Ukraine," *Consortium News*, 12 June 2015.

441 J. Carden, "Congress Has Removed a Ban on Funding Neo-Nazis From Its Year-End Spending Bill," *The Nation*, 14 January 2016.

that "White supremacy and neo-Nazism are unacceptable and have no place in our world."[442] In September 2019, a testimony was presented before the House Committee on Homeland Security cautioning that the "Azov Battalion has actively recruited foreign fighters motivated by white supremacy and neo-Nazi beliefs, including many from the West, to join its ranks and receive training, indoctrination, and instruction in irregular warfare."[443]

Washington—in every year since 2013—voted against the annual UN resolution "combatting glorification of Nazism" to defend the Western Ukrainians who glorified the fascists who had collaborated with Hitler as freedom fighters. In November 2021, the U.S. and Ukraine were the only two countries in the world to vote against the resolution combatting the glorification of Nazism. Washington argued that the resolution was Russian propaganda designed to denigrate Ukraine's independence movement.

A Far-Right Veto Against Peace

After the coup in February 2014, the formalities of democracies continued as elections were held, although any elected Ukrainian leader would have to adjust to the realities of where the power actually resides. Aligning with the nationalists gave Kiev a powerful ally as opposed to a powerful adversary. But by aligning with the nationalists, peace with Donbas and Russia became impossible. Washington, which had also been critical of the Minsk-2 agreement had found its reliable allies among the nationalists. As aptly argued by Professor John Mearsheimer: "The Americans will side with the Ukrainian right. Because the Americans, and the Ukrainian right, both do not want Zelensky cutting a deal with the Russians that makes it look like the Russians won."[444]

Ukrainian President Petro Poroshenko went through an astounding transformation from an opponent of Ukrainian nationalism to one of its leading advocates. Zelensky ran on a political platform in

---

442 R. Kheel, "Congress bans arms to Ukraine militia linked to neo-Nazis," *The Hill*, 27 March 2018.

443 A. H. Soufan, "Global Terrorism: Threats to the Homeland, Testimony to be presented before the House Committee on Homeland Security," 10 September 2019.

444 A. Maté, "Siding with Ukraine's far-right, U.S. sabotaged Zelensky's mandate for peace," *Aaron Maté* (Substack blog), 10 April 2022.

which he warned against dividing Ukraine with ethnic hatred against fellow Ukrainians and Russia. But then, as the Ukrainian Minister of Transportation predicted, Zelensky would also align himself with the far right:

> Each new president of Ukraine begins his cadence with the conviction that he is the one who can conduct a constructive dialogue with Moscow, and that he has been given the role of peacemaker, who will do business and develop good relations.... And every president of Ukraine has ended up becoming a de facto follower of Bandera and fighting the Russian Federation.[445]

The Minsk-2 agreement of February 2015 which intended to end the war in Donbas by granting the region autonomy, was fiercely resisted by the far-right nationalists who were determined to fight and reject peace agreements. The BBC reported in August 2015 that a clear majority of 265 MPs out of 450 had supported the first reading of the decentralisation bill to grant more autonomy to Donbas. This sparked a violent veto by the far right, it then reported: "Protesters led by the populist Radical Party and the ultra-nationalist Svoboda (Freedom) party—who oppose any concession to the Russian-backed separatists" clashed with riots police that resulted in the death of a national guard member and over 100 injured.[446] Poroshenko subsequently began to abandon his efforts to implement the Minsk-2 agreement. A similar scenario played out in August 2021 as Zelensky entertained the idea of pursuing the Steinmeier formula to end the conflict in Donbas, which resulted in violent clashes with far-right groups outside the presidential office.[447]

Zelensky had won the presidential election in April 2019 with the pledge to make peace, running on a peace platform including establishing talks with Donbas, restoring normal relations with Russia, and implementing the Minsk-2 peace agreement. In an astonishing

---

445 N. N. Petro, *The Tragedy of Ukraine*, 90.

446 "Ukraine crisis: Deadly anti-autonomy protest outside parliament," *BBC*, 31 August 2015.

447 "Right-Wing Protesters Clash With Police Outside Ukrainian President's Office," *RFE/RL*, 14 August 2021.

landslide victory of 73 percent of the vote, Zelensky achieved an immense Ukrainian mandate to resolve its conflict with Donbas and Russia. Following his election victory, Zelensky declared his intentions: "I think that we will have personnel changes. In any case we will continue in the direction of the Minsk [peace] talks and head towards concluding a ceasefire."[448]

However, the nationalists and the U.S. had established significant influence, to the extent that they had a powerful political veto in Kiev. By 2020, the paramilitary militias in Ukraine constituted about 102,000 men, which was about 40 percent of the entire Ukrainian armed forces.[449] These paramilitary organisations were infused heavily with nationalists from Western Ukraine, and they were armed and trained by Western powers. Subsequently, the nationalists and NATO countries gained significant influence over the political decisions in Kiev.

The Combating Terrorism Center at West Point, the prestigious U.S. military academy, published an analysis of how the fascist group in Ukraine collaborated with right-wing extremists in the U.S. The report also recognised that the fascists were fiercely opposed to any peaceful settlement that entailed concessions:

> These groups have bitterly opposed any suggestion of compromise with Russia over Donbas through the Normandy negotiating process and were prominent at another rally witnessed by the author in Kyiv in the fall of 2019 to oppose concessions floated by President Volodymyr Zelensky.[450]

The far right eventually overturned Zelensky's peace mandate with the "no capitulation" campaign which portrayed implementing the Minsk-2 Agreements as treason. After Zelensky became president, a protest was arranged in Kiev on 6 October 2019; approximately

448 "Ukraine election: Comedian Zelensky wins presidency by landslide," *BBC*, 22 April 2019.

449 P. K. Dutta, S. Granados, and M. Ovaska, "On the edge of war," *Reuters*, 26 January 2022.

450 T. Lister, "The Nexus Between Right-Wing Extremists in the United States and Ukraine, 30.

10,000 people rallied against President Zelensky's plan to end the war, which was denounced as "capitulation."[451]

Ukrainian far-right groups refused to follow Zelensky's orders to pull back heavy weapons from the front-line city of Zolote in accordance with the disengagement plan. Zelensky responded on 26 October 2019 by visiting the region to assert his authority. Upon Zelensky's arrival, the nationalist soldiers openly rejected his orders to remove the heavy weapons, and one of the soldiers warned or threatened Zelensky with protests if he attempted to carry these orders out. To no avail, Zelensky told the soldiers: "I'm the president of this country. I'm 41 years old. I'm not a loser. I came to you and told you: remove the weapons."[452] The humiliating encounter was recorded, and the video spread across the internet, revealing that President Zelensky had limited power vis-à-vis the far right as he could do nothing but complain.

As the video spread, threats against Zelensky immediately followed. Russia scholar Stephen Cohen argued in 2019 that Zelensky was not allowed to deal directly with Putin as nationalist opponents used the threat of violence as a veto: "They have said that they will remove and kill Zelensky if he continues along this line of negotiating with Putin." Cohen opined that the U.S. had a veto over Kiev as Zelensky could not negotiate with Moscow "unless America has his back. Maybe that won't be enough, but unless the White House encourages this diplomacy, Zelensky has no chance of negotiating an end to the war, so the stakes are enormously high."[453] Washington did not offer support for Zelensky's peace mandate, resulting in Kiev returning to a confrontational stance. After failing to assert control over the far-right groups in the military, Zelensky had to align himself closer with the nationalists.[454]

Sofia Fedyna, a Ukrainian lawmaker, even seemingly threatened the life of Zelensky as she stated: "Mr. President thinks he is immortal....

---

451 A. Korniienko, "Thousands rally in Kyiv against Zelensky's plan to end war with Russia," *Kyiv Post*, 6 October 2019.

452 O. Grytsenko, "'I'm not a loser': Zelensky clashes with veterans over Donbas disengagement," *Kyiv Post*, 28 October 2019.

453 A. Maté, "Ukrainegate impeachment saga worsens U.S.-Russia Cold War." *The Grayzone*, 13 November 2019.

454 J. Melanovski, "Ukrainian President Zelensky deepens alliance with far right," *World Socialist Web Site*, 30 April 2021.

A grenade may explode there, by chance. And it would be the nicest if this happened during Moscow's shelling when someone comes to the front line wearing a white or blue shirt."[455] Andriy Biletsky, the head of National Corps and the Azov Battalion, told President Zelensky that if he tried to remove them from the front line then "there will be thousands there instead of several dozen."[456] Biletsky was not punished and by 2023 Zelensky even posted a picture on his Telegram account of himself together with Biletsky. Biletsky had earlier declared his vision for Ukraine: "The historic mission of our nation in this critical moment is to lead the White Races of the world in a final crusade for their survival. A crusade against the Semite-led Untermenschen."[457]

An even more direct death threat came from Dmitri Yarosh, the leader of Right Sector, a far-right extremist group. Yarosh warned in May 2019, shortly after Zelensky's election victory, that fulfilling his campaign promises would have dire consequences: "He will be hanged from a tree on [Khreshchatyk Avenue], if he betrays Ukraine and the people who died during the Revolution and the War. And it is very important that he understands this."[458] Dmitri Yarosh was not arrested, instead he was promoted in November 2021 to become the advisor to the Commander-in-Chief of the Ukrainian Armed Forces, while simultaneously being the head of the "Ukrainian Volunteer Army." In December 2021, Zelensky also delivered the Hero of Ukraine award to Dmytro Kotsyubaylo, a leader of the fascist group Right Sector.

Zelensky's peace initiative of "a massive national dialogue" lasted until 2020. The initiative was largely led by Sergei Sivokho, a friend and former colleague of Zelensky. Even prior to 2014, Sivokho had worked to reconcile Ukrainians as the country was polarising and tearing itself apart. Sivokho and the peace initiative were hardly mentioned in the Western media, where the prevailing narrative was that Ukraine was united under the Maidan government and the militia in Donbas were agents of Russia. Zelenky supported Sivokho's

---

455 O. Grytsenko, "'I'm not a loser': Zelensky clashes with veterans over Donbas disengagement," *Kyiv Post*, 28 October 2019.

456 Ibid.

457 T. Parfitt, "Ukraine crisis: the neo-Nazi brigade fighting pro-Russian separatists," *The Telegraph*, 11 August 2014.

458 J. Baud, *Operation Z* (Paris: Max Milo, 2022).

"National Platform for Reconciliation and Unity," although 70 nationalists interrupted the introductory presentation of the initiative and assaulted Sivokho as he was accused of treason. Zelensky bowed to the pressure and violence of the nationalists, and two weeks later Sivokho was fired from his government position.[459]

The Western political media establishment provided a cover for the rising influence of the far-right by pointing to Zelensky's Jewish background as evidence that it was all Russian propaganda. While Zelensky was not ideologically inclined to support fascists, he had to adjust to the realities of where much of the power resided. The Ukrainian Jewish oligarch Igor Kolomoisky was the main financier of both Zelensky and the neo-Nazi Azov Battalion. Washington also made efforts to whitewash Nazi collaborators as freedom fighters with a video by Radio Free Europe/Radio Liberty, which argued that Stepan Bandera can be considered either a hero or a villain while leaning decisively in favour of the hero narrative. Some Western media, such as *Deutsche Welle*, were more critical and recognised that the slogan "Slava Ukraini" [Glory to Ukraine] originates from the fascist Stepan Bandera and the OUN, which is often supplemented with the Hitler salute. The slogan was adopted by far-right groups and then gradually became mainstream within the Ukrainian military. After the Russian invasion in 2022, Western leaders also began to repeat the fascist chant to display their support for Ukraine.

After failing to implement his peace mandate, Zelensky's approval ratings began to falter. A poll from the Kyiv International Institute of Sociology in October 2021 revealed that Zelensky's approval had been reduced to merely 24 percent.[460] Zelensky faced a dilemma as he would either lose his public support and the prospect of peace or have to face the far-right nationalist groups. In 2021, Zelensky even accused one of the far-right nationalist groups of planning a coup.[461]

The *New York Times* published an article from two weeks before the Russian invasion of Ukraine, arguing that the nationalists who had

---

459 N. N. Petro, "The last Ukrainian peacemaker: Sergei Sivokho remembered The last Ukrainian peacemaker: Sergei Sivokho remembered," *Responsible Statecraft*, 23 October 2023.

460 "Socio-political moods of the population of Ukraine," *Kyiv International Institute of Sociology*, 19 October 2021.

461 A.E. Kramer, "Armed Nationalists in Ukraine Pose a Threat Not Just to Russia," *The New York Times*, 10 February 2022.

been armed against Russia also threatened the government in Kiev. The article recognised that the far-right nationalists presented a double-edged sword as they could deter Russia, but they also deterred Zelensky from negotiating with Russia: "Mr. Zelensky would be taking extreme political risks even to entertain a peace deal, which is why he is so careful not to talk about possible avenues for negotiations."[462]

NATO Prepares Ukraine for War

In 2014 and shortly after the coup, NATO advisors assisted Ukraine in evaluating its security and defence sector, which eventually led to NATO endorsing the Comprehensive Assistance Package for Ukraine in 2016. The purpose of the Comprehensive Assistance Package was to "consolidate and enhance NATO's assistance for Ukraine" and "reform its Armed Forces according to NATO standards and to achieve their interoperability with NATO forces by 2020."[463] The U.S. Defence Intelligence Agency acknowledged in a report in 2017 that "The Kremlin is convinced the United States is laying the groundwork for regime change in Russia, a conviction further reinforced by the events in Ukraine."[464]

Ukraine began to build a NATO-trained army of 700,000 soldiers plus a million in reserve. Only the U.S. and Turkey among all the NATO countries had a larger army than Ukraine, making it a powerful frontline-state. The objective of using Ukrainians as a proxy to fight Russia had been advocated by George Soros in 1993, foreseeing a new world order where NATO would be the dominant institution. As Soros suggested, Western societies would find it difficult to accept large casualties among their own soldiers, which is why eastern Europeans should be used, since:

> the combination of manpower from Eastern Europe with the technical capabilities of NATO would greatly enhance the military potential of the Partnership because it would

---

462 Ibid.

463 NATO, "Comprehensive Assistance Package for Ukraine," July 2016.

464 "Russia Military Power: Building a military to support great power aspirations," *Defense Intelligence Agency*, 6 July 2017, 15.

> reduce the risk of body bags for NATO countries, which is the main constraint on their willingness to act.[465]

The U.S. considered Ukraine as a key instrument to weaken Russia as a strategic rival. In 2019, the U.S. *Army Quadrennial Defence Review Office* funded a 325-page long report developed by the RAND Corporation, a think tank funded by the U.S. government and renowned for its close ties with the intelligence community. The RAND report had the title: "Extending Russia: Competing from Advantageous Ground" and explored ways to provoke Russia "to overextend itself militarily or economically or causing the regime to lose domestic and/or international prestige and influence."[466]

The RAND report identified Ukraine as a region where Russia is "bleeding" and recognises opportunities: "Providing more U.S. military equipment and advice could lead Russia to increase its direct involvement in the conflict and the price it pays for it. Russia might respond by mounting a new offensive and seizing more Ukrainian territory," although the report also recognises the dilemma of provoking a Russian incursion: "While this might increase Russia's costs, it would also represent a setback for the United States, as well as for Ukraine."[467] The threat of NATO expansion is also deemed helpful to instigate tensions between Russia and Ukraine: "While NATO's requirement for unanimity makes it unlikely that Ukraine could gain membership in the foreseeable future, Washington pushing this possibility could boost Ukrainian resolve while leading Russia to redouble its efforts to forestall such a development."[468] The strategy of using Ukraine as a proxy to weaken Russia gave rise to explicit comparisons to Afghanistan:

> Expanding U.S. assistance to Ukraine, including lethal military assistance, would likely increase the costs to Russia, in both blood and treasure, of holding the Donbass

---

465 G. Soros, "Toward A New World Order: The Future of NATO," *Open Society Foundations*, 1 November 1993.

466 J. Dobbins, R. S. Cohen, N. Chandler, B. Frederick, E. Geist, P. DeLuca, F. E. Morgan, H. J. Shatz, and B. Williams, *Extending Russia: Competing from Advantageous Ground* (Santa Monica, CA: RAND Corporation, 24 April 2019), iii.

467 Ibid., xv.

468 Ibid., 99.

> region. More Russian aid to the separatists and an additional Russian troop presence would likely be required, leading to larger expenditures, equipment losses, and Russian casualties. The latter could become quite controversial at home, as it did when the Soviets invaded Afghanistan.[469]

So the strategy of weakening Russia had to be carefully "calibrated" as the objective was to slowly bleed Russia while avoiding starting a full-scale war:

> Providing lethal aid to Ukraine would exploit Russia's greatest point of external vulnerability. But any increase in U.S. military arms and advice to Ukraine would need to be carefully calibrated to increase the costs to Russia of sustaining its existing commitment without provoking a much wider conflict in which Russia, by reason of proximity, would have significant advantages.[470]

In early 2017, U.S. Senators John McCain and Lindsay Graham visited Ukrainian troops near the Donbas frontline to call for an escalation against Russia. Senator John McCain informed the Ukrainian troops: "I believe you will win. I am convinced you will win and we will do everything we can to provide you with what you need to win." Senator Lindsay Graham similarly told the Ukrainian troops: "Your fight is our fight. 2017 will be the year of offense." He continued: "All of us will go back to Washington and we will push the case against Russia. Enough of a Russian aggression. It is time for them to pay a heavier price."[471]

In 2019, Oleksii Arestovich, a popular advisor to President Zelensky, predicted the Russian invasion that would occur three years later. Arestovich believed that Ukraine had to join NATO, otherwise, it would gradually be absorbed by Russia. The price for joining NATO would be a major war with Russia. Arestovich explained that the threat of Ukraine's accession to NATO would "provoke Russia to launch a

469 Ibid., 99.

470 Ibid., 136.

471 D. M. Herszenhorn, "U.S. senators praise Ukrainian marines, slam Putin," *Politico*, 2 January 2017.

large-scale military operation against Ukraine" to ensure that "NATO would be reluctant in accepting us." Arestovich argued that the current path of Ukraine towards NATO would make the likelihood of a Russian invasion "99.9 percent" certain and that the "period between 2020-2022 was the most critical." Arestovich predicted "a large-scale war with Russia and joining NATO as a result of the defeat of Russia. The coolest thing." Victory would be ensured as this was a NATO proxy war: "In this conflict, we will be very actively supported by the West—with weapons, equipment, assistance, new sanctions against Russia and the quite possible introduction of a NATO contingent, a no-fly zone etc. We won't lose, and that's good."[472]

NATO was also preparing for war against Russia in the Baltic States. In September 2020, the U.S. placed multiple-launch rocket systems for a live-fire exercise with tactical missiles in Estonia—merely 70 miles from the Russian border. In May 2021, another NATO military exercise included the launch of 24 missiles to simulate an attack on the Russian air defence system.[473] They continued to insist that this was not provoking Russia, although the U.S. would certainly have reacted fiercely to such provocations on its own borders.

Moscow was convinced that the U.S. remained committed to its objective after the coup in Kiev to replace the Russian Black Sea Fleet in Crimea. In 2021, Ukraine accelerated its adoption of NATO standards.[474] The U.S. had begun work on upgrading Ukrainian ports in 2019 to fit U.S. warships.[475] In February 2021, Ukraine and NATO announced plans to construct two new naval bases on Ukraine's Black Sea coast. Ukrainian Prime Minister Denys Shmyhal announced at NATO headquarters in Brussels that the UK is "helping us financially" to construct the naval bases. At the joint press conference, NATO Secretary General Jens Stoltenberg confirmed that the Black Sea would be a key priority for NATO:

---

472 A. Arestovich, "Voennoe Obozrenie" [Military Review], *Apostrof TV*, 18 February 2019.

473 B. Deveraux, "Rocket Artillery can keep Russia out of the Baltics," *War on the Rocks*, 20 May 2021.

474 H. Shelest, "Defend. Resist. Repeat: Ukraine's lessons for European defence," *ECFR*, 9 November 2022.

475 P. Mcleary, "U.S. Upgrades Ukrainian Ports To Fit American Warships," *Breaking Defense*, 3 July 2019.

> I think we have to understand that the Black Sea is of strategic importance for NATO and the NATO allies—our littoral states, Turkey, Bulgaria and Romania. And then we have two close and highly valued partners in the region, Ukraine and Georgia.[476]

NATO's plans to expand its military presence on Ukraine's Black Sea coast were reaffirmed by General Tod Wolters, NATO's supreme allied commander and head of the U.S. European Command. Wolters argued that NATO must develop an "enhanced forward presence" in the Black Sea region in cooperation with Georgia and Ukraine.[477]

From March to June 2021, one of the largest U.S.-led military exercises in decades was launched which included the Baltic and Black Sea region. "Defender Europe 2021" included 28,000 troops from 27 different nations that signalled support for Ukraine. Arestovich, the advisor of Zelensky and representative in the Trilateral Contact Group in Donbas, referred to the military exercise as preparation for war with Russia: "Their meaning is that in the waters from the Baltic to the Black Seas, a war with Russia is being worked out—well, let's put it bluntly, the topic of an armed confrontation with Russia."[478]

In June and July 2021, the U.S. and Ukraine organised the largest naval exercise in decades, Sea Breeze 2021, which consisted of 32 ships, 40 aircrafts and 5000 soldiers from 24 countries in the Black Sea. The military exercise aimed to display NATO-Ukrainian solidarity and "with the goal of bringing Ukraine up to NATO standards."[479] The exercise almost caused Russia to fire upon a British warship that deliberately entered what Russia considers to be its territorial water. From Moscow's perspective, these actions were interpreted as a message to Moscow that NATO countries were behind Ukraine as a de facto member, and that both NATO and Ukraine were challenging Russia's control over Crimea.

---

476 J. Vandiver, "Ukraine plans Black Sea bases as U.S. steps up presence in region," *Start and Stripes*, 10 February 2021.

477 Ibid.

478 "In Kiev, they announced the development of a scenario of a war with Russia with NATO," *Teller Report*, 2 April 2021.

479 R. Goncharenko, "Ukraine, U.S. Black Sea drills raise tensions," *Deutsche Welle*, 29 June 2021.

On 21 June 2021, the UK signed a naval agreement with Ukraine on board the British Destroyer *HMS Defender* in the port of Odessa. The agreement included the UK constructing a new naval base on the Black Sea and another base on the Sea of Azov. Two days later, the *HMS Defender* sailed through the territorial waters of Crimea in a display of power under the auspices of upholding "freedom of navigation." Russia claims it fired warning shots and dropped bombs in the path of the *HMS Defender*. The incident had a profound impact on Moscow, which was becoming convinced that the NATO countries were determined to use Ukraine to project force against Russia as opposed to pursuing peace.

The incrementalism of making Ukraine a de facto NATO member continued with the Rapid Trident military exercise from September to October 2021 to enhance the interoperability between NATO and Ukraine.[480] Ukrainian Brigadier General Vladyslav Klochkov argued that the military exercise was "an important step toward Ukraine's European integration. It will strengthen the operational capabilities of our troops, improve the level of interoperability between units and headquarters of the Armed Forces of Ukraine, the United States, and NATO partners."[481]

While Ukraine and Russia were sending troops toward the border of Donbas, NATO appeared to throw fuel on the fire. In June 2021, NATO pushed the prospect of membership for Ukraine: "We reiterate the decision made at the 2008 Bucharest Summit that Ukraine will become a member of the Alliance."[482]

In the same month, June 2021, Kurt Volker, the former U.S. Ambassador to NATO and former U.S. Special Representative for Ukraine Negotiations from 2017 to 2019, opposed peace and reconciliation with Russia. Volker wrote that "Success is confrontation" in terms of what should be the objectives for an upcoming summit between President Joe Biden and President Vladimir Putin, which was organised to find peace in Ukraine and to restore stability and predictability in U.S.-Russian relations. Volker argued that the best

---

480 C. Menegay and A. Valles, "U.S., NATO, Ukraine enhance interoperability with Rapid Trident exercise," *U.S. Army*, 21 September 2021.

481 Ibid.

482 North Atlantic Council, "Brussels Summit Communiqué, North Atlantic Treaty Organization," 14 June 2021.

outcome for the summit was confrontation as any accommodation of Russia was tantamount to appeasement:

> It is surely not in the interests of the U.S., the EU, NATO, and other allies to see a summit in which Putin leaves convinced that he has blunted the United States and faces no consequences for his behavior. It would send a signal globally that authoritarians can get away with aggressive acts at home and abroad, and that the U.S. and the West will not take any meaningful action to stop them. This is why the Summit is riskier for Biden than Putin: any outcome that seems reassuring and benign on the surface actually works in Putin's favor. For the U.S., therefore, the best possible outcome is not one of modest agreements and a commitment to "predictability," but one of a lack of agreements altogether. Success is confrontation.[483]

The preparedness for war against Russia was evident across the American leadership. Evelyn Farkas, a former U.S. Deputy Assistant Secretary of Defence for Russia, Ukraine, Eurasia in the Obama administration, and former senior advisor to the Supreme Allied Commander in NATO, published an op-ed on 11 January 2022 with the title: "The U.S. Must Prepare for War Against Russia over Ukraine":

> We must not only condemn Russia's illegal occupations of Ukraine and Georgia, but we must demand a withdrawal from both countries by a certain date and organize coalition forces willing to take action to enforce it.... The horrible possibility exists that Americans, with our European allies, must use our military to roll back Russians—even at the risk of direct combat.[484]

In August 2021, the U.S. and Ukraine signed the U.S.-Ukraine Strategic Defence Framework, which formalised Ukraine as a de facto

---

483 K. Volker, "What Does a Successful Biden-Putin Summit Look Like? Not What You Think," *CEPA*, 2 June 2021.

484 E. Farkas, "The U.S. Must Prepare for War Against Russia Over Ukraine," *Defense One*, 11 January 2022.

NATO member state by translating NATO procurement into a bilateral U.S.-Ukrainian agreement. In November 2021, Moscow saw a war on the horizon as the U.S. and Ukraine signed the "U.S.-Ukraine Charter on Strategic Partnership" that committed the U.S. to Ukraine's "full integration into European and Euro-Atlantic institutions," to develop the Ukrainian army, deepen cooperation in the Black Sea, and provide "unwavering commitment" to reintegrating Crimea into Ukraine. Henri Guaino, a top adviser to former president Nicolas Sarkozy, warned that the charter "convinced Russia that it must attack or be attacked."[485]

Russia Demands Security Guarantees

By the end of 2021, Russia decided to set a red line backed up by the threat of military force. Moscow sent Washington a draft treaty in December 2021 outlining the conditions to restore security and stability in Europe. The draft treaty demanded that NATO would expand no further to the east, and commit Washington to not establish any military bases in Ukraine. In a second draft, Moscow also demanded that NATO would withdraw the troops and equipment it had moved into Eastern Europe since 1997.

The draft treaty largely reiterated commitments the West had already signed and agreed to in the 1990s. Both the agreements for pan-European security according to the Charter of Paris for a New Europe in 1990 and the founding document for the OSCE in 1994 were based on the principles of indivisible security in a Europe without any dividing lines. Furthermore, the NATO-Russia Founding Act of 1997 explicitly prohibited NATO from placing permanent troops in the new member states.

However, the U.S. and NATO rejected Russia's security demands; even discussing them was presented as dangerous appeasement. The negotiations did not progress as Washington was categorically against providing any limitations on NATO expansion and Biden's own proposals did not address the key Russian security concerns. Yet, one concession on U.S. military expansionism appeared to be offered to Moscow as Biden assured Putin that "Washington had no intention of deploying offensive strike weapons in Ukraine." However, Washington

485 C. Caldwell, "The War in Ukraine May Be Impossible to Stop."

appeared to change its mind with regard to accepting any limitations on deploying offensive strike weapons in Ukraine.[486] In response to Moscow's demand for security guarantees and warnings against crossing its red lines, President Biden responded "I don't accept anyone's red line."[487]

Any dissenting efforts to address Russian security concerns were swiftly shut down. The head of the German Navy, Vice Admiral Kay-Achim Schönbach, was forced to resign in January 2022 after arguing: "the Crimea Peninsula is gone: It will never come back—this is a fact"; and that the West should address Russian security concerns with respect.[488] Even after Russia invaded, the acceptance of criticism remained low. The head of Germany's armed forces, General Eberhard Zorn, was fired from his position after he argued in an interview with *Focus Magazine* in September 2022 that Ukraine "can win back places or individual areas of the frontlines, but not push Russia back over a broad front."[489] Furthermore, General Zorn had warned that continuing the war could risk that Russia might open a second front. U.S. General Ben Hodges criticised the analysis of German General Zorn, and a few months later Zorn was removed from his position.

To prevent the war, German Chancellor Olaf Scholz met with President Zelensky on 19 February 2022 in which he argued that "Ukraine should renounce its NATO aspirations and declare neutrality as part of a wider European security deal between the West and Russia."[490] Kiev rejected Germany's proposal and instead hinted towards further escalation. At the Munich Security Conference in February 2022, merely days before the Russian invasion, President Zelensky implied that Ukraine might develop nuclear weapons as the Budapest Memorandum had been breached.

---

486 R. McGovern, "Biden Reneged—Now Russian Army Will Talk," *AntiWar*, 30 December 2022.

487 "Biden Says He'll Make It 'Very Difficult' For Russia To Attack Ukraine," *RFE/RL*, 4 December 2021.

488 "German navy chief quits after Putin, Crimea gaffes," *Deutsche Welle*, 22 January 2022.

489 "Germany replaces the head of the Bundeswehr armed forces," *Deutsche Welle*, 13 March 2023.

490 "Vladimir Putin's 20-Year March to War in Ukraine—and How the West Mishandled It," *The Wall Street Journal*, 1 April 2022.

George Beebe, the former head of Russia analysis at the CIA, cautioned in December 2021 that Moscow "feels threatened" by the growing U.S. military actions in Ukraine to the extent this could pressure Russia into invading. Beebe argued that NATO membership for Ukraine was still distant, although the rapidly growing U.S. military cooperation with Kiev was making Ukraine a de facto NATO member. The U.S. was providing Ukraine with vast amounts of military equipment, training its army, and even upgrading Ukraine's ports to fit U.S. warships. Moscow was pressured by the U.S. military build-up on its borders to the extent that the risks Russia faced by invading were outweighed by the risks of not invading. As Beebe argued: "That relationship [U.S.-Ukraine] will be far stronger and deeper, and the United States military will be more firmly entrenched inside Ukraine two to three years from now. So inaction on [the Kremlin's] part is risky."[491]

This analysis of a pending war was largely confirmed by Moscow, as the Russian ambassador to Washington published an article in the *Foreign Policy* journal on 30 December 2021 with a direct warning:

> Everything has its limits. If our partners [the U.S. and NATO countries] keep constructing military-strategic realities imperilling the existence of our country, we will be forced to create similar vulnerabilities for them. We have come to the point when we have no room to retreat. Military exploration of Ukraine by NATO member states is an existential threat for Russia.[492]

On 26 December 2021, Putin warned that more than two decades of NATO expansionism towards Russian borders had pushed Russia into a corner. Putin seemingly implied that diplomatic efforts had been exhausted: "We have nowhere to retreat.... They have pushed us to a line that we can't cross. They have taken it to the point where we simply must tell them: 'Stop!.'" Russia's Foreign Minister Sergey Lavrov resorted to the same language: "We reached our boiling point."

---

491 "Russia's Proposal To Redraw European Security 'Unacceptable,' U.S. Says," *Radio Free Europe / Radio Liberty*, 18 December 2021.

492 A. Antonov, "An Existential Threat to Europe's Security Architecture?," *Foreign Policy*, 30 December 2021.

On 26 of January 2022, the U.S. and NATO rejected Russia's key demands for security guarantees. Washington insisted that they knew that a Russian invasion was forthcoming, yet any limitations on the U.S. and NATO were rejected. U.S. Secretary of State Anthony Blinken answered unmistakably: "there is no change; there will be no change" when asked if there could be any changes to NATO expansion.[493]

Linking NATO closer with Ukraine under a leadership committed to retaking Crimea by force also put pressure on Russia to act before the NATO-Ukraine military partnership deepened further. In a press conference following a meeting with the Hungarian Prime Minister, Putin warned about a possible great war in Europe:

> Listen attentively to what I am saying. It is written into Ukraine's doctrines that it wants to take Crimea back, by force if necessary. This is not what Ukrainian officials say in public. This is written in their documents.... Imagine that Ukraine is a NATO country and starts these military operations. What are we supposed to do? Fight against the NATO bloc? Has anyone given at least some thought to this? Apparently not.[494]

In a meeting with Macron in early February, Putin reiterated that "if Ukraine is in NATO and if they decided to take back Crimea using military means... European countries will automatically be in a military conflict with Russia."[495]

Conclusion

Russia went to war in February 2022 once it became convinced that diplomatic efforts were futile and exhausted. There was a recognition that Russia may have been walking into a trap as the U.S. and other NATO countries had prepared for a long proxy war. Yet, after eight years of sabotaging the Minsk-2 agreement, the assumption

493 A. Blinken, "Secretary Antony J. Blinken at a Press Availability," *U.S. Department of State*, 26 January 2022.

494 V. Putin, "News conference following Russian-Hungarian talks," *President of Russia*, 1 February 2022.

495 D. M. Herszenhorn and G. Leali, "Defiant Putin mauls Macron in Moscow," *Politico*, 7 February 2022.

in Moscow was seemingly that a display of force would convince Ukraine and the West to make peace. Irrespective of how the West would react to Russia using military force, the assumption was that if war was unavoidable then it was important to strike first.

9.

The Russian Invasion of 2022

RUSSIA SEEMINGLY considered its invasion of Ukraine in 2022 to be a pre-emptive attack to push through a peace agreement it could not achieve through diplomacy. Nonetheless, it was a war of aggression with unpredictable consequences. It also became a proxy war as the NATO countries saw the opportunity to fight and degrade Russia using Ukrainian soldiers. The proxy war became extremely dangerous as effectively it was the main frontline in the struggle for the future world order. The opposing sides in a conflict are willing to take greater risks when strategic rivalries are defined by total victory or defeat.

The main objective of the West is to revive its weakening position in the world and restore its collective hegemony under U.S. leadership. Defeating Russia would remove the key rival in Europe and weaken China, which enables the collective West to restore the so-called rules-based international order. However, a defeat in Ukraine would discredit NATO in Europe and intensify the emergence of a multipolar world. In the words of Polish Prime Minister Mateusz Morawiecki: "If we lose Ukraine, we will lose the world for decades. The defeat in Ukraine could be the beginning of the end of the golden age of the West."[496] President Biden similarly cautioned that rising conflicts meant the world order had "run out of steam" and argued for revitalising U.S. leadership and hegemony for "a new world order."[497]

496 Eastern Herald, "Polish Prime Minister Morawiecki Has Warned of the Beginning Of The End Of The West's Golden Age," *The Eastern Herald*, 18 April 2023.

497 J. Biden, "Remarks by President Biden at a Campaign Reception," *The White House*, 20 October 2023.

President Vladimir Putin also defined the conflict in Ukraine as being about world order, framing the conflict as a struggle between unipolarity as a source of conflict and multipolarity as a system of mutual constraints:

> This is not a territorial conflict and not an attempt to establish regional geopolitical balance. The issue is much broader and more fundamental and is about the principles underlying the new international order. Lasting peace will only be possible when everyone feels safe and secure, understands that their opinions are respected, and that there is a balance in the world where no one can unilaterally force or compel others to live or behave as a hegemon pleases even when it contradicts the sovereignty, genuine interests, traditions, or customs of peoples and countries.[498]

The Information War: An "Unprovoked" Russian Invasion

Mobilising popular opinion for a war against the world's largest nuclear power and rejecting peace negotiations requires the conflict to be ideologically framed as a struggle between good and evil. The consistent talking point among the Western political media elites has been to deny that Russia is motivated by legitimate security concerns, and instead assert that Russia's invasion of Ukraine was "unprovoked."

If the public were to believe that Russia was provoked into invading, then logic would suggest that a diplomatic solution could be reached, and any weapon supplies will only escalate the violence. However, this logic is turned on its head by framing Russia's invasion as unprovoked and an effort to acquire more territory or to "rebuild the Soviet Union." Arming Ukraine and prolonging the war is then logical to alter the cost/benefit calculations of Russian military opportunism. Any diplomatic solution would then merely appease and embolden Russia and other states to engage in similar hostilities in the future.

The mantra from NATO was therefore that the war could end anytime if Russia withdraws its soldiers, while for Russia the war is

498 V. Putin. "Valdai International Discussion Club meeting," *President of Russia*, 5 October 2023.

believed to be nothing less than an existential threat and cannot be lost. The narrative of an "unprovoked" invasion was therefore imperative to sustain a proxy war against Russia in which NATO sent powerful weaponry, the Europeans sacrificed their economies, and the rest of the world was pressured to isolate Russia.

The narrative that the invasion was not provoked was weak from the onset as the world's largest military alliance expanded towards Russian borders. Great powers are very sensitive about other major powers on their borders, especially Russia as its history exemplifies, to a large extent, a need to establish buffers against Western invaders. One can predict with great certainty that the U.S. would react similarly with war if Russia or China sought to establish a military alliance with Mexico and place their weaponry on the American border. Indeed, the U.S. threatened nuclear war in 1962 if the Soviets did not remove their nuclear weapons from Cuba. The hypothesis that the world order was not based on common rules was tested in January 2022 as Moscow suggested it could respond to the U.S. militarisation of Ukraine by sending Russian soldiers and weapon systems to Cuba and Venezuela. The U.S. National Security Advisor Jake Sullivan responded: "If Russia were to move in that direction, we would deal with it decisively."[499]

The narrative of an "unprovoked" invasion subsequently demanded strict information control due to almost 30 years of evidence that Russia considers NATO expansion to be the principal threat to Russia. In the information war this was later dismissed as "Russian propaganda." Dissenters who argued that the Russian invasion was not "unprovoked" could be accused of legitimising and supporting the war, thus justifying censorship from the public discussion and cancellation.

Following Russia's annexation of Crimea in 2014, Professor John Mearsheimer argued "the United States and its European allies share most of the responsibility for the crisis. The taproot of the trouble is NATO enlargement."[500] After Russia invaded in 2022, none other than Pope Francis suggested that "In Ukraine, it was other states that

499 "Press Briefing by Press Secretary Jen Psaki and National Security Advisor Jake Sullivan," *The White House*, 13 January 2022.

500 J. J. Mearsheimer, "Why the Ukraine crisis is the West's fault: The liberal delusions that provoked Putin," *Foreign Affairs* 93, no. 5 (2014): 1.

created the conflict" and added that the "barking of NATO at the door of Russia" may have provoked the Russian invasion of Ukraine.[501] Even the neoconservative hawk, Robert Kagan asserted that "to insist that the invasion was entirely unprovoked is misleading" as "Russian decisions have been a response to the expanding post–Cold War hegemony of the United States and its allies in Europe."[502] In May 2023, the U.S. Director of National Intelligence Avril Haines also concluded at a hearing of the Senate Armed Services Committee that the goals of Moscow were "to consolidate control over the occupied territory in the eastern and southern Ukraine, and ensuring that Ukraine will never become a NATO ally."[503]

By removing NATO provocations from the equation, the invasion could be attributed solely to Russian malice and its internal dysfunction. Another common narrative was that Putin was seeking to restore the Soviet Union and prevent Ukrainian democracy and freedom from spreading to Russia. The year was now 1938 and Putin was the new Hitler, thus Russia would move on to invade the rest of Eastern Europe if the West would fail to stop Putin in Ukraine. The war propaganda in the West thus referred to an unhinged Russian dictator seeking to eliminate Ukraine's sovereignty to restore a Russian empire. On the day of the Russian invasion, President Biden asserted:

> This was never about genuine security concerns on their part. It was always about naked aggression, about Putin's desire for empire by any means necessary—by bullying Russia's neighbors through coercion and corruption, by changing borders by force, and, ultimately, by choosing a war without a cause.[504]

The EU Foreign Policy Chief and top diplomat, Josep Borrell, dismissed the role of diplomacy as he argued the war would be won

---

501 F. X. Rocca and E. Gershkovich, "Pope Says NATO Might Have Provoked Russian Invasion of Ukraine," *The Wall Street Journal*, 3 May 2022.

502 R. Kagan, "The Price of Hegemony: Can America Learn to Use Its Power?," *Foreign Affairs*, May/June 2022.

503 AFP, "Putin Focused On Consolidating Ukraine Gains: U.S. Intel," *The Defense Post*, 5 May 2023.

504 "Remarks by President Biden on Russia's Unprovoked and Unjustified Attack on Ukraine," *The White House*, 24 February 2022.

on the battlefield and began arming Ukraine with the "European Peace Facility."[505] Similarly, NATO Secretary General Jens Stoltenberg argued that "weapons are the way to peace." The rejection of diplomacy and pursuit of victory on the battlefield was evident as Norway even awarded the Nobel Peace Prize to the Ukrainian Oleksandra Matvijtsjuk, who argued that compromise with Russia is not peace.[506] Former British Prime Minster Boris Johnson also opined that the West should not worry about escalation because the Russian invasion was unprovoked: "How can we seriously worry about provoking [Putin] when we have seen what he will do without the slightest provocation?." Johnson also dismissed the threat of escalating to nuclear war with Russia as even if there was a nuclear war "the Ukrainians will probably fight on and win anyway."[507]

After Russia invaded Ukraine in February 2022, the political media elites across the West insisted for the next 18 months that NATO expansion had nothing to do with Russia's decision to go to war. The reference to NATO expansion was dismissed as Russian propaganda providing a cover for seizing territory to restore the Russian or Soviet Empire. However, in September 2023, NATO Secretary General Jens Stoltenberg perhaps inadvertently admitted: "So he [Putin] went to war to prevent NATO, more NATO, close to his borders." The context of Stoltenberg's comments was his gloating that Russia had started the war to prevent NATO expansion but instead they got more NATO on its borders:

> President Putin declared in the autumn of 2021, and actually sent a draft treaty that they wanted NATO to sign, to promise no more NATO enlargement. That was what he sent us. And [it] was a pre-condition for not invad[ing] Ukraine. Of course we didn't sign that. The opposite happened. He wanted us to sign that promise, never to enlarge NATO. He wanted us to remove our military infrastructure in all Allies

---

505 "Foreign Affairs Council: Remarks by High Representative Josep Borrell upon arrival," *European Union External Action*, 11 April 2022.

506 "Fredsprisvinner: Kompromiss med Russland er ikke fred" [Peace-prize winner: Compromise with Russia is not peace], *NRK*, 10 December 2022.

507 K. Walla, "Boris Johnson: Stop worrying about Putin and 'focus entirely on Ukraine'," *Atlantic Council*, 1 February 2023.

> that have joined NATO since 1997, meaning half of NATO, all the Central and Eastern Europe, we should remove NATO from that part of our Alliance, introducing some kind of B, or second class membership. We rejected that. So he went to war to prevent NATO, more NATO, close to his borders. He has got the exact opposite. He has got more NATO presence in eastern part of the Alliance and he has also seen that Finland has already joined the Alliance and Sweden will soon be a full member.[508]

Russia's Plan of a Limited Intervention and NATO Sabotage of Peace Negotiations

Russia's invasion of Ukraine can be viewed in Clausewitzian terms, as a continuation of politics by other means. After Kiev's failure to implement the Minsk-2 agreement and NATO's reluctance to accommodate Russian security concerns, Moscow decided that all peaceful means had been exhausted. Threats are assessed by capabilities and intentions. The capabilities Russia faced increased rapidly as a powerful Ukrainian army was armed and trained by the West while incrementally being converted into a de facto NATO member. The intentions also appeared threatening as Kiev and NATO seemed fixed on a military solution to Donbas and even retaking Crimea. With these growing threats, the risks associated with a Russian military intervention were eventually seen to be outweighed by the risk of inaction.

The subsequent decision to use military force was framed as a "special military operation," partly due to the limited objective of pressuring Kiev to accept Moscow's demands. Russia's invasion indicated that the objective was to impose a settlement on Ukraine as this could not be achieved by diplomacy. Russia initially entered Ukraine with an army of approximately 150,000 troops, which were far too few to conquer and occupy Ukraine.

Steven Myers, who previously served on the U.S. State Department's Advisory Committee on International Economic Policy under two Secretaries of State, argued that Russian military tactics were

---

508 J. Stoltenberg, "Opening remarks," *NATO*, 7 September 2023.

"completely inconsistent with conquest" as the agenda was to keep Ukraine out of NATO.[509] Furthermore, the Russian military avoided attacks on critical infrastructure and was restrained to limit civilian casualties. The restraints by the Russian army in the early stages of the war reflected the limited objectives of pressuring Ukraine into negotiations without creating excessive animosity within the Ukrainian population as this would also make it difficult for Kiev to negotiate. The extent of Russian military assigned to Ukraine was organised to put pressure on Ukraine and the West; it was not sufficiently robust as an invasion army capable of occupying large parts of Ukrainian territory. However, this allowed NATO to put forward the narrative of a weak and backwards Russian army that could be defeated by the Ukrainians.

In the first weeks of the war, there were three attempts to negotiate Ukrainian neutrality to end the war before unleashing more excessive destruction. All efforts were close to success before being torpedoed by the U.S. and the UK. From a strategic perspective, Washington had an interest in preventing Ukraine's neutrality, while some carnage would enable the U.S. to weaken Russia and ensure a permanent Russia-Ukraine divorce. The U.S. sank Russia's objective of a brief and limited intervention by sabotaging peace negotiations and instead pushed for a long war.

On 25 February 2022, the day after the Russian invasion, President Zelensky argued: "Today we heard from Moscow that they still want to talk. They want to talk about Ukraine's neutral status.... We are not afraid to talk about neutral status."[510] If Kiev had agreed to neutrality and thus end its efforts to join NATO, the war would likely have been very short—as intended. On the next day, 26 February, Zelensky reaffirmed his preparedness to negotiate about Ukraine's neutrality: "If talks are possible, they should be held. If in Moscow they say they want to hold talks, including on neutral status, we are not afraid of this. We can talk about that as well."[511] The day after, on 27

509 J. Bacon and J. L. Oritz, "'Zelensky is in a box': Some experts say Ukraine won't win the war," *USA Today*, 27 July 2023.

510 V. Zelensky, "Address by the President to Ukrainians at the end of the first day of Russia's attacks," *President of Ukraine: Official website*, 25 February 2022.

511 P. Polityuk, "Ukraine ready for talks with Russia on neutral status—official," *Reuters*, 25 February 2022.

February, Moscow and Kiev announced they would hold peace talks "without preconditions" in Belarus.[512] Later, Zelensky even called for a "collective security agreement" that would also include Russia to mitigate the mutual security concerns that have sparked the war.[513]

In the West, there were expressions of concern about the prospect of a peace agreement and incentives were offered to keep the war going. On 25 February 2022, the first day after the Russian invasion, even as Zelensky agreed to discuss neutrality, U.S. spokesperson Ned Price announced Washington rejects any peace talks without preconditions as he insisted the U.S. could not accept diplomacy before Russia withdrew all its forces from Ukraine:

> Now we see Moscow suggesting that diplomacy take place at the barrel of a gun or as Moscow's rockets, mortars, artillery target the Ukrainian people. This is not real diplomacy… If President Putin is serious about diplomacy, he knows what he can do. He should immediately stop the bombing campaign against civilians, order the withdrawal of his forces from Ukraine, and indicate very clearly, unambiguously to the world, that Moscow is prepared to de-escalate.[514]

The Europeans also provided incentives for prolonging the war. On 27 February, the same day that Russia and Ukraine announced peace talks, the EU approved 450 million Euros in military aid to Ukraine in a forceful display of support, which reduced the incentives for Kiev to negotiate with Moscow.[515] As would be recognised later in the war by EU foreign policy chief Josep Borrell, the war would end "in a matter of days" without military support from the West.[516] The subsequent and ongoing claim by both the EU and the U.S. was that military aid should strengthen Kiev's power at the negotiating table,

---

512 S. Raskin and L. Brown, "Ukraine and Russia to meet for peace talks 'without preconditions,' Zelensky says," *New York Post*, 27 February 2022.

513 M. Hirsh, "Hints of a Ukraine-Russia Deal?," *Foreign Policy*, 8 March 2022.

514 U.S. Department of State, "Department Press Briefing," 25 February 2022.

515 J. Deutsch and L. Pronina, "EU Approves 450 Million Euros of Arms Supplies for Ukraine," *Bloomberg*, 27 February 2022.

516 M. McMahon, "'If we don't support Ukraine, Ukraine will fall in a matter of days,' says Josep Borrell," *Euronews*, 5 May 2023.

yet neither the EU nor the U.S. advocated for negotiations for the following year and a half. Instead, peace negotiations were actively sabotaged.

A second effort was made to negotiate a quick end to the conflict in early March, led by Israeli Prime Minister Naftali Bennett. The Israeli Prime Minister said that Zelensky had contacted him and requested peace talks with Putin.[517] According to Bennett, Putin was mainly preoccupied with the threat of NATO expansion and was therefore willing to make "huge concessions" by abandoning objectives such as the demilitarisation of Ukraine. Putin asked Bennett to tell Zelensky that the invasion would end if Zelensky would accept to remain outside of NATO, and Zelensky accepted these terms stipulating that Ukraine would not join NATO.[518] Bennett proposed that Ukraine could pursue the Israeli model of a strong independent army capable of defending itself instead of relying on NATO, which was acceptable to both Putin and Zelensky. Bennett claimed that "both sides very much wanted a ceasefire," and thus "there was a good chance of reaching a ceasefire."

However, Bennett argued that the West intervened and "blocked" the peace agreement. While Germany and France were pragmatic, the UK and the U.S. were hawkish and wanted to use the opportunity of war to fight and weaken Russia. According to Bennett, the West blocked the peace agreement as there was a "decision by the West to keep striking Putin" instead of pursuing peace. On 21 March 2022, U.S. spokesperson Ned Price suggested that a diplomatic settlement was not entirely up to Ukraine as it was also a conflict about world order:

> [T]his is a war that is in many ways bigger than Russia, it's bigger than Ukraine.... The key point is that there are principles that are at stake here that have universal applicability everywhere, whether in Europe, whether in the Indo-Pacific, anywhere in between. And those are the core principles that President Putin has sought to violate and flout and that our Ukrainian partners, backed by the international community, have sought to defend—the principle that each and every

517 N. Bennett, "Bennett speaks out," videotaped interview with Naftali Bennett, 4 Feb. 2023, 4:51:31, https://youtu.be/qK9tLDeWBzs?si=OVzKMzo7Z3AYNgBT.

518 Ibid.

> country has a sovereign right to determine its own foreign policy, has a sovereign right to determine for itself with whom it will choose to associate in terms of its alliances, its partnerships, and what orientation it wishes to direct its gaze. In this case, Ukraine has chosen a democratic path, a path—a Western-looking path, and that is something that, clearly, President Putin was not willing to countenance.[519]

A third effort to reach a peace agreement began in late March, as Turkey took the role of a mediator to negotiate peace between Ukraine and Russia. The main obstacle to peace was overcome as Zelensky offered neutrality in the negotiations.[520] Moscow and Kiev were therefore, yet again, close to a peace agreement. The tentative peace agreement was confirmed by Fiona Hill, a former official at the U.S. National Security Council, and Angela Stent, a former National Intelligence Officer for Russia and Eurasia. Hill and Stent penned an article in *Foreign Affairs* in which they outlined the main terms of the agreement. The article recognised that NATO expansionism had been the source of the conflict. Almost the entire political media elite across the West had asserted, in unison, that Russia's military actions had nothing to do with NATO expansionism and that it was not possible to negotiate with Putin. The article by Hill and Stent was an admission of the contrary:

> According to multiple former senior U.S. officials we spoke with, in April 2022, Russian and Ukrainian negotiators appeared to have tentatively agreed on the outlines of a negotiated interim settlement: Russia would withdraw to its position on February 23, when it controlled part of the Donbas region and all of Crimea, and in exchange, Ukraine would promise not to seek NATO membership and instead receive security guarantees from a number of countries.[521]

---

519 U.S. Department of State, "Department Press Briefing," 21 March 2022.

520 Guardian, "Ukraine has offered neutrality in talks with Russia—what would that mean?," *The Guardian*, 30 March 2022.

521 F. Hill and A. Stent, "The World Putin Wants How Distortions About the Past Feed Delusions About the Future," *Foreign Affairs*, September/October 2022.

Later, Putin revealed the draft agreement for a peace treaty that had been reached between Russia and Ukraine. The title of the draft agreement, "The Treaty on the Permanent Neutrality and Security guarantees for Ukraine," outlined that Ukraine would introduce "permanent neutrality" to its constitution.

However, on 9 April 2022, British Prime Minister Boris Johnson went to Kiev in a rush to sabotage the agreement. The killings in Bucha were cited as the reason for cancelling the peace negotiations. Reports from Ukraine claimed that the UK and U.S. had convinced Zelensky to abandon the peace agreement by offering Ukraine the weapons they required to defeat Russia on the battlefield.[522] Ukrainian media reported that Johnson came to Kiev with two messages:

> The first is that Putin is a war criminal, he should be pressured, not negotiated with. And the second is that even if Ukraine is ready to sign some agreements on guarantees with Putin, they [the UK and U.S.] are not.[523]

The Turkish negotiators confirmed that the West did not want peace as the U.S. and UK had established an opportune situation in which they could weaken Russia by fighting with Ukrainians as a proxy. Turkish Foreign Minister Mevlut Cavusoglu argued some NATO states wanted to extend the war to bleed Russia of its strength. Cavusoglu clarified:

> After the talks in Istanbul, we did not think that the war would take this long.... But following the NATO foreign ministers' meeting, I had the impression that there are those within the NATO member states that want the war to continue—let the war continue and Russia gets weaker. They don't care much about the situation in Ukraine.[524]

---

522 C. Echols, "Diplomacy Watch: Did Boris Johnson help stop a peace deal in Ukraine?," *Responsible Statecraft*, 2 September 2022.

523 R. Romaniuk, "Possibility of talks between Zelenskyy and Putin came to a halt after Johnson's visit—UP sources," *Ukraniska Pravda*, 5 May 2022.

524 R. Semonsen, "Former Israeli PM: West Blocked Russo-Ukraine Peace Deal," *The European Conservative*, 7 February 2023.

Numan Kurtulmus, the deputy chairman of Erdogan's political party, confirmed that Zelensky was ready to sign the peace agreement before the U.S. intervened:

> This war is not between Russia and Ukraine, it is a war between Russia and the West. By supporting Ukraine, the United States and some countries in Europe are beginning a process of prolonging this war. What we want is an end to this war. Someone is trying not to end the war. The U.S. sees the prolongation of the war as in its interest.[525]

Retired German General Harald Kujat, the former head of the German Bundeswehr and former chairman of the NATO Military Committee, confirmed that Johnson had sabotaged the peace negotiations to fight a proxy war with Russia. Kujat confirmed that an agreement was almost been reached in which "Ukraine had pledged to renounce NATO membership and not to allow any foreign troops or military installations to be stationed," while "Russia had apparently agreed to withdraw its forces to the level of February 23, i.e. before the attack on Ukraine began." However, General Kujat also confirmed that "British Prime Minister Boris Johnson intervened in Kiev on the 9th of April and prevented a signing. His reasoning was that the West was not ready for an end to the war"[526] According to Kujat, the West demanded what was tantamount to a Russian capitulation: "Now the complete withdrawal is repeatedly demanded as a prerequisite for negotiations."[527] General Kujat explained that this position was due to the U.S. war plans against Russia:

> Perhaps one day the question will be asked who did not want to prevent this war… Their declared goal is to weaken Russia politically, economically and militarily to such a degree that they can then turn to their geopolitical rival,

525 "Son dakika... Numan Kurtulmuş CNN TÜRK'te: (Rusya-Ukrayna) Birileri savaşı bitirmemek için çabalıyor" [Last minute... Numan Kurtulmuş on CNN TÜRK: (Russia-Ukraine) Someone is trying not to end the war]. *CNN Turk*, 18 November 2022.

526 J. Helmer, "Whr. Gen. Kujat: Ukraine War is Lost, Germany Now Faces an Angry Russia… Alone," *Veterans Today*, 25 January 2023.

527 Ibid.

> the only one capable of endangering their supremacy as a world power: China… No, this war is not about our freedom… Russia wants to prevent its geopolitical rival USA from gaining a strategic superiority that threatens Russia's security.[528]

Niall Ferguson at *Bloomberg* also cited sources in the U.S. and UK governments who favoured that "the conflict to be extended and thereby bleed Putin," as "the only end game now is the end of Putin regime."[529] Washington believed that the war could be used in a wider geopolitical campaign as weakening Russia and toppling Putin would send a strong signal to China. In the imperial tradition of having other nations fight their wars, retired U.S. General Keith Kellogg similarly argued in March 2023 that "if you can defeat a strategic adversary not using any U.S. troops, you are at the acme of professionalism." Kellogg further explained that using Ukrainians to fight Russia "takes a strategic adversary off the table" and thus enables the U.S. to focus on its "primary adversary which is China." NATO Secretary General Stoltenberg also argued that defeating Russia and using Ukraine as a bulwark against Russia "will make it easier" for the U.S. "to focus also on China… if Ukraine wins, then you will have the second biggest army in Europe, the Ukrainian army, battle-hardened, on our side, and we'll have a weakened Russian army, and we have also now Europe really stepping up for defense spending."[530]

The accusations and reports about the sabotage of the peace agreements to use Ukraine as a proxy to weaken Russia were never confirmed by London or Washington. Yet, the rhetoric that ensued suggests the British and Americans were setting the state for a prolonged proxy war. In April 2022, after Kiev withdrew from the peace negotiations in Istanbul, Johnson argued that "I think it's very hard to see how the Ukrainians can negotiate with Putin" and advocated instead to "keep going with the strategy" of supplying weapons to

---

528 "Russland will verhandeln!" [Russia wants to negotiate!], *Emma,* 4 March 2023.

529 N. Ferguson, "Putin Misunderstands History. So, Unfortunately, Does the U.S.," *Bloomberg*, 22 March 2022.

530 T. O'Conner, "So, if the United States is concerned about China and wants to pivot towards Asia, then you have to ensure that Putin doesn't win in in Ukraine," *Newsweek*, 21 September 2023.

Ukraine. In June 2022, Johnson argued in an address to the G7 and NATO that "now is not the time to settle and encourage the Ukrainians to settle for a bad peace" and instead argued for "strategic endurance."[531] In September 2022, Johnson argued yet again against a peace deal with Russia as it was necessary to stay the course in Ukraine since Moscow's position was weakening.[532] Later, Johnson published an op-ed in the *Wall Street Journal* arguing against any negotiations: "The war in Ukraine can end only with Vladimir Putin's defeat."[533] In October 2022, President Zelensky invoked a decree of the National Security and Defence Council of Ukraine making it illegal to hold negotiations with President Putin. Any political settlement would require the removal of President Putin from power. NATO's effort to prolong the Ukraine War for regime change in Russia was gaining momentum.

China proposed a 12-point peace plan in February 2023 to start negotiations. Both Russia and Ukraine responded to some extent positively to the proposal and its principles. Ukraine's foreign minister, Dmitri Kuleba, expressed Ukraine's preparedness to discuss the proposal. On the Russian side, President Putin also affirmed that the proposal presented a good point of departure for negotiations. However, the U.S. expressed "deep concerns" and its firm opposition to the Chinese-brokered ceasefire. National Security Council spokesman John Kirby argued that "we don't support calls for a ceasefire right now" as a ceasefire "basically ratifies what they've been able to grab inside Ukraine and gives them time and space to prepare for future operations, and that's just not going to be acceptable."[534] In June 2023, Secretary of State Anthony Blinken repeated the rejection of a ceasefire as Washington was pushing Kiev for a counter-offensive:

> [A] ceasefire that simply freezes current lines in place and enables Putin to consolidate control over the territory he's

531 E. Webber, "Boris Johnson warns against seeking 'bad peace' in Ukraine," *Politico*, 23 June 2022.

532 "Boris Johnson warns against a Ukraine-Russia peace deal," *BBC*, 22 September 2022.

533 B. Johnson, "For a Quicker End to the Russia War, Step Up Aid to Ukraine," *Wall Street Journal*, 9 December 2022.

534 T. Hains, "NSC's Kirby: Ukraine Should Reject Any Russian-Chinese Ceasefire Plan," *Real Clear Politics*, 20 March 2023.

> seized, and then rest, re-arm, and re-attack—that is not a just and lasting peace. It's a Potemkin peace. It would legitimize Russia's land grab. It would reward the aggressor and punish the victim.[535]

The U.S. rejection and sabotage of peace negotiations became a growing problem as world opinion, especially outside of NATO countries, was not supportive of the West's proxy war against Russia. Washington thus sponsored its own peace summits, first held in Denmark and thereafter another in Saudi Arabia. However, Russia was not invited to these peace summits and its security concerns about NATO expansion were not addressed. Their principal objective was to sow divisions within the BRICS countries (Brazil, Russia, India, China, and South Africa); Kiev explicitly stated that the objective was to organise the world around Ukraine. Therefore, the peace summits were alliance-building initiatives.

Weakening or Destroying Russia by Fighting to the Last Ukrainian

The American political leadership announced objectives ranging from weakening Russia to regime change and the breakup of Russia. On 24 February 2022, the day of the Russian invasion of Ukraine, President Biden announced the goal of sanctions was not to deter but to weaken Russia and undermine Putin's authority:

> no one expected the sanctions to prevent anything from happening.... this is going to take time. And we have to show resolve so he [Putin] knows what's coming and so the people of Russia know what he's brought on them. That's what this is all about.[536]

In his State of the Union Address on 1 March 2022, President Biden announced the objective to "sap [Russia's] economic strength

535 U.S. Department of State, "Russia's Strategic Failure and Ukraine's Secure Future," 2 June 2023.

536 J. Biden, "Remarks by President Biden on Russia's Unprovoked and Unjustified Attack on Ukraine," *The White House*, 24 February 2022.

and weaken its military for years to come."[537] U.S. Secretary of Defence Lloyd Austin outlined the U.S. objective in the Ukraine War as weakening its strategic adversary:

> We want to see Russia weakened to the degree that it can't do the kinds of things that it has done in invading Ukraine.... So it [Russia] has already lost a lot of military capability. And a lot of its troops, quite frankly. And we want to see them not have the capability to very quickly reproduce that capability.[538]

Shortly thereafter, in a speech about Ukraine in Warsaw, President Biden yet again suggested that regime change was necessary in Russia: "For God's sake, this man cannot remain in power." However, the White House later walked back Biden's remarks about regime change. U.S. Senator Lindsay Graham was more explicit in his support for regime change and even advocated assassinating the Russian president: "The only way this ends is for somebody in Russia to take this guy out," as there was "no off-ramp" which would enable Putin to remain in power. When criticised for his remarks, Graham doubled down by stating "let's take out Putin" otherwise China would be emboldened.[539]

The spokesperson of Prime Minister Boris Johnson, also made explicit reference to regime change by arguing "the measures we're introducing, that large parts of the world are introducing, are to bring down the Putin regime." James Heappey, the UK Minister for the Armed Forces, similarly wrote in the *Daily Telegraph:*

> His failure must be complete; Ukrainian sovereignty must be restored, and the Russian people empowered to see how little he cares for them. In showing them that, Putin's days as President will surely be numbered and so too will those

537 J. Biden, "Remarks by President Biden in State of the Union Address," *The White House*, 1 March 2022.

538 G. Carbonaro, "U.S. Wants Russia 'Weakened' So It Can Never Invade Again," *Newsweek*, 25 April 2022.

539 J. Lemon, "'Let's Take Out Putin': Graham Doubles Down on Ukraine War 'Off-Ramp'," *Newsweek*, 8 May 2022.

> of the kleptocratic elite that surround him. He'll lose power and he won't get to choose his successor.[540]

The decision by the Europeans to have the International Criminal Court issue an arrest warrant for President Putin under his alleged responsibility for war crimes could also be interpreted as a call for regime change, as any diplomacy would then become almost impossible with a Putin-led Russian government.

In the first week of the Russian invasion in February 2022, former Secretary of State Hillary Clinton argued on MSNBC that the U.S. should treat Ukraine as another Afghanistan: "I think that [Afghanistan] is the model that people are now looking toward."[541] Leon Panetta—the White House chief of staff under Bill Clinton, the U.S. Secretary of Defence, and CIA director under Barack Obama—argued in March 2022: "We are engaged in a conflict here, it's a proxy war with Russia, whether we say so or not.... The way you get leverage is by, frankly, going in and killing Russians."[542]

Chas Freeman, the former U.S. Assistant Secretary of Defence for International Security Affairs and Director for Chinese Affairs at the U.S. State Department, acknowledged but criticised what he referred to as a U.S. proxy war against Russia in Ukraine. According to Freeman, the hawks in Washington had decided that "we will fight to the last Ukrainian," which implies policies are aimed at prolonging rather than ending the war:

> the United States is not part of any effort to negotiate an end to the fighting. To the extent that there is mediation going on, it seems to be by Turkey, possibly Israel, maybe China. That's about it. And the United States is not in the room. Everything we are doing, rather than accelerating an end to the fighting and some compromise, seems to be aimed at prolonging the fighting, assisting the Ukrainian

540 J. Heappey, "Ukrainians are fighting for their freedom, and Britain is doing everything to help them," *The Telegraph*, 26 February 2022.

541 "Transcript: The Rachel Maddow Show, 2/28/22, Guests: Hillary Clinton, Alexander Prokhoren," *MSNBC*, 1 March 2022.

542 L. Panetta, "U.S. Is in a Proxy War With Russia: Panetta," *Bloomberg*, 17 March 2022.

> resistance—which is a noble cause, I suppose, but that will result in a lot of dead Ukrainians as well as dead Russians.[543]

U.S. Congressman Dan Crenshaw advocated continuing the proxy war by supplying weapons to Ukraine as "investing in the destruction of our adversary's military, without losing a single American troop, strikes me as a good idea."[544] Republican Senator Lindsey Graham similarly argued that the U.S. was in a favourable position as it could fight Russia to the last Ukrainian: "I like the structural path we're on here. As long as we help Ukraine with the weapons they need and the economic support, they will fight to the last person."[545] The Republican leader, Mitch McConnell, cautioned against conflating the idealism of helping Ukraine with the reality of U.S. objectives in the proxy war:

> President Zelenskyy is an inspiring leader. But the most basic reasons for continuing to help Ukraine degrade and defeat the Russian invaders are cold, hard, practical American interests. Helping equip our friends in Eastern Europe to win this war is also a direct investment in reducing Vladimir Putin's future capabilities to menace America, threaten our allies, and contest our core interests.... Finally, we all know that Ukraine's fight to retake its territory is neither the beginning nor end of the West's broader strategic competition with Putin's Russia.[546]

The following year, as American support for the war began to dwindle, Polish President Andrzej Duda argued in favour of continued U.S. engagement stating that they now had the opportunity to fight Russia with Ukrainian soldiers rather than American soldiers: "Right now, Russian imperialism can be stopped cheaply, because

---

543 A. Maté, "U.S. fighting Russia 'to the last Ukrainian': Veteran U.S. diplomat," *The Grayzone*, 24 March 2022.

544 L. Lonas, "Crenshaw, Greene clash on Twitter: 'Still going after that slot on Russia Today'," *The Hill*, 11 May 2022.

545 A. Maté, "U.S., UK sabotaged peace deal because they 'don't care about Ukraine': fmr. NATO adviser," *The Grayzone*, 27 September 2022.

546 M. McConnell, "McConnell on Zelenskyy Visit: Helping Ukraine Directly Serves Core American Interests," *Mitch McConnell official website*, 21 December 2022.

American soldiers are not dying."[547] On 21 September 2023, Mitch McConnell reiterated the wider strategic significance of America's war against Russia in a tweet: "American support for Ukraine is not charity. It's in our own direct interests—not least because degrading Russia helps to deter China."

Senator Mitt Romney also informed his countrymen that sending weapons to Ukraine was "the best national defense spending I think we've ever done" because it is a relatively small amount to pay and "we're losing no lives in Ukraine." In return for this investment "We're diminishing and devastating the Russian military for a very small amount of money... a weakened Russia is a good thing." Senator Richard Blumenthal reassured Americans that "we're getting our money's worth on our Ukraine investment" because "for less than 3 percent of our nation's military budget, we've enabled Ukraine to degrade Russia's military strength by half." Besides weakening Russia and sending a message to China, the U.S. was able to "restore faith and confidence in American leadership—moral and military. All without a single American service woman or man injured or lost."[548]

In addition to weakening Russia and pursuing regime change, others sought the even greater goal of destroying Russia itself by breaking up the country. On 23 June 2022 a U.S. government body overseen by the Congress, the Commission on Security and Cooperation in Europe also known as the Helsinki Commission, launched a discussion on "decolonizing Russia." The premise for the forum was that Russia is not a country, but an empire that the U.S. must break up by supporting separatist movements within the country.[549] Plotting how to balkanise Russia occurred under the guise of supporting "anti-colonial" and "pro-sovereignty" movements, which thus made dismantling Russia a "moral and strategic imperative."

One of the most active speakers at the event, published an article in *The Atlantic* a month before with the same title: "Decolonize Russia." He similarly argued that: "The West must complete the

---

547 M. A. Thiessen, "Why should conservatives support Ukraine? I asked a populist leader in Europe," *The Washington Post*, 10 August 2023.

548 R. Blumenthal, "Zelenskyy doesn't want or need our troops. But he deeply and desperately needs the tools to win," *CT Post*, 29 August 2023.

549 Commission on security and cooperation in Europe (CSCE), "Decolonizing Russia: A Moral and Strategic Imperative," 23 June 2022.

project that began in 1991. It must seek to fully decolonize Russia.... Until Moscow's empire is toppled, though, the region—and the world—will not be safe."[550]

The goal of destroying Russia was further promoted by politicians such as Anna Fotyga, a member of the EU Parliament and the former Minister of Foreign Affairs of Poland. Fotyga called for sowing divisions within Russia: "We should put more focus on the regions and nations of the Russian Federation, their capacities, and their perspectives for sovereignty." The West's objective, according to Fotyga, should be to break up Russia into smaller states: "We should be aware that the dissolution of the Russian Federation might bring certain difficulties and risks, as with any transition period. However, those risks will be far less dangerous than leaving this aggressive empire unchanged."[551]

These initiatives can be considered a continuation of discussions in the U.S. starting in the 1990s, which advocated that the breakup of the Soviet Union should be followed by the breakup of Russia. Former U.S. Defence Minister, Robert Gates, recalled in his memoirs that Dick Cheney "wanted to see the dismantlement not only of the Soviet Union and the Russian Empire but of Russia itself, so it could never again be a threat to the rest of the world."[552] These ideas were further popularised by the influential Zbigniew Brzezinski who advocated in 1997 the establishment of "A loosely confederated Russia—composed of a European Russia, a Siberian Republic, and a Far Eastern Republic... a decentralized Russia would be less susceptible to imperial mobilization.[553]

An American-led War with a Military and Economic Battlefield

The role of the U.S. and NATO on the military battlefield became more pronounced as both sides continued to climb the escalation ladder. NATO pursued its usual incrementalism/salami tactics by

550 C. Michel, "Decolonize Russia," *The Atlantic*, 27 May 2022.

551 A. Fotyga, "The dissolution of the Russian Federation is far less dangerous than leaving it ruled by criminals," *Euractiv*, 27 January 2023.

552 R. M. Gates, *Duty: Memoirs of a Secretary at War* (New York: Knopf Doubleday Publishing Group, 2014).

553 Z. Brzezinski, "A Geostrategy for Eurasia," *Foreign Affairs* 76, no. 5 (1997).

providing increasingly more powerful and long-distance weapons as one red line after the other was crossed. Biden declined in March 2022 to send F-16 fighter jets capable of carrying nuclear weapons as "that's called World War III."[554] Yet, by August 2023, Biden approved that Denmark and Netherlands could send the F-16s.

Once the ammunition depots of NATO countries reached critically low levels, the UK began to send depleted uranium and the U.S. began sending cluster ammunition. Even Germany sent leopard tanks, which was especially controversial given the history of German tanks on the eastern front. A neo-Nazi group even attacked the Belgorod region within Russia with American armoured vehicles. NATO soldiers also appeared in large numbers in Ukraine, albeit as volunteers serving under the Ukrainian flag; their presence was necessary to assist with the technical management of the new weaponry. Former NATO Secretary General, Anders Rasmussen, suggested that individual NATO countries could "assemble a coalition of the willing" to intervene in Ukraine.[555]

In September 2023, the U.S. considered supplying Ukraine with 200-mile-range ATACMS missiles that could be used to attack deep inside Russia. Washington had previously argued they had received assurances from Kiev that American weapons would not be used to strike inside Russian territory. When asked if it was "okay if those missiles allow Ukraine to attack deep into Russian territory," U.S. Secretary of State Anthony Blinken responded: "In terms of their targeting decisions, it's their decision, not ours."[556] The U.S. eventually shipped ATACMS secretly to launch a surprise attack on Russia.[557]

Ukraine also relied heavily on Western intelligence for the targets of these weapons. Reports by *The New York Times* revealed that U.S. intelligence was used to kill Russian generals and helped to locate and strike the *Moskva* warship in the Black Sea.[558] U.S. National Security

---

554 S. Nelson, "'That's called World War III': Biden defends decision not to send jets to Ukraine," *New York Post*, 11 March 2022.

555 P. Wintour, "NATO members may send troops to Ukraine, warns former alliance chief," *The Guardian*, 7 June 2023.

556 A. Blinken, "Secretary Antony J. Blinken With Jonathan Karl of ABC This Week," U.S. Department of State, 10 September 2023.

557 L. Seligman, P. McLeary, and A. Ward, "Ukraine uses secretly shipped U.S. missiles to launch surprise strike," *Politico*, 17 October 2023.

558 H. Cooper, E. Schmitt, and J. E. Barnes, "U.S. Intelligence Helped Ukraine

Advisor Jake Sullivan and Under Secretary of State for Political Affairs Victoria Nuland openly stated U.S. support for attacks on Crimea. As the West shipped large amounts of armoured vehicles, weapons and ammunition in preparation to Ukraine's summer offensive in 2023, Nuland also revealed that the U.S. had been involved in planning the offensive.

The involvement of the NATO became incrementally more brazen. A source in the Ukrainian general staff even told *The Economist* that they were pressured by the West to do attacks they were not prepared for: "We simply don't have the resources to do the frontal attacks that the West is imploring us to do."[559] It seems reasonable to assume that the U.S. strategy of fighting Russia would be different when fighting with Ukrainian soldiers as opposed to when doing so with their own soldiers. For example, the *Washington Post* reported that "Ukraine incurred major casualties against Russia's well-prepared defenses" and that The U.S. and UK "anticipated such losses but envisioned Kyiv accepting the casualties as the cost of piercing through Russia's main defensive line."[560]

There was possibly more profound involvement by NATO in the attacks on Russia, although the West's political media establishment tended to initially blame Russia for attacking itself: for attacking its own Nord Stream pipelines, and for continuously bombing the nuclear power plant under Russian control in occupied Zaporizhzhia, although Russia never bombed the nuclear powerplants under Kiev's control. It was similarly suggested that Russia might attack the Kremlin with drones in a false flag operation. In the absence of support by evidence or logic, the political media establishment commonly suggests such actions do not require further explanation as it is straight out of the "Russian playbook."

On the economic battlefield, the West also imposed unprecedented sanctions against Russia that were aimed at destroying its economy, financial system, and currency. The French Finance Minister Bruno Le Maire confirmed that the West is "waging an all-out economic and

---

Strike Russian Flagship, Officials Say," *The New York Times*, 5 May 2022.

559 "Ukraine's sluggish counter-offensive is souring the public mood," *The Economist*, 20 August 2023.

560 J. Hudson and A. Horton, "U.S. intelligence says Ukraine will fail to meet offensive's key goal," *The Washington Post*, 17 August 2023.

financial war on Russia" to "cause the collapse of the Russian economy."[561] *The New York Times* reported that the sanctions had the objective of fuelling unrest in Russia and that regime change was at the top of everyone's mind. The sanctions "ignited questions in Washington and in European capitals over whether cascading events in Russia could lead to regime change, or rulership collapse, which President Biden and European leaders are careful to avoid mentioning."[562] The reference to the president of the Russian Federation as a war criminal and even indicting Putin at the International Criminal Court, signalled that the West was reducing its own room for diplomatic maneuverer.

The destruction of the Nord Stream pipelines delivered a blow to Russian energy revenues in Europe. While there has not been any solid evidence of culpability, the issue of *cui bono* and most traces lead to the U.S. Following the Western-backed Orange Revolution in Ukraine in 2004 that installed a pro-West/anti-Russian government, it became evident that the reliability of gas transit was adversely affected by the political instability. Germany sought to ensure a reliable and cheap supply of gas to fuel its energy-intensive industries by constructing the first Nord Stream gas pipeline connecting Germany directly to Russia through the Baltic Sea. The dilemma for the U.S. was that the more it sought to decouple Ukraine from Russia, the more Germany established independent relations with Russia by circumventing Eastern Europe. Historically, a key objective for the UK and then the U.S. has been to prevent the economic integration of Germany and Russia as a rival pole of power.

After the Western-backed coup in Kiev in 2014 the same problem emerged again. Conflicts between Ukraine and Russia returned with a vengeance and the reliability of energy supplies diminished. The solution was the agreement reached in 2015 to construct Nord Stream 2 to further increase the capacity of Russia to deliver gas to Germany while circumventing Eastern Europe. Without reliable gas supplies, Germany and Europe faced the possibility of deindustrialising and seeing their key industries flee to the U.S. Washington's efforts to obstruct the construction of Nord Stream 2 included political pressure

561 E. Wong and M. Crowley, "With Sanctions, U.S. and Europe Aim to Punish Putin and Fuel Russian Unrest," *The New York Times*, 4 March 2022.

562 Ibid.

and even sanctioning the companies of its European allies who participated in the project.

The RAND Corporation wrote a report in 2019 sponsored by the Army Quadrennial Defense Review Office about how to extend and weaken Russia. The report outlined the goal of cutting Russia's energy ties to Europe and "A first step would involve stopping Nord Stream 2."[563] In July 2020, then-U.S. Secretary of State Mike Pompeo argued: "We will do everything we can to make sure that that pipeline doesn't threaten Europe."[564]

Tensions between Ukraine and Russia escalated throughout 2021 and the threats against Nord Stream intensified. U.S. Senator Tom Cotton announced in May 2021 that "there is still time to stop it.... Kill Nord Stream 2 now, and let it rust beneath the waves of the Baltic."[565] On 14 January 2022, U.S. National Security Adviser Jake Sullivan also threatened the pipeline: "We have made clear to the Russians that pipeline is at risk if they move further into Ukraine."[566] Senator Ted Cruz similarly used very direct language calling for stopping Nord Stream: "This pipeline must be stopped and the only way to prevent its completion is to use all the tools available to do that."[567]

As NATO rejected Russia's demands for security guarantees in the weeks before the Russian invasion, the threats became unmistakable. On 7 February 2022, President Biden stood next to German Chancellor Scholz at a press briefing, warning that if Russia invades Ukraine, then "there will be no longer a Nord Stream 2. We will bring an end to it." When asked by a journalist how he would end a project under German control, Biden responded: "I promise you, we will be able to do that."[568]

U.S. spokesperson, Ned Price, was explicit: "I want to be very clear: if Russia invades Ukraine one way or another, Nord Stream 2

563 RAND, "Extending Russia: Competing from Advantageous Ground," *RAND Corporation*, 24 April 2019, p.62.

564 "Pompeo Says U.S. Will 'Do Everything' To Stop Nord Stream 2 Project," *RFE/RL*, 30 July 2020.

565 T. Cotton, "Kill Russia's Nord Stream 2, Let it Ruse in the Baltic," *Tom Cotton official website*, 19 May 2021.

566 "At this hour with Kate Bolduan," *CNN*, 14 January 2022.

567 T. Cruz, "President Biden and the Democrats have Imperiled Ukraine and Put Europe on the Brink of War," *Ted Cruz official website*, 7 February 2022.

568 S. Sarkar, "'There Will No Longer Be a Nord Stream 2': Fingers Pointed Towards Biden after Gas Pipeline Blasts," *News18*, 30 September 2022.

will not move forward."[569] Undersecretary of State for Policy, Victoria Nuland, used the exact same words: "If Russia invades Ukraine, one way or another, Nord Stream 2 will not move forward."[570]

On 26 September 2022, the German-Russian Nord Stream pipelines were destroyed in an underwater explosion, which also had a massive impact on the environment. The former Foreign Minister of Poland, Radek Sikorski, tweeted "Thank you, USA" accompanied by a picture of the destroyed pipeline. The next day, on 27 September 2022, leaders from Poland, Norway, and Denmark attended a ceremony in Poland to mark the opening of the new Norway-Poland Baltic Pipe that was constructed to reduce Europe's dependence on Nord Stream.

U.S. Secretary of State Antony Blinken even celebrated the destruction of Nord Stream, saying it presented "a tremendous opportunity. It's a tremendous opportunity to once and for all remove the dependence on Russian energy." Blinken also offered to assist Western Europe by replacing Russian gas with much more expensive American energy. Victoria Nuland weighed in with: "I am, and I think the Administration is, very gratified to know that Nord Stream 2 is now, as you like to say, a hunk of metal at the bottom of the sea."[571]

While celebrating the destruction of the pipeline, the U.S. and NATO initially blamed Russia for attacking its own pipeline. NATO Secretary General Jens Stoltenberg seemingly threatened war by suggesting such attacks could trigger NATO's Article 5 of collective defence. However, the disinformation about Russia's responsibility for destroying a key pillar of Europe's energy infrastructure, against Russia's own interests, ended with the report of Pulitzer Prize-winning investigative journalist Seymour Hersh. Based on information gleaned from his sources, Hersh's report argued that the U.S.—with the cooperation of Norway—had attacked the gas pipelines.[572] These allegations were rejected by Washington, yet its narrative changed nonetheless as Washington began to blame a rogue "pro-Ukrainian group" for the

569 "Nord Stream 2 won't happen if Russia invades Ukraine: U.S.," *Deutsche Welle*, 27 January 2022.

570 "If Russia invades Ukraine, Nord Stream 2 pipeline will not move forward: U.S.," *Wion*, 28 January 2022.

571 I. Van Brugen, "Sergei Lavrov Accuses U.S. of Nord Stream Pipeline Attack," *Newsweek*, 2 February 2023.

572 S. Hersh, "How America Took Out The Nord Stream Pipeline," *Seymour Hersh* (Substack blog), 8 February 2023.

attack. While Russia was suddenly no longer the suspect in the West, the focus was shifted away from the U.S.

The entire story of the greatest attack on European security architecture and what could be categorised as environmental terrorism then disappeared from the media. It was suggested that politicians and the media should not speculate and instead let the investigators do their job, yet no independent investigation was forthcoming. Sweden announced in October 2022 that it would not establish a joint investigation team with allies such as Germany or share its findings due to national security. After being blocked from participation in the investigations, Russia put forward a resolution to the UN Security Council calling for establishing an international independent investigative commission into the September 2022 attacks on the Nord Steam pipelines. The Western countries rejected an independent international investigation and blocked the UN resolution.

Then, in June 2023, *The Washington Post* reported that leaks revealed the U.S. had intelligence indicating a Ukrainian plot to attack Nord Stream, despite the improbability of such a Ukrainian action being undertaken without Washington's awareness and approval. Whether there was U.S. or Ukrainian involvement in the attack, in either case, the U.S. would have known all along that Russia was not the culprit. Nonetheless, Washington lied to its own public and the international community with disinformation that risked a nuclear war with Russia.[573]

By the summer of 2023, it became evident that the Ukrainian counteroffensive had failed and there was increasing commentary from the political media establishment to address the failing narrative of Ukraine winning. Media reports began to blame Ukraine for the failure while there were also efforts to establish favourable measurements to present the proxy war in positive terms. Case in point, the *New York Times* reported that "American officials say they fear that Ukraine has become casualty averse, one reason it has been cautious about pressing ahead with the counteroffensive." The huge losses for minimal territorial gains discouraged the Ukrainians, although the Americans did not have the same considerations as they were fighting Russia with Ukrainian soldiers. A new narrative by the *Washington*

573 S. Harris and S. Mekhennet, "U.S. had intelligence of detailed Ukrainian plan to attack Nord Stream pipeline," *The Washington Post*, 6 June 2023.

Post replaced the notion of a Ukrainian victory with measurements of the war's advantage to the U.S.:

> Meanwhile, for the United States and its NATO allies, these 18 months of war have been a strategic windfall, at relatively low cost (other than for the Ukrainians). The West's most reckless antagonist has been rocked. NATO has grown much stronger with the additions of Sweden and Finland. Germany has weaned itself from dependence on Russian energy and, in many ways, rediscovered its sense of values. NATO squabbles make headlines, but overall, this has been a triumphal summer for the alliance.[574]

At this point, a victory narrative is required as Ukraine cannot realistically defeat Russia on the battlefield. The strongest narrative is obviously to claim that Russia has failed in its objective to annex all of Ukraine to recreate the Soviet Empire and thereafter conquer Europe. This narrative enables NATO to claim victory. However, such an approach also requires NATO to distance its own war objectives from those of Ukraine. Case in point, Sean Bell, a former Royal Air Force Air Vice-Marshal and Ministry of Defence staffer, argued in September 2023 that the war had significantly degraded the Russian military to the point it "no longer poses a credible threat to Europe." Bell therefore concluded that "the Western objective of this conflict has been achieved" and "The harsh reality is that Ukraine's objectives are no longer aligned with their backers."[575] Hence, the West may part ways with Ukraine as the Ukrainians have exhausted their ability to fight and weaken Russia, and thus lost their value in the proxy war.

Conclusion

With the use of unprecedented war propaganda, NATO was able to convince the public it was not part of the war and that the Russian

574 D. Ignatius, "The West feels gloomy about Ukraine. Here's why it shouldn't," *The Washington Post*, 18 July 2023.

575 S. Bell, "The West remains committed to Ukraine's counteroffensive—but there's scepticism over Zelenskyy's ultimate objectives," *Sky News*, 9 September 2023.

invasion had been unprovoked. However, to understand the war it is necessary to acknowledge that it has three participants: NATO, Russia, and Ukraine, with their respective objectives. NATO under U.S. leadership explicitly seeks to defeat Russia to end its great power status. The common definition of defeat is to destroy Russia's military and wreck its economy to impose a Western settlement in Ukraine. Beyond this objective, the definition of Russian defeat tends to vary across the West and has been defined more broadly by some in terms of regime change in Russia and dismembering Russia itself.

Russia considers the war to be an existential threat and has acted accordingly. Within Russia, there were disagreements regarding the urgency of the threat from NATO and the subsequent need to respond. However, once Russia invaded and the West demonstrated its intention to defeat Russia, the country coalesced around the Kremlin. The initial objective was to impose neutrality on Ukraine, although as the war escalated to a war of attrition Russia annexed territory thus complicating possible peaceful solutions.

Ukraine obviously also considers the war to be an existential threat, although different factions within Ukraine may turn on each other. Zelensky's initial instinct was to make peace with Russia, although he gave into American and British pressure to prolong the war. The moderates are unhappy with Zelensky for allowing the U.S. to dictate the development of the war by—for example—launching the disastrous offensive in the summer of 2023 while the far right will not accept negotiations. The need to preserve cohesion within Ukraine thus limits the room for manoeuvre.

Irrespective of the outcome of the war, the unipolar world order has come to an end. The war has demanded NATO solidarity, yet the Europeans are not content with how their position has weakened vis-à-vis the U.S. The rest of the world did not support Russia's invasion of Ukraine, yet they also did not support NATO's proxy war against Russia. Much of the world is therefore seeking to reduce their reliance on the U.S. and diversify their economic ties. For the foreseeable future, Russia will develop a more powerful army on its western borders, while its economic connectivity will be directed to the east.

10.

A Eurasian-Westphalian World Order

BEFORE THE EMERGENCE of the Western-centric world in the 16th century, the ancient Silk Road had connected China, India, Central Asia, the Middle East, and Europe through a network of trade routes from the 2nd century BC to the 15th century AD. The Silk Road facilitated cultural exchange and international trade which led to the emergence of new economic centres and the rise of powerful empires. The Silk Road also contributed to the growth of the Roman Empire by providing the Romans with new technologies and ideas of Chinese provenance, such as papermaking, medical technologies and gunpowder that significantly impacted the development of Western civilisation. The Silk Road was an early model of globalisation, although it did not result in a common world order as the civilisations of the world were primarily connected by nomadic intermediaries.

The demise of the ancient Silk Road was largely caused by the decline of the nomadic Mongol Empire in 14th century and the rise of European maritime power during the Age of Exploration starting in the 15th century. The rise of the European maritime powers entailed reconnecting the world through European trade-post empires. The endurance of the collective hegemony of Western maritime powers relied on preserving divisions across Eurasia to control the arteries of trade, and for centuries, preventing the emergence of a Eurasian world order was a key strategy. However, after five centuries of Western dominance, the unique world order it produced by controlling the vast Eurasian continent from the maritime periphery is coming to an end.

A Eurasian world order is now finally emerging as the international distribution of power continues to shift from the West to the East, and the legitimacy of the Western-centric world order has been severely weakened. Railways enabled Russia to take the role as the successor to the Mongolian nomads as the last custodian of the Eurasian land corridor, while China is seeking to revive the ancient Silk Road with economic connectivity. A powerful Eurasian gravitational pull is thus reorganising the supercontinent and the wider world.

The West's trade-post empires eventually evolved into colonial empires and imperial powers, although following the same format of controlling economic connectivity. The hegemonic maritime powers capable of dominating the seas, such as the UK and then the U.S., rely on divisions across Eurasia. In contrast, the Eurasian powers enhance their power by increasing connectivity to reduce excessive dependence on the maritime hegemon. The principal objective is to create a favourable symmetry of interdependence by becoming less reliant on the West. The geoeconomics of multipolarity thus supports rules of civilisational distinctiveness as the foundation for sovereign equality.

Russia and China as Eurasian Powers

Russia and China are the key actors spearheading a more balanced international distribution of power. Adam Smith acknowledged that the rise of Western maritime powers transformed the world. The discovery of America and a passage to the East Indies were, according to Smith, the "two greatest and most important events recorded in the history of mankind."[576] However, he also recognised that the immense concentration of power in Europe resulted in these two events having a huge human cost to the natives:

> To the natives however, both of the East and West Indies, all the commercial benefits which can have resulted from those events have been sunk and lost in the dreadful misfortunes which they have occasioned. These misfortunes, however, seem to have arisen rather from accident than from anything in the nature of those events themselves. At the particular

576 A. Smith, *An Inquiry into the nature and causes of the Wealth of Nations*, (Edinburgh: Adam and Charles Black, 1863), 282

> time when these discoveries were made, the superiority of force happened to be so great on the side of the Europeans that they were enabled to commit with impunity every sort of injustice in those remote countries.[577]

Smith anticipated, however, that a more benign and just world could emerge under a more evenly distributed balance of power:

> Hereafter, perhaps, the natives of those countries may grow stronger, or those of Europe may grow weaker, and the inhabitants of all the different quarters of the world may arrive at that equality of courage and force which, by inspiring mutual fear, can alone overawe the injustice of independent nations into some sort of respect for the rights of one another. But nothing seems more likely to establish this equality of force than that mutual communication of knowledge and of all sorts of improvements which an extensive commerce from all countries to all countries naturally, or rather necessarily, carries along with it.[578]

Russia became a key rival to Britain and then the U.S. as its extensive Eurasian geography threatened to unravel the primacy of maritime corridors. Historically, Russia has continuously struggled to regain access to maritime corridors. Russia's civilisational cradle was Kievan Rus with its convenient location on the Dniper River. The disintegration of Kievan Rus in the 13th century and the Mongol invasion that followed shortly thereafter resulted in Russia being severed from the arteries of international trade for centuries. Russia's enduring challenge has been to obtain adequate access to warm-water ports and maritime corridors enjoyed by the other Europeans. Limiting Russia's access to maritime corridors thus became a strategy by Western maritime powers such as Sweden, the UK, and the U.S. to weaken Russia.

The rise of Russia in the 19th century threatened to completely alter the world order by unravelling naval power as the foundation for the international distribution of power. The 19th century was marked by intense geopolitical rivalries among the major European powers,

577 Ibid.
578 Ibid.

and one of the most significant and enduring rivalries was between Britain and Russia. This rivalry was rooted in their competing imperial ambitions, territorial expansion, and competition for influence in regions crucial to their strategic interests. The British-Russian rivalry was especially unique as the Russians threatened to upend the significance of controlling the seas by connecting the Eurasian landmass with land corridors. Eurasian Russia thus threatened to unravel British dominance and the entire world order based on the primacy of Western maritime powers.

The British first became aware of the Russian threat as a Eurasian land power during the French Revolutionary Wars when the Russian Tsar briefly aligned with Napoleon and sent a Cossack army through Central Asia to reach British India.[579] However, the campaign did not produce any results as Tsar Paul I was assassinated in 1801, which ended the agreement with Napoleon and the Cossack army was subsequently ordered to return to Russia. While the immediate threat was gone, the British took note of a wider trend as Russia began to expand its influence towards the maritime periphery of the vast Eurasian continent.

Russia's victory in the Russian-Persian War (1826–1828) resulted in the Treaty of Turkmenchay, in which Persia ceded substantial territories to Russia, including parts of present-day Armenia, Azerbaijan, and Georgia. Russia's victory and territorial acquisition raised Britain's concerns as it enabled Russia to expand its territorial control and influence along the Black Sea with the possibility of wrestling Constantinople from the Ottomans. Furthermore, the Russo-Persian War reduced British influence in the region as it had been unable to provide decisive support, which incentivised Persia to look towards Russia instead as the leading regional power. The risk of a Russian-Persian conquest of British India became a growing concern for Britain.

The British and French subsequently assisted the Ottoman Empire by going to war against Russia, with the Russians suffering a humiliating defeat in the Crimean War (1853–1856). Russia's defeat further weakened its naval power and subsequent access to the seas,

---

579 D. S. Van der Oye, "Russia, Napoleon and the Threat to British India," in J. M. Hartley, P. Keenan, and D. Lieven (eds.), *Russia and the Napoleonic Wars* (London: Palgrave Macmillan, 2015).

although it also incentivised Russia to embrace technologies that augmented its ability to control land corridors. The lesson from the Crimean War was that Russian industries and infrastructure were too underdeveloped, and the remedy was rapid industrialisation and the construction of railroads to connect its vast territory. By 1879, roads and railways had become a key component of Russia's expansion into Central Asia as infrastructure translated into a sphere of influence.[580] In what became known as the Great Game, Russia and Britain were fighting for power in Central Asia as Russia expanded towards British India. Yet, the Great Game eventually came to an end with the Pamir Boundary Commission protocols of 1895, which made Afghanistan a buffer state between the Russian Empire as a land power and the British Empire as a sea power. Tensions rose again as Russia built the trans-Siberian Railroad to extend and cement its power on the Pacific Coast as Russia began expanding south to Port Arthur in China.

In the late 19th century, Russia's Finance Minister, Sergei Witte, began to develop ideas for a Eurasian political economy in accordance with the ideas of Alexander Hamilton and Friedrich List. Russia industrialised quickly and enjoyed rapid economic growth. Instead of remaining economically underdeveloped at the periphery of Europe and Asia, Russia could position itself at the centre of a larger Eurasian region connected by land corridors. Witte wanted to end Russia's role as an exporter of natural resources to Europe as it resembled "the relations of colonial countries with their metropolises."[581] By pivoting to Asia, the Russians hoped to offset their unfavourable position in Europe.

A Eurasian identity also began to develop as an alternative to Russia's futile efforts to be accepted in Europe. Since the early 18th century under Peter the Great, Russia had equated modernisation to the Europeanisation of Russia, which exacerbated existing schisms in Russian identity and society.[582] In the late 19th century, Fyodor Dostoyevsky argued that Russia's problems derived from its

---

580 H. T. Cheshire, "The Expansion of Imperial Russia to the Indian Border," *The Slavonic and East European Review,* 1934.

581 T. H. Von Laue, "A Secret Memorandum of Sergei Witte on the Industrialization of Imperial Russia," *The Journal of Modern History* 26, no.1 (1954): 66.

582 G. Diesen, *Russian Conservatism: Managing Change under Permanent Revolution* (London: Routledge, 2021).

continuous futile efforts to adjust to Europe where Russians would never be welcomed:

> Russians are as much Asiatics as European. The mistake of our policy for the past two centuries has been to make the people of Europe believe that we are true Europeans.... We have bowed ourselves like slaves before the Europeans and have only gained their hatred and contempt. It is time to turn away from ungrateful Europe. Our future is in Asia. True, Europe is our mother, but instead of mixing in her affairs we shall serve her better by working at our new orthodox idea, which will eventually bring happiness to the whole world. Meanwhile it will be better for us to seek alliances with the Asiatics.[583]

Mackinder's "heartland theory," which has greatly influenced British and American policy, subsequently analysed the threat of Russia becoming a Eurasian power as it represented a struggle between maritime powers and land powers. Mackinder considered the development of railways as key to this occurrence as it enabled Russia to emulate the nomadic skills of the Scythians, Huns, and Mongols that were required to control the vast continent: "the Russian army in Manchuria is as significant evidence of mobile land power as the British army in South Africa was of sea power." [584] Mackinder observed that "railways acted chiefly as feeders to ocean-going commerce," although transcontinental railways could rival and displace maritime transportation corridors:

> A generation ago steam and the Suez Canal appeared to have increased the mobility of sea-power relatively to land-power. Railways acted chiefly as feeders to ocean-going commerce. But trans-continental railways are now transmuting the conditions of land-power, and nowhere can they have such effect as in the closed heart-land of EuroAsia, in

583 A. Dostojevskij, *Fyodor Dostoyevsky: A Study* (Honolulu: University Press of the Pacific, 2001), 260.

584 H. J. Mackinder, "The Geographical Pivot of History," *The Geographical Journal* 170, no. 4 (1904): 434.

> vast areas of which neither timber nor accessible stone was available for road-making.[585]

Suddenly, it appeared that the military and economic imperative of controlling the world seas could be overturned: "The heartland is the region to which under modern conditions, sea power can be refused access."[586] The key objective of the British, and later the Americans, was therefore to prevent the emergence of a hegemon or a group of states capable of dominating Europe and Eurasia that could threaten the dominant maritime power.

With British support, the Japanese eventually defeated Russia in 1905 and pushed back its influence. From thereon, Russia began to destabilise and eventually ceased its existence as a state when the Bolsheviks took power following the revolution of 1917.

However, in the early 20th century, exiled Russian Eurasianists such as Trubetskoi and Savitsky continued to develop ideas of a Eurasian order that were deeply influenced by Mackinder. In the 1920s, Russian conservative Eurasianists envisioned a completely different path than that pursued by the Soviet Union. A Eurasian political economy was considered anti-hegemonic in opposition to the dominance of maritime powers. While the pursuit of hegemony by maritime powers, such as Britain and the U.S., required a divide-and-conquer tactic across the Eurasian continent, a Eurasian political economy required cooperation among the major civilisations to function:

> Eurasia has previously played a unifying role in the Old World. Contemporary Russia, absorbing this tradition, must resolutely and irrevocably abandon the old methods of unification belonging to an outlived and overcome era, such as those of violence and war.[587]

These ideas were suppressed during the Soviet era, while Russia in the liberal era of Yeltsin primarily sought economic integration with

---

585 Ibid.

586 H. J. Mackinder, *Democratic Ideals and Reality: A Study in the Politics of Reconstruction* (London: Constable, 1919), 86.

587 P. Savitsky, "The Geographical and Geopolitical Foundations of Eurasianism, Orient und Occident," no. 17, Moscow, 1933.

the West. Once it became evident that Russia would not be included in a Greater Europe after the Cold War but instead relegated to a permanently weakened and subservient supplier of natural resources, Eurasianist ideas made a powerful return. The Western-backed coup in Ukraine in 2014 convinced Russia to abandon its ambitions to construct a Greater Europe and instead to embrace the Greater Eurasian Partnership. Even the former Russian Foreign Minister Igor Ivanov, who had been a leading advocate for Greater Europe, acknowledged that the initiative had been utopian and that a necessary shift towards the Greater Eurasian Initiative had begun.[588]

The Greater Eurasia Initiative entails repositioning Russia from the dual periphery of Europe and Asia to the centre of a larger super-region. Russia aims to reduce its dependence on the West by seeking greater economic connectivity with the East in terms of technologies, industries, transportation corridors and finance. By positioning itself at the centre of a Greater Eurasia, the world would become more dependent on Russia while Russia would reduce its reliance on any one state or region. A favourable symmetry of interdependence would be the source of Russia's position as an independent pole of power in a multipolar world.

The Western-backed coup in Kiev and the death of Greater Europe occurred at the same time as China had outgrown the U.S.-dominated international economic architecture and thus was seeking to create alternatives. China therefore became the indispensable partner of Russia due to its capability and intention to challenge the U.S.-dominated international economic system.

The Rise of China

The rise of Western hegemony led to China's destruction. The rise of British imperial power in Asia in the 19th century had been obstructed by Chinese autarchy. Interdependence was unsustainable as Britain was reliant on China for products such as silk, tea, and ceramics, while a largely self-sufficient China only required gold and precious metals. The British therefore pursued the illegal export of

---

588 I. Ivanov, "The Sunset of Greater Europe," Speech at the 20th Annual International Conference of the Baltic Forum, "The U.S., the EU and Russia—the New Reality," Riga, 12 September 2015.

opium to China to restore a trade balance. After being defeated in the Opium Wars in the mid-19th century and losing much sovereign control, China was subjugated to extreme economic asymmetries and subsequently suffered what has been termed the century of humiliation as its wealth and position in the world diminished.

China's recovery and rise went through several stages of development. The century of humiliation ended with the Communist Revolution in 1949 as Mao asserted Chinese sovereignty over the next three decades. In 1978, China began to embrace market reforms and pursued a policy of "peaceful rise" in which China focused on internal development without attracting unwanted attention from the U.S. Three decades later, the Global Financial Crisis of 2008–09 revealed the unsustainable debt and thus the unsustainability of the U.S.-led economic system. China's next step was to assert itself in the international economy and challenge U.S. hegemony.

China's peaceful rise required a dual process insofar as, while China integrated itself into the structures and rules of the international order, the U.S. as the dominant state in the international economic system had to be willing to reform and accommodate China's rise.[589] However, Washington remained unwilling to accommodate China adequately, despite having permitted it to accede to the WTO, as it undermines the mechanisms of U.S. primacy within institutions such as the IMF, World Bank and Asian Development Bank. China subsequently began to create a parallel international economic architecture. International institutions that no longer reflect the international distribution of power eventually began to decline. Back in 1990, Deng Xiaoping had told members of the Central Committee that China would eventually become a pole in a multipolar world:

> The situation in which the United States and the Soviet Union dominated all international affairs is changing. Nevertheless, in the future when the world becomes three-polar, four-polar or five-polar, the Soviet Union, no matter how weakened it may be and even if some of its republics withdraw from it, will still be one pole. In the so-called multi-polar world,

589 B. Buzan, "The Security Dynamics of a 1+4 World," in E. Aydinli and J. N. Rosenau (eds.), *Globalization, Security, and the Nation State: Paradigms in Transition* (Albany: SUNY Press, 2005), 5.

> China too will be a pole. We should not belittle our own importance: one way or another, China will be counted as a pole. Our foreign policies remain the same: first, opposing hegemonism and power politics and safeguarding world peace; and second, working to establish a new international political order and a new international economic order.[590]

China has, to some extent, replicated the three-pillared American System of the early 19th century, in which the U.S. developed a manufacturing base, physical transportation infrastructure, and a national bank to counter British economic hegemony and subsequent intrusive political influence. China has similarly decentralised the international economic infrastructure by developing leading technological ecosystems, associated with the Fourth Industrial Revolution, launched the Belt and Road Initiative (BRI) in 2013, and developed new financial instruments of power in terms of development banks and de-dollarisation. China's desire to revive the ancient Silk Road revealed the desire to reduce reliance on Western maritime transportation corridors that had marked the beginning of 500 years of Western dominance.

After years of industrial policies aimed at catching up with the West, China began to pursue technological leadership. In 2015, it launched the *Made in China 2025*, a state-led industrial policy aiming to make China the world leader in the main high-tech industries. The industrial policy was further developed with the *China Standards 2035 plan* to set global standards for the next generation of technologies. China's "Digital Silk Road" seeks to connect the wider world with Chinese technologies and strategic industries. China's 5G technology is recognised to be the digital nervous system for the "Internet of Things," self-driving cars, and other technologies of the Fourth Industrial Revolution. The U.S. responded by launching an economic war against China to sabotage its industrial rise which has intensified its technological and industrial decoupling from American supply chains.

Russia similarly developed an independent digital ecosystem that is not vulnerable to pressures and economic coercion from the West. In areas of limited capabilities, Russia prioritises technological

590 X. Deng, "The international situation and economic problems," *The Selected Works of Deng Xiaoping* 3, no. 3 (1990).

cooperation with China but still aims for technological sovereignty to avoid excessive dependence. Russia and China cooperate on key technologies within artificial intelligence, communications, e-commerce and the "Internet of Things." Agreements have been signed for joint high-tech research centres. Russia has even decoupled from common space exploration with the West in favour of China. On 9 March 2021, the Russian Space Agency Roscosmos and the China National Space Administration (CNSA) signed a Memorandum of Understanding to build a moon base.

The ambitious Belt and Road Initiative connects the world physically with China through land corridors (Belt) and maritime corridors (Road). President Xi first announced the land-based Silk Road initiative in Kazakhstan in September 2013, and he then launched the maritime-based Silk Road at the Indonesian Parliament in October 2013. China is building formidable military forces to push back against the U.S. island chains to contain China, while simultaneously constructing land corridors to make itself less vulnerable to maritime corridors controlled by the U.S. The island chains are a reference to two militarised island chains off the coast of China, which the U.S. used to contain the Soviet Union and China in the early 1950s. The first island chain stretches from Japan, Ryukyu Islands, Taiwan, Philippines, Malaysia and Indonesia. The second island chain stretches from Japan, the Northern Mariana Islands, Guam, Micronesia, Palau and Indonesia. The then U.S. Secretary of State John Foster Dulles defined the two island chains and their purpose in 1952.[591]

Russia is unavoidably a key partner in the economic integration of Eurasia. Besides the land corridors, the Russian Northern Sea Route along the Arctic is a new transportation corridor that is faster and cheaper than the alternative maritime routes, and outside the control of the U.S. In 2018, China released its first white paper on the Arctic in which the Arctic corridor was referred to as the "Polar Silk Road."

China also takes a leadership position in decoupling from the U.S.-led financial system that has been globally dominant since Bretton Woods. China is the largest participant in the BRICS New Development Bank which was founded in 2014. It also launched the Asian Infrastructure Investment Bank (AIIB) in 2015 as a competitor

591 J. F. Dulles, "Security in the Pacific," *Foreign Affairs* 30, no.2 (1952).

to the World Bank and the Asian Development Bank. Washington warned its allies not to join, yet in the end all its major allies except Japan joined the initiative. China also developed the China International Payment System (CIPS) in 2015 to reduce reliance on the SWIFT system which was increasingly being used as a political weapon. Russia similarly developed the Financial Messaging System of the Bank of Russia (SPFS) as an alternative system to SWIFT, and several major Russian banks joined the CIPS system.

De-dollarisation is perhaps the initiative most threatening to U.S. hegemony. China is attempting to increase the use of the yuan in international trade and encourages settlements via the use of national currencies. China also developed the Digital Currency Electronic Payment (DCEP) that uses blockchain technology to circumvent dependence on banks. The digitalisation of China's national currency is expected to generate demand and elevate its attractiveness vis-à-vis the U.S. dollar. Russia supports the de-dollarisation and after the sanctions of 2022, began to reject dollars and euros for its exports. Since the Ukrainian War, both Russia and China have intensified their efforts to reduce their dollar reserves and accumulate more gold.

Russia's diversification away from the U.S.-led financial system has included creation of the Eurasian Development Bank (EDB) of the Eurasian Economic Union to organise the post-Soviet space. Rather than engaging in zero-sum rivalry, China and Russia began to harmonise the financial arrangements of the Eurasian Economic Union and the Belt and Road Initiative under the sponsorship of the Shanghai Cooperation Organisation (SCO). By expanding the SCO in 2017 to include both India and Pakistan, China could expand the region of its economic leadership while—at the same time—reassuring Russia, as the inclusion of other large powers would make it more difficult for China to translate into economic leadership into dominance.[592]

Russia and China have somewhat different formats and preferences for Eurasian integration, yet neither of the two can pursue their Eurasian integration without the cooperation of the other. Unlike in the 19th and 20th centuries, Russia has neither the capacity nor intention to assert hegemony in Eurasia, thus its objective is to be a

592 I. Gatev and G. Diesen, "Eurasian encounters: The Eurasian economic union and the Shanghai Cooperation Organisation," *European Politics and Society* 17, no. 1 (2016): 133–50.

balancer that facilitates multipolarity. This entails an acceptance that China will be the leading economy in Eurasia, although Russia will not accept Chinese dominance. The difference between China playing a leading role and exerting dominance is ensured by the diversification of Eurasian economic connectivity via countries such as India, Iran, Turkey and others to accommodate more centres of power. China will still be the leading power but unable to impose its dictate.

The basics of geoeconomics is to skew the symmetry of economic interdependence by reducing one's own dependence and increasing the reliance of others on oneself. Seemingly becoming aware of Hamiltonian economics to skew the symmetry of interdependence, the President of the European Commission Von der Leyen observed: "In the last decades China has become an economic powerhouse and a key global player. It is now reducing its dependency on the world while increasing the world's dependency on itself."

World Adjustment from Unipolar Conflicts to Multipolar Peace

The U.S. conflict with Russia and China threatens to make the entire world a chessboard for geopolitics. The U.S. has been unwilling to accommodate either Russia or China in a multipolar world order, and instead aims to weaken both. NATO expansionism is the key U.S. instrument for weakening Russia, while it seeks to weaken China by abandoning the One-China Policy by pushing for Taiwan's secession. The Ukrainian War has intensified the transition to a multipolar Eurasian World Order. While Washington offers allies the opportunity to weaken a common adversary, the price for the allies is to cede some sovereignty to the U.S. such as control over foreign policy.

However, the Ukrainian War demonstrated that this anti-Russian alliance severely weakened Europe. Reviving the militarised dividing lines in Europe may have unified the NATO states, but it predictably made the continent less secure and thus more reliant on Washington, while a mutually acceptable post-Cold War settlement with Russia could have revived the relevance of Europe as an independent pole of power. Conventional wisdom suggests that the Ukrainian War will augment European support for U.S. leadership as solidarity is required to confront a common external enemy. Yet, the systemic pressures of a multipolar international system suggest the opposite. To restore strategic autonomy, the Europeans will, at some point, need to adjust to the new balance of power by reducing their excessive dependence on Washington.

Western solidarity was a phenomenon that occurred during the bipolar era due to the Soviet threat, and during the unipolar era, the Europeans aspired for collective hegemony in which the EU would be an equal partner of the U.S. In the years before the Ukrainian War, the EU began to formulate the objective of "strategic autonomy" and "European sovereignty." In a multipolar world, these objectives require a diversification of partnerships as excessive dependence on the U.S. will subordinate the Europeans politically. The U.S. has a greater ability to subordinate the Europeans during conflicts as security dependence can be converted to economic and political loyalty. However, Washington's pressure to decouple Europe from Russia, China, Iran, and other adversaries of the U.S. will fuel animosity as the Europeans become increasingly irrelevant as an appendage of the U.S.

If the Ukrainian War is fought to the last Ukrainian, then it will also be fought to the last Euro. Germany, the economic powerhouse of Europe, exemplified the humiliating subordination to the U.S. The German political media elites remained largely silent about the attack on its critical energy infrastructure, even more so when it became evident that Russia was not responsible. While Russia was able to divert its energy exports to the East, the Europeans suffered from de-industrialisation and economic crisis. The energy-intensive industries of Germany became more reliant on more expensive American energy which reduced their competitiveness. Making matters worse, Washington's Inflation Reduction Act of 2022 created great incentives for uncompetitive European industries to move across to the U.S. French Economy Minister Bruno Le Maire, who less than a year earlier had called for the destruction of the Russian economy, warned that the U.S. was de-industrialising Europe with the Inflation Reduction Act. The EU Commissioner for the Internal Market, Thierry Breton, went even further and called the U.S. de-industrialisation of Europe an "existential challenge" to Europe.[593] Germany's energy partnership

593 T. Moller-Nielsen, "U.S. protectionism poses 'existential challenge' to Europe, say EU leaders," *The Brussels Times*, 30 November 2022.

with Russia and France's ambitions of EU strategic autonomy were effectively over, as Europe increasingly became a "vassal" of America as Macron had previously cautioned.

The ideological European elites can continue to act against their own strategic interests for only so long before new political forces replace them. Populists in both the U.S. and Europe increasingly express the desire to abandon hegemony and accept a more moderate position in the international system. Furthermore, many of these voices are also opposed to the excesses of liberalism and are consequently ideologically sympathetic to Russia. The West revived the ideological dividing lines after the Cold War by attempting to reorganise the world along the heuristics of liberalism versus authoritarianism. The excesses of neoliberalism alienated conservatives as liberalism decoupled itself from the nation-state, and many populists began to see the world as being split along a national-patriotism versus cosmopolitan-globalism divide in which Russia transitioned from being an adversary to an ally.[594]

The World Reduces Dependence on the West

The West was unable to isolate Russia as approximately 85 percent of the world population resides in countries that did not send weapons to Ukraine and did not impose sanctions on Russia. The new multipolar international community thus ensured that the West could not defeat Russia on the battlefield or destroy the Russian economy through sanctions. The Singaporean diplomat and former president of the UN Security Council, Kishore Mahbubani, remarked that most people in the world desire to live in a multipolar world, which is why they oppose sanctions against Russia. A Western victory over Russia risks a return to Western hubris and unipolar ambitions, thus Mahbubani argued "a Russian defeat would not be in the interests of the Global South" as they want to live in a multipolar world: "Many countries in the South who still retain memories of the once-dominant

594 G. Diesen, "Russia as an international conservative power: the rise of the right-wing populists and their affinity towards Russia," *Journal of Contemporary European Studies* 28, no. 2 (2020).

West know the West will once again become arrogant and insufferable if it defeats Russia completely."[595]

While the West considered its sanctions against Russia to be righteous and necessary to preserve the rules and norms of the international system, much of the world was taken aback by its blatant violation of key rules and norms as the West severed Russia from the allegedly apolitical SWIFT transaction system and seized the reserves of the Russian central bank. The rule of law was seemingly suspended as Russians saw their assets frozen without due process. Furthermore, Western states also threatened secondary sanctions against states that did not abide by the West's unilateral sanctions.

The aggressive efforts to deprive other states of their sovereignty and independent foreign policy were not limited to economic sanctions. Case in point, leaked cables revealed that U.S. diplomats were angered by Pakistan's "aggressive neutrality" over the war in Ukraine and threatened Pakistan with "isolation" if Prime Minister Imran Khan remained in power. Washington therefore pressed for the removal of Pakistan's democratically elected Prime Minister as he failed to toe the line, thereby destabilising a nuclear power.[596]

India is seemingly more aware that "allies" do not necessarily share the same interests. The U.S. has an interest in encouraging a Sino-Indian split by fuelling tensions between China and India, as this would weaken the former and subordinate the latter to U.S. through required security guarantees. However, India benefits in terms of security and prosperity by making peace and pursuing economic connectivity in its neighbourhood. The mentality in Washington can be summarised by an article in the *New York Times* with the title "In Wake of Recent India-China Conflict, U.S. Sees Opportunity." As the U.S. seeks to replicate the alliance system of Europe in Asia, the *New York Times* recognises:

> [The] U.S. attempt[s] to create an Asian version of the North Atlantic Treaty Organization directly aimed at counterbalancing its interests… Still, the United States and India

595 Modern Diplomacy, "Kishore Mahbubani: "A Russian defeat would not be in the interests of the Global South'," *Modern Diplomacy*, 23 March 2023.

596 R. Grim and M. Hussain, "Pakistan Confirms Secret Diplomatic Cable Showing U.S. Pressure to Remove Imran Khan," *The Intercept*, 16 August 2023.

> have not signed a formal alliance. India, which for years has maintained a stance of nonalignment, has been reluctant to engage. But the Himalayan crisis is helping change that.[597]

India's position is strengthened by integrating its economy with Russia as it develops a more balanced Eurasia that is not excessively dependent on China. In contrast, joining a U.S.-led anti-China alliance would subordinate India to the U.S. India subsequently did not take the European path of making itself a frontline state. Instead, India integrated its economy closer to the Russian economy during the war. At the onset of the war, Russia's export of crude oil to India was minimal, but by November 2022, Russia had become India's leading oil supplier. The systemic incentives for a balanced multipolar Eurasia manifested itself in the International North-South Transportation Corridor (INSTC) linking Russia, Iran, and India, which also enhanced cooperation in technologies, industry, and finance. The north-south format is an initiative that ensures Eurasian connectivity does not become excessively China-centric without becoming an anti-China initiative. India and Russia are even contemplating the construction of oil tankers and the development of energy insurance companies to permanently immunise themselves from the West's economic coercion. As a result, the economic influence it took the West centuries to build would falter, and the ability of Washington to pressure New Delhi into a U.S.-led alliance would diminish.

Taiwan may also be forewarned by the lesson the Europeans' preparedness to be frontline states against U.S. adversaries has provided. The U.S. incremental abandonment of its official One-China Policy has the predictable consequence of instigating a hostile Chinese response, which the U.S. will exploit to mobilise the region under U.S. leadership. This can be instrumental for a U.S. policy of containment or to fight a proxy war to weaken China akin to what was done in Ukraine. The extent to which Taiwan aligns with U.S. interests thus becomes a greater concern for the region. Despite its purported support for Taiwan, in Washington, plans to destroy Taiwan's largest chip manufacturer TSMC are openly discussed, to prevent the semiconductor factories from falling into China's hands in the event of a possible

597 P. Verma, "In Wake of Recent India-China Conflict, U.S. Sees Opportunity," *The New York Times*, 3 October 2020.

invasion. Taiwan's Defence Minister, Chiu Kuo-Cheng, warned the Americans that Taiwan would not accept an American attack on its strategic industries. While the threat to attack Taiwan's industries is not official U.S. policy, it is nonetheless a reminder of the potential cost of excessive dependence on a declining hegemon.

The U.S. seeks to organise the East-Asia region into a U.S.-led alliance, which would replicate Australia's transition into a U.S. ally against China. For years, consecutive Australian Prime Ministers have insisted that Australia would not choose between the U.S. and China. Nonetheless, through the usual U.S. incrementalism, Australia became a frontline state against China, and Beijing began to respond. Former Australian Prime Minister Paul Keating was very vocal about his displeasure with the new path of Australia and criticised the efforts of expanding NATO to Asia to confront China:

> Exporting that malicious poison to Asia would be akin to Asia wishing the plague upon itself.... Of all the people on the international stage the supreme fool among them is Jens Stoltenberg, the current Secretary-General of NATO. Stoltenberg by instinct and by policy, is simply an accident on its way to happen. Stoltenberg, in his jaundiced view, overlooks the fact that China represents twenty percent of humanity and now possesses the largest economy in the world. And has no record of attacking other states, unlike the United States, whose bidding Stoltenberg is happy to do.[598]

The alternative to unipolarity achieved and secured through the strategy of divide-and-conquer is a multipolar Eurasian world order. The prospect for peace under Eurasian multipolarity became evident with China's peace offensive in the Middle East. While U.S. power depends on a perpetual conflict that weakens Iran and makes Saudi Arabia dependent, China and Russia are not advancing an alliance system as it does not serve their interests to divide Eurasia into rival blocs. A key challenge for China and Russia is to deepen economic connectivity with both Iran and Saudi Arabia without alienating the

598 P. Karp, "Paul Keating labels Nato chief a 'supreme fool' and 'an accident on its way to happen'," *The Guardian*, 9 July 2023.

other. This created strategic incentives are created for resolving disputes and building trust. China's mediation leading to the normalisation of Saudi-Iran relations in March 2023 demonstrated that a multipolar approach could be a superior format to promote peace. As the dividing lines in the Middle East could come to an end, the former director of Mossad recognised the danger of Israel being the last country in the region left in an anti-Iranian alliance, and thus asked if "the time has come for Israel also to seek a different policy towards Iran.'[599] China and Russia even avoid forming a formal alliance with each other as the Chinese would alienate Europe and Russia would alienate India, and possibly incentivise the establishment of counter-alliances.

The transition to economic and political multipolarity thus becomes an increasingly attractive proposition for most of the world. The evolution and expansion of the BRICS grouping to 11 members in August 2023 was a clear signal that multipolar realities will assert themselves even against the fierce opposition of the West. The West's unilateral sanctions that weaponize dependence on Western technologies, currencies, international payment systems, and insurance systems caused economic pain across the world and diminished food security. Brazil, Russia, India, China, and South Africa already had a greater GDP than the G7 in terms of purchasing power parity (PPP) before the expansion. By creating alternatives to the Western-centric international economic system, the BRICS has turned economic coercion by the West into its surrender of its market share.

BRICS expansion by admitting Saudi Arabia, Iran, Ethiopia, Egypt, Argentina, and the United Arab Emirates further accelerated a new world order. With a list of over 40 countries that want to join BRICS as a non-Western institution to introduce multipolarity, it will be difficult to reorganise the world back under the hegemony of the collective West. BRICS+ is anti-hegemonic and not anti-Western; the objective is to create a multipolar system and not to assert an alternative collective dominance over the West. Unlike the U.S.-led alliance systems that divide countries into weakened adversaries and obedient allies, the BRICS grouping pursues security *with* other members rather than *against* non-members. Case in point, both Saudi Arabia and Iran joined to mitigate their rivalry in the region, and both Egypt and

599 E. Gjevori, "Israel: Former Mossad chief urges rapprochement with Iran," *Middle East Eye*, 16 March 2023.

Ethiopia joined who have disputes over the Nile River. BRICS thus demonstrates some qualitative differences from the imperial alliance system of divide and conquer.

Westphalian Conservatism

Conservatism focuses on civilisational distinctiveness and can therefore be considered an antidote to encroaching universalism. After the Napoleonic Wars fuelled by liberal internationalism, the Congress of Vienna restored a more conservative European order that constrained revolutionary liberal ideals that undermined sovereignty. The principle of non-interference is strengthened if it is accepted that each state has its own distinctive path to development rather than being coerced into emulating the hegemon.

The new Eurasian World Order is seemingly based on conservative principles. China is led by the Chinese Communist Party, although the ideology of a Marxist world revolution is long gone. China embraces economic nationalist policies akin to Alexander Hamilton and Friedrich List, and a conservative Confucianist philosophy to preserve traditional values and civilizational distinctiveness as the foundation of its nation-building. While communists seek to uproot and transcend history, conservatives use shared history as an anchor of domestic cohesion. China's Foreign Minister, Wang Yi argued:

> The unique features of China's diplomacy originate in the rich and profound Chinese civilisation… the idea of peace as of paramount importance and harmony without uniformity, as well as the personal conduct of treating others in a way that you would like to be treated, and helping others succeed in the same spirit as you would want to succeed yourself. These traditional values with a unique oriental touch provide an endless source of invaluable cultural asset for China's diplomacy.[600]

In the 1980s, a new cultural conservatism began to emerge in China at the same time as classical conservatism began to be discarded

600 Y. Wang, "Exploring the Path of Major-Country Diplomacy with Chinese Characteristics," *Foreign Affairs Journal*, no. 10 (2013): 14.

in the West under the Reagan and Thatcher administrations.[601] Confucianism supports conservative ideas devoted to preserving the group, such as social integration, stability and harmonious relationships, require respect for tradition and social hierarchy. Confucian values have a wider appeal in East Asia as they are also found in states such as Japan and Korea. The rapid and disruptive economic developments in China over the past decades created a demand for tradition as an anchor of stability, thus Confucianism ensures that morality and harmony are not lost on the path to modernity.[602] While China and other states in Asia become more liberal, their governments tend to embrace conservative policies to strengthen the group to maintain a balance.

Xi Jinping launched China's Global Civilisation Initiative to support conservatism in the international system The Global Civilisation Initiative aims to build a global network for inter-civilization dialogue and cooperation that promotes mutual understanding and equality among civilisations. Translated into the language of world order, the aim is to restore and improve the Westphalian sovereign system based on sovereign equality, which entails repudiating the system of universalism that legitimises a hierarchical ordering of superior civilisations versus inferior civilisations. Emphasising respect for the diversity of world civilizations cements the principle of non-interference.

As liberal hegemony continues to falter, there is a risk that the world will descend into conflict and competition for global dominance. The idea of replacing U.S. hegemony with Chinese hegemony is unlikely to unify a world community that aspires to multipolarity. China's Global Civilisation Initiative can be considered an effort to reassure and reorganise the world towards multipolarity. Universalism lends support to hegemonic ideologies, while the call for respecting civilisational distinctiveness strengthens the foundation for sovereign equality as a key component of a multipolar Westphalian system.

---

601 S. H. Cha, "Modern Chinese Confucianism: The Contemporary Neo-Confucian Movement and its Cultural Significance," *Social Compass* 50, no. 4 (2003): 482.

602 D. Bell, *Confucian Political Ethics* (Princeton: Princeton University Press, 2010).

The argument for civilizational distinctiveness was a key component of China's President Xi Jinping's speech proposing the Global Civilization Initiative:

> A single flower does not make spring, while one hundred flowers in full blossom bring spring to the garden... We advocate the respect for the diversity of civilizations. Countries need to uphold the principles of equality, mutual learning, dialogue and inclusiveness among civilizations, and let cultural exchanges transcend estrangement, mutual learning transcend clashes, and coexistence transcend feelings of superiority.[603]

China has not displayed hegemonic intentions in which it would seek to prevent diversification and multipolarity, rather the Global Civilisation Initiative signals that Beijing is content with merely being the leading economy as the "first among equals." Case in point, Russian efforts to diversify its economic connectivity in Greater Eurasia have not been opposed by Beijing, which has made Moscow more comfortable with China's economic leadership in the region. This represents a very different approach from the hegemonic model of Washington's divide-and-rule strategy, in which the U.S. attempts to decouple economic partnerships between Russia, Germany, China, India, Turkey, Iran, Central Asia, and others.

Conservatism is also the preferred path for Russia. After centuries of history full of disastrous revolutionary disruptions, various competing identities emerged in Russia, which undermines unity. Russian conservative Nikolai Berdyaev acknowledged that "the development of Russia has been catastrophic" as its history was divided into periods with little continuity, which created conflicting ideas about Russia's identity and thus the lack of a common vision of its future:

> There have been five periods in Russian history and each provides a different picture. They are: the Russia of Kiev; Russia in the days of the Tartar yoke; the Russia of Moscow;

603 J. Xi, "Join Hands on the Path Towards Modernization," *China Institutes of Contemporary International Relations*, 15 March 2023.

> the Russia of Peter the Great; and Soviet Russia. And it is quite possible that there will be yet another new Russia.[604]

As Berdyaev correctly predicted, Soviet Russia was replaced with liberal Russia of the 1990s, before returning to conservatism that aimed to bring together the all the various periods under one common historical narrative with a united national consciousness. Russia embraces conservatism, seeing its distinctive thousand-year history as the source of unity and sets the conditions for a unique path to modernity.

States can establish international unity on the need to preserve their distinctive culture and thus pursue a unique path to modernity. The need to preserve the defining features of the group as a balance to unfettered individualism does not translate into universalism as each state has different features to conserve. American conservatism can appear paradoxical as it seeks to preserve the liberal ideals of its foundation and constitution. Russian conservatism can similarly appear contradictory as it must salvage what it can from its revolutionary past and incorporate it into the national narrative. It may seem contradictory to decorate the Kremlin with both the cross and the red star, although these are both periods that define Russian history. Similarly, Russia's history as a European and an Asian power can both be united under the umbrella of Eurasianism. Attempting to set back the clock and erase part of its history is in itself a revolutionary act that will spawn incompatible identities that seek to eviscerate each other.

Russia's national objective to bring all Russians under the same tent conforms with its objective to develop an international system based on civilisational diversity as the foundation for sovereign equality. President Putin outlined Eurasian integration as an initiative to support civilisational diversity:

> I want to stress that Eurasian integration will also be built on the principle of diversity. This is a union where everyone maintains their identity, their distinctive character and their political independence… We expect that it will become our

---

604 N. Berdyaev, *The Russian Idea* (London: Geoffrey Bles Ltd., 1947), 3.

> common input into maintaining diversity and stable global development.[605]

Preserving civilization distinctiveness is also seen as a way to avoid of concepts such as a "clash of civilizations" and the purported "superiority of civilizations." Danilevsky cautioned in 1869 against a single path to modernisation with a view to create a universal civilisation:

> The danger consists not of the political domination of a single state, but of the cultural domination of one cultural-historical type.... The issue is not whether there will be a universal state, either a republic or a monarchy, but whether one civilization, one culture, will dominate, since this would deprive humanity of one of the necessary conditions for success and perfection—the element of diversity.[606]

Fyodor Dostoyevsky similarly argued in 1873 that Russia could not contribute anything of value to the world if it merely emulated the West:

> Embarrassed and afraid that we have fallen so far behind Europe in our intellectual and scientific development, we have forgotten that we ourselves, in the depth and tasks of the Russian soul, contain in ourselves as Russians the capacity perhaps to bring new light to the world, on the condition that our development is independent.[607]

Civilizational diversity is imperative as it, much like biodiversity, makes the world more capable of absorbing shocks and handling crises: "Universalism, if realized, would result in a sharp decline of

---

605 V. Putin, "Meeting of the Valdai International Discussion Club," *Government of the Russian Federation*, 19 September 2013.

606 N. Danilevsky, *Russia and Europe: The Slavic World's Political and Cultural Relations with the Germanic-Roman West* (Bloomington: Slavica Publishers, 2013), 76.

607 F. Dostoevsky, *F. M. Dostoevskii: Polnoe Sobranie Sochinenii v 30 TT* [*Collected Works of Dostoevsky in 30 Volumes*] (Nauka, Leningrad: Academy of Sciences, 1986), 260.

the complexity of the global society as a whole and the international system in particular. Reducing complexity, in turn, would dramatically increase the level of systemic risks and challenges."[608] Russia's Foreign Minister Sergei Lavrov opined:

> As regards the content of the new stage in humankind's development, there are two basic approaches to it among countries. The first one holds that the world must gradually become a Greater West through the adoption of Western values. It is a kind of "the end of history." The other approach—advocated by Russia—holds that competition is becoming truly global and acquiring a civilizational dimension; that is, the subject of competition now includes values and development models. The new stage is sometimes defined as "post-American."[609]

Denouncing liberalism as the organising principle of world order, Putin argued ahead of the G20 meeting in June 2019:

> The liberal idea has become obsolete. It has come into conflict with the interests of the overwhelming majority of the population… Deep inside, there must be some fundamental human rules and moral values. In this sense, traditional values are more stable and more important for millions of people than this liberal idea, which, in my opinion, is really ceasing to exist.[610]

The West could also benefit greatly from returning to a more conservative Westphalian world order. The objection to intrusive claims of universalism is also fundamental to Western civilization. In ancient Greece, the cradle of Western civilization, it was recognised that universalism and uniformity weakened the vigour and resilience

608 A. Kortunov, "False Conflict: Universalism and Identity," *Valdai Discussion Club*, 11 October 2017.

609 S. Lavrov, "Russia and the World in the 21st Century," *Russia in Global Affairs*, July/September 2008.

610 L. Barber, H. Foy, and A. Barker, "Vladimir Putin says liberalism has 'become obsolete,'" *Financial Times*, 28 June 2019.

that defined the Hellenic idea. The benign cooperation and competition between various Greek city-states were the source of a diversity of ideas and a vitality that elevated Greek civilization. Integration into one political system would entail losing the diversity of philosophy, wisdom, and leadership that incentivized experimentation and advancement. The U.S. state system was founded on similar ideas before the federal concentration of power deprived the states of much of their autonomy.

Universalism has been incentivised by the concentration of power in the West, which meant the Westernisation of the world. As power and the ability to influence continue to shift from the West to the East, the West will have an incentive to revive the idea of preserving civilisational distinctiveness. While the West will have less ability to influence others and others will have more ability to influence the West.

Conclusion

It can be concluded that restoring a Westphalian world order not only requires a multipolar distribution of economic power, it also demands respect for civilizational diversity to ensure that the principle of indivisible security is preserved. Toward this end, the international order should counteract nefarious claims of civilizational superiority clothed in the benign rhetoric of universal values and development models. Through this prism, the U.S. efforts to divide the world into democracy versus authoritarianism can be considered a recipe for hegemony and sovereign inequality rather than harmony and human progress. Xi Jinping has thus repudiated the U.S. hegemonic model, and instead advanced the Westphalian argument that states must "refrain from imposing their own values or models on others."

The new Westphalia can, for the first time, truly be a world order by including non-Western nations as sovereign equals, which is already the foundation for equality under international law according to the United Nations Charter. One should therefore not be surprised by the positive response from the majority of the world to the proposal of replacing intrusive bullying with cooperation based on equality and mutual respect.

11.

Conclusion: Interregnum—Transition, Uncertainty and Disorder

THE UKRAINE WAR was a predictable consequence of an unsustainable world order and became a battleground for charting a future world order of either global hegemony or Westphalian multipolarity. The objectives to defeat Russia militarily, economically, or politically by isolating it in the world all failed. The reaction by NATO has been continuous escalation and theatrics. As Ukraine has been devastated by untold suffering and its inability to achieve its military goals has become an acknowledged fact, the only possible solution to the conflict is for the West to recognise Russia's legitimate security concerns and thus mitigate the security dilemma. Its difficulty in so doing is because this would entail the end the era of liberal hegemony.

Russian security concerns could be ignored in the 1990s as Russia was weak and declining, and the Russians had to adjust to their increasingly unfavourable and difficult position as they did not have other partners. Three decades later, the strategic situation for Russia had become intolerable as NATO's expansion to Ukraine is believed to be an existential threat. However, the international distribution of power has become vastly different. New centres of power have emerged across the world that share Russia's ambitions to construct a multipolar Westphalian world order. Unipolarity had already come to an end and the world was amid a transition to multipolarity when Russia invaded Ukraine in February 2022. The war intensified the global decoupling from the West, which openly presented the war as an all-or-nothing struggle for world order.

Irrespective of the outcome of the war, it has already led to the graveyard of liberal hegemony. Security as defined by the West entails restoring military superiority, expanding military alliances, increasing joint military exercises, exercising freedom of navigation along the coastline of rival powers, and weaponizing economic interdependence. In service to that end, democracy, civil society and human rights have been instrumentalised and weaponised.

Hegemony did not mitigate great power rivalry; instead, it enabled the dominant power to act without regard for others, replacing diplomacy with the language of ultimatums. What was sold to the public as "pro-Ukrainian" policies and "helping Ukraine" entailed toppling their democratically elected government without majority support from Ukrainians; supporting an "anti-terror operation" against Ukrainian citizens in the East; purging its political opposition and dismantling its democracy; empowering far-right militant groups; sabotaging peace agreements supported by Kiev; and pressuring the Ukrainian armed forces to launch a devastating counter-offensive that had little to no chance of succeeding.

It is difficult to imagine a peaceful end to the Ukraine War. As NATO emptied its weapon storages and Ukraine has been exhausted by casualties, there will—predictably—be proposals for a ceasefire to freeze the conflict. A temporary ceasefire without a political settlement would be unacceptable for Russia, fearing that NATO would likely attempt to repeat what was done with the Minsk Agreement—to yet again use the peace agreement to buy time to rearm Ukraine and thus continue the fight another day. Ideally, the humanitarian tragedy should have been a motivation to put an end to the war that has taken so many Ukrainian and Russian lives.

A political solution to the war demands that NATO expansionism and the collapse of the pan-European security architecture be addressed as the underlying *casus belli* of the war. The Europeans should be most concerned about war on their continent and its further devastating economic repercussions. The Europeans should therefore push the hardest to revive diplomacy and possibly revisit Russia's demands for security guarantees made in late 2021—and even consider offering neutrality for Ukraine. However, what the Europeans want is of less significance as the Euro-Atlantic decisions are primarily made in Washington. This was true before the war, and even more so after the war. Even though the U.S. prefers to focus on China as its principal challenger, the defeat or weakening of Russia is seen as an important step to also defeat China. Moscow may calculate that Russia can seize more territory when Ukraine finally collapses, which puts mounting pressure on Washington to make a deal before the strategic environment worsens. Even at this point in time, NATO must either accept a humiliating defeat or enter directly into what could escalate quickly to a nuclear war.

The Ukraine War that threatens to destroy the planet in a nuclear holocaust is a symptom of a wider crisis in the international system. After enjoying hegemony for five centuries and constructing and imposing global rules to serve Western interests, there is now a spectacular realignment of power in the world. The global majority seeks multipolarity in accordance with a Westphalian world order, while the West, under Washington's leadership, attempts to restore its dominant position in the world. The U.S. has accurately identified China and Russia as the main challengers that have created a gravitational pull to reorganise the world order towards multipolarity. Unable to bring down China and Russia by economic means, the conflicts for the future world order will continue to be militarized. The fear of nuclear war appears to be gone, and wars between the great powers are no longer unimaginable. As the world is transitioning between unipolarity and multipolarity; common rules are largely absent.

Former Prime Minister of Australia, Kevin Rudd, cautioned in 2012 that the rise of China meant that the West would be confronted with a world that would no longer be under its control:

> Very soon we will find ourselves at a point in history when, for the first time since George III, a non-Western, non-democratic state will be the largest economy in the world. If this is the case, how will China exercise its power in the future international order? Will it accept the culture, norms and structure of the postwar order? Or will China seek to change it? I believe this is the single core question for the

first half of the twenty-first century, not just for Asia, but for the world.[611]

A traumatic experience is awaiting the West as it must adjust to a multipolar international distribution of power and rules that are seen to be set or influenced by non-Western powers. However, it does not appear that the U.S. will accept a peaceful transition to a Westphalian world order. The absence of political imagination in Washington has produced a world view in which chaos is the only alternative to U.S. global dominance.

U.S. Secretary of State Anthony Blinken delivered a eulogy for the world order of liberal hegemony in September 2023 as he recalled an era of remarkable progress through economic interdependence political liberalism and human rights at the centre. But then Blinken acknowledged the end of the order: "what we're experiencing now is more than a test of the post-Cold War order. It's the end of it." China and Russia are named as the main culprits for ending the era of liberal hegemony. Viewing the world as divided between good and evil, Blinken insisted that "Beijing and Moscow are working together to make the world safe for autocracy." Rather than envisioning a transition to a balanced multipolar Westphalian world order, Blinken envisioned a struggle against both China and Russia under America's global leadership.

If this continues to be the view of the West, we will witness a great tragedy for humankind.

---

611 K. Rudd, "West is unprepared for China's rise," *The Australian*, 14 July 2012.

Bibliography

Abrahms, M. M. "Does Ukraine Have Kompromat on Joe Biden?" *Newsweek.* 8 August 2023.

Adams, B. *America's Economic Supremacy*. New York: Macmillan, 1900.

Adler, E., and M. Barnett. "A Framework for the Study of Security Communities.' In *Security Communities,* edited by E. Adler and M. Barnett, 29–65. Cambridge: Cambridge University Press, 1998.

AFP. "Putin Focused On Consolidating Ukraine Gains: U.S. Intel." *The Defense Post*, 5 May 2023.

Albright, M. K. *Madam Secretary.* New York: Miramax Books, 2004.

Allen, J., and A. Parnes. *Shattered: Inside Hillary Clinton's Doomed Campaign*. New York: Crown Publishing Group, 2017.

Angell, N. *The Great Illusion: A Study of the Relation of Military Power to National Advantage*. London: W. Heinemann, 1913.

Antonov, A. "An Existential Threat to Europe's Security Architecture?" *Foreign Policy*, 30 December 2021.

Arendt, H. *The Origins of Totalitarianism.* New York: Harcourt Inc, 1951.

Arestovich, A. "Voennoe Obozrenie" [Military Review]. *Apostrof TV*, 18 February 2019.

Arms Control Association. "Opposition to NATO Expansion." *Arms Control Today*. 26 June 1997. https://www.armscontrol.org/act/1997-06/arms-control-today/opposition-nato-expansion.

Aron, R. *Peace and War: A Theory of International Relations*. Garden City: Doubleday, 1966.

Asch, R. *The Thirty Years War: The Holy Roman Empire and Europe 1618–1648*. London: Palgrave Macmillan, 1997.

Bacon, J., and J. L. Oritz. "'Zelenskyy is in a box': Some experts say Ukraine won't win the war." *USA Today News*, 27 July 2023.

Baer, G. W. *One Hundred Years of Sea Power: The U.S. Navy, 1890–1990.* Stanford: Stanford University Press, 1996.

Baker, J. A. "Russia in NATO?" *Washington Quarterly* 25, no. 1 (2002): 93–103.

Baker, P. "Obama Said to Resist Growing Pressure From All Sides to Arm Ukraine." *The New York Times*, 10 March 2015

Baldwin, D. A. *Economic Statecraft.* Princeton: Princeton University Press, 1985.

Barber, L., H. Foy, and A. Barker. "Vladimir Putin says liberalism has 'become obsolete'." *Financial Times*, 28 June 2019.

Barnett, T. P. *The Pentagon's New Map: War and Peace in the Twenty-First Century*. New York: Penguin, 2004.

Baruch, L. *Intangibles: Management, Measuring and Reporting*. Washington D.C.: Brookings Institution Press, 2001.

Baud, J. *Operation Z.* Paris: Max Milo, 2022.

Bauman, Z. "Times of Interregnum." *Ethics & Global Politics* 5, no. 1 (2012): 49–56.

BBC. "Boris Johnson Warns Against a Ukraine-Russia Peace Deal." *BBC*, 22 September 2022.

———. "Ukraine Crisis: Deadly Anti-autonomy Protest Outside Parliament." *BBC*, 31 August 2015.

———. "Ukraine Crisis: Transcript of leaked Nuland-Pyatt call." *BBC*, 7 February 2014.

———. "Ukraine Election: Comedian Zelensky Wins Presidency by Landslide." *BBC*, 22 April 2019.

———. "Ukraine's Revolution and the Far Right." *BBC*, 7 March 2014.

Bell, C. *The Royal Navy, Seapower and Strategy Between the Wars.* London: Palgrave, 2000.

———. "Thinking the Unthinkable: British and American Naval Strategies for an Anglo-American War, 1918–1931." *The International History Review* 19, no. 4 (1997): 789–808.

Bell, D. *Confucian Political Ethics.* Princeton: Princeton University Press, 2010.

Bell, S. "The West Remains Committed to Ukraine's Counteroffensive—But There's Scepticism over Zelenskyy's Ultimate Objectives." *Sky News*, 9 September 2023.

Bellant, R. *Old Nazis, The New Right, and The Republican Party*. Boston: South End Press, 1991.

Beorn, W. W. *The Holocaust in Eastern Europe: At the Epicenter of the Final Solution.* London: Bloomsbury Publishing, 2018.

Berdyaev, N. *The Russian Idea*. London: Geoffrey Bles Ltd., 1947.

Bennett, Naftali. "Bennett Speaks Out." YouTube, 4 February 2023. Video, 4:51:31. https://www.youtube.com/watch?v=qK9tLDeWBzs.

Bernays, E. *Propaganda.* New York: Liveright, 1928.

Bertrand, N. "Putin: The Deterioration of Russia's Relationship with the West is the Result of Many 'Mistakes'." *Business Insider*, 11 January 2016.

Biden, J. "Remarks by President Biden at a Campaign Reception." *The White House*, 20 October 2023

———. "Remarks by President Biden in State of the Union Address." *The White House*, 1 March 2022.

———. "Remarks by President Biden on Russia's Unprovoked and Unjustified Attack on Ukraine." *The White House,* 24 February 2022.

Blair, T. "Doctrine of the International Community." Speech presented at the Economic Club of Chicago, 22 April 1999.

Blumenthal, R. "Zelenskyy Doesn't Want or Need Our Troops. But He Deeply and Desperately Needs the Tools to Win." *CT Post*, 29 August 2023.

Blinken, A. "Secretary Antony J. Blinken at a Press Availability.' U.S. Department of State, 26 January 2022.

———. "Secretary Antony J. Blinken with Jonathan Karl of ABC This Week." Interview by Office of the Spokesperson. U.S. Department of State, 10 September 2023.

Bolton, A. "GOP Senator: Congress Must Find Out What Trump Knew of Russian Bounties, and When." *The Hill*, 29 June 2020.

Booth, K., and N. J. Wheeler. *The Security Dilemma: Fear, Cooperation and Trust in World Politics*. Basingstoke: Palgrave Macmillan, 2008.

Borger, J. "Russian Hostility 'Partly Caused by West,' Claims Former U.S. Defence Head." *The Guardian*, 9 March 2016.

Borrell, J. "The Gardeners have to go to the Jungle. Europeans have to be much more Engaged with the Rest of the World. Otherwise, the Rest of the World Will Invade Us." *European Union External Action*, 13 October 2022.

Broers, M., P. Hicks, and A. Guimera (eds.). *The Napoleonic Empire and the New European Political Culture*. New York: Springer, 2012.

Brown, A., *The Human Factor: Gorbachev, Reagan, and Thatcher, and the End of the Cold War*. Oxford: Oxford University Press, 2020.

Brown, J. D. *Japan, Russia and Their Territorial Dispute: The Northern Delusion.* New York: Routledge, 2016.

Brzezinski, Z. "A Geostrategy for Eurasia." *Foreign Affairs* 76, no. 5 (1997): 50–64.

———. *The Choice: Global Domination or Global Leadership.* New York: Basic Books, 2009.

———. *The Grand Chessboard: American Primacy and its Geopolitical Imperatives.* New York: Basic Books, 1997.

Buchanan, P. J. *A Republic, Not an Empire: Reclaiming America's Destiny.* Washington D.C.: Regnery Publishing, 1999.

Bull, H. *The Anarchical Society: A Study of World Order in World Politics.* New York: Palgrave Macmillan, 1977.

Bull, H. *The Anarchical Society: A Study of Order in World Politics*. London: Bloomsbury Publishing, 2012.

Bundesbank. "EMS: Bundesbank Council meeting with Chancellor Schmidt (assurances on operation of EMS)" [declassified 2008]. Bundesbank Archives, N2/267, 30 November 1978.

Burds, J. "The Early Cold War in Soviet West Ukraine, 1944–1948." *The Carl Beck Papers in Russian & East European Studies* no. 1505, 2001.

Burns, W. J. *The Back Channel: A Memoir of American Diplomacy and the Case for Its Renewal*. New York: Random House, 2019.

———. "Nyet Means Nyet: Russia's NATO Enlargement Redlines." *Wikileaks*, 1 February 2008.

Bush, G. W., "Address Before a Joint Session of the Congress on the State of the Union." Speech presented at the State of the Union, Washington D.C., *The American Presidency Project*, 29 January 1991.

———, "Address Before a Joint Session of the Congress on the State of the Union." Speech presented at the State of the Union, Washington D.C., *The American Presidency Project*, 28 January 1992.

———. "Address to the Nation Announcing Allied Military Action in the Persian Gulf." *The American Presidency Project*, 16 January 1991.

———. "The National Security Strategy of the United States of America." *The White House*, 1 June 2002.

Butt, Y., and T. Postol. "Upsetting the Reset: The Technical Basis of Russian Concern Over NATO Missile Defence." *Federation of American Scientists*, FAS Special Report No. 1, September 2011.

Buzan, B. "Economic structure and international security: The limits of the liberal case." *International Organization* 38, no. 4 (1984): 597–624.

———. "The Security Dynamics of a 1+4 World." In *Globalization, Security, and the Nation State: Paradigms in Transition*. Edited by E. Aydinli and J. N. Rosenau, 177–198. Albany: State University of New York Press, 2005.

Caldwell, C. "The War in Ukraine May Be Impossible to Stop. And the U.S. Deserves Much of the Blame." *The New York Times*, 31 May 2022.

Carbonaro, G. "U.S. Wants Russia "Weakened" So It Can Never Invade Again." *Newsweek*, 25 April 2022.

Carden, J. "Congress Has Removed a Ban on Funding Neo-Nazis From Its Year-End Spending Bill." *The Nation*, 14 January 2016.

Carpenter, T. G. "America's Ukraine Hypocrisy." *CATO Institute*, 6 August 2017.

Carpenter, T. G., and B. Conry. *NATO Enlargement: Illusions and Reality*. CATO Institute, 1998.

Cha, S. H. "Modern Chinese Confucianism: The Contemporary Neo-Confucian Movement and its Cultural Significance." *Social Compass* 50, no. 4 (2003): 481–491.

Charap, S. "The U.S. Approach to Ukraine's Border War Isn't Working. Here's What Biden Should Do Instead." *Politico*, 19 November 2021.

Charap, S., and S. Boston. "The West's Weapons Won't Make Any Difference to Ukraine." *Foreign Policy*, 21 January 2022.

Chatham House. "Myths and Misconceptions in the Debate on Russia." *Chatham House*, 13 May 2021.

Cheshire, H. T. "The Expansion of Imperial Russia to the Indian Border." *The Slavonic and East European Review* 13, No. 37 (1934): 85–97.

Clark, C. "Release of 'Twitter Files' revs GOP's pursuit of Big Tech, Dem collusion." *The Washington Times*, 4 December 2022.

Clark, N. "Fools No More." *The Guardian,* 19 April 2008.

Clark, W. K. *A Time to Lead: For Duty, Honor and Country.* New York: Palgrave Macmillan, 2007.

Clinton, B. "Remarks to Multinational Audience of Future Leaders of Europe." Speech given in Brussels, Belgium. *U.S. Diplomatic Mission to Germany*, 9 January 1994.

Clover, C. "Clinton Vows to Thwart New Soviet Union." *Financial Times*, 7 December 2012.

CNN. "At This Hour with Kate Bolduan." *CNN*, 14 January 2022.

———. "Son dakika... Numan Kurtulmuş CNN TÜRK'te: (Rusya-Ukrayna) Birileri savaşı bitirmemek için çabalıyor" [Last minute... Numan Kurtulmuş on CNN TÜRK: (Russia-Ukraine) Someone is trying not to end the war]. *CNN Turk*, 18 November 2022.

Cohen, S. "'We Are Not Beginning a New Cold War, We Are Well into It': Stephen Cohen on Russia-Ukraine Crisis." *Democracy Now*, 17 April 2014.

———. *Soviet Fates and Lost Alternatives: From Stalinism to the New Cold War*. New York: Columbia University Press, 2009.

Congressional Record, Proceedings and Debates of the 89th Congress, Volume 111, Part 7, 28 April 1965 to 10 May 1965.

Cooper, R, "The New Liberal Imperialism." *The Guardian*, 7 April 2002.

Cooper, H., E. Schmitt, and J. E. Barnes. "U.S. Intelligence Helped Ukraine Strike Russian Flagship, Officials Say." *The New York Times*, 5 May 2022.

Cotton, T. "Kill Russia's Nord Stream 2, Let it Ruse in the Baltic." *Tom Cotton official website*, 19 May 2021.

Cousins, N. *The Pathology of Power*. New York: Norton, 1987.

Cox, R. W. "Social Forces, States and World Orders: Beyond International Relations Theory." In *Neorealism and Its Critics.* Edited by R.O. Keohane, 204–255. New York: Columbia University Press, 1986.

Cruz, T. "President Biden and the Democrats have Imperiled Ukraine and put Europe on the Brink of War." *Ted Cruz official website*, 7 February 2022.

CSCE. "Decolonizing Russia: A Moral and Strategic Imperative." *Commission on Security and Cooperation in Europe*, 23 June 2022.

Cumings, B. "Trilateralism and the New World Order." *World Policy Journal* 8, no. 2 (1991): 195–222.

Daalder, I., and J. Lindsay. "An Alliance of Democracies." *The Washington Post*, 23 May 2004.

Danilevsky, N. *Russia and Europe: The Slavic World's Political and Cultural Relations with the Germanic-Roman West*. Bloomington: Slavica Publishers, 2013.

Das, B. "'Old, Dangerous, Rich': S. Jaishankar's not-so-kind description of George Soros." *Business Today*, 18 February 2023.

Davidson, G., and P. Davidson. *Economics for a Civilized Society*. New York: Norton, 1988.

Davis, R.T. "Should NATO Grow? A Dissent." *The New York Review*, 21 September 1995.

"Defense Planning Guidance" [DPG]. *Militarist Monitor*, 18 February 1992.

Deng X. "The International Situation and Economic Problems." *The Selected Works of Deng Xiaoping* 3, no. 3 (1990).

Dennekamp, G. J. "De Hoop Scheffer: Poetin werd radicaler door NAVO" [De Hoop Scheffer: Putin became more radical because of NATO]. *NOS*, 7 January 2018.

Deudney, D., and G. J. Ikenberry. "The Unravelling of the Cold War Settlement." *Survival: Global Politics and Strategy* 51, no. 6 (2009): 39–62.

Deutsch, J., and L. Pronina. "EU Approves 450 Million Euros of Arms Supplies for Ukraine." *Bloomberg*, 27 February 2022.

Deveraux, B. "Rocket Artillery can Keep Russia out of the Baltics." *War on the Rocks*, 20 May 2021.

DIA. "Russia Military Power: Building a Military to Support Great Power Aspirations." *Defense Intelligence Agency*, 6 July 2017.

Diamond, L. J. "Three Paradoxes of Democracy." *Journal of Democracy* 1, no. 3 (1990): 48–60.

Dibb, P. "NATO's 'Expansionist Policy' Fuels Fear." *Financial Review*, 17 June 1999.

Diesen, G. *EU and NATO Relations with Russia: After the Collapse of the Soviet Union*. London: Routledge, 2015.

———. "Russia as an international conservative power: the rise of the right-wing populists and their affinity towards Russia." *Journal of Contemporary European Studies* 28, no. 2 (2020): 182–196.

———. *Russian Conservatism: Managing Change under Permanent Revolution*. London: Routledge, 2021.

———. *Russia's Geoeconomic Strategy for a Greater Eurasia*. London: Routledge, 2017.

———. *The Think Tank Racket*. Atlanta: Clarity Press, 2023.

Diesen, G., and S. Wood. "Russia's Proposal for a New Security System: Confirming Diverse Perspectives." *Australian Journal of International Affairs* 66, no. 4 (2012): 450–467.

Dorfman, Z. "CIA-trained Ukrainian Paramilitaries May Take Central Role if Russia Invades." *Yahoo News*, 13 January 2022.

Dostoevsky, F. *A Writer's Diary—Volume 2: 1877-1881*. Illinois: Northwestern University Press, 1997.

———. *Polnoe Sobranie Sochinenii v 30 TT* [*Collected Works of Dostoevsky in 30 Volumes*]. Nauka/Leningrad, 1986.

Dostoyevsky, A. *Fyodor Dostoyevsky: A Study*. Honolulu: University Press of the Pacific, 2001.

Doyle, M. W. "Kant, Liberal Legacies, and Foreign Affairs." *Philosophy & Public Affairs* 12, no. 3 (1983): 205–235.

Du Bois, W.E.B. "Neuropa: Hitler's New World Order." *The Journal of Negro Education* 19, no. 3 (1941): 380–386.

Dulles, J. F. "Security in the Pacific." *Foreign Affairs* 30, no. 2 (1952): 175–187.

Dutta, P. K., S. Granados, and M. Ovaska. "On the edge of war." *Reuters*, 26 January 2022.

DW. "German Navy Chief Quits After Putin, Crimea Gaffes." *Deutsche Welle*, 22 January 2022.

———. "Germany Replaces the Head of the Bundeswehr Armed Forces." *Deutsche Welle*, 13 March 2023.

———. "Nord Stream 2 Won't Happen if Russia Invades Ukraine: U.S." *Deutsche Welle,* 27 January 2022.

Eastern Herald. "Polish Prime Minister Morawiecki Has Warned Of The Beginning of the End of the West's Golden Age." *The Eastern Herald,* 18 April 2023.

Echols, C. "Diplomacy Watch: Did Boris Johnson Help Stop a Peace Deal in Ukraine?' *Responsible Statecraft*, 2 September 2022.

Economist. "Ukraine's sluggish counter-offensive is souring the public mood." *The Economist*, 20 August 2023.

Emma. "Russland will verhandeln!" [Russia wants to negotiate!], *Emma,* 4 March 2023.

English, C. "Ukrainians See More Value in Ties With Russia Than U.S." *Gallup*, 15 February 2008.

EUEA. "Foreign Affairs Council: Remarks by High Representative Josep Borrell upon arrival." *European Union External Action*, 11 April 2022.

EurLex. "Journal of the European Community 1990. Minutes of proceedings of the sitting of Thursday 22 November 1990." *European Union EurLex official website*, No. C 324/186, 22 November 1990.

Euronews. "Ukraine War to be "Decided on the Battlefield." NATO official says." *Euronews*, 12 July 2022.

European Council. "15th EU-Russia Summit." *European Council*, 10 May 2005.

European Parliament. "Ukraine: The Minsk Agreements Five Years On." European Parliament, March 2020.

European Union. "EU-Ukraine Association Agreement—The Complete Texts." *European External Action Service*, 2013.

Farkas, E. "The U.S. Must Prepare for War Against Russia Over Ukraine." *Defense One*, 11 January 2022.

Ferguson, N. "Putin Misunderstands History. So, Unfortunately, Does the U.S." *Bloomberg*, 22 March 2022.

Fischer, J. "From Confederacy to Federation: Thoughts on the Finality of European Integration." Speech presented at the Humboldt University, Berlin, 12 May 2000.

Fotyga, A. "The Dissolution of the Russian Federation is Far Less Dangerous than Leaving it Ruled by Criminals." *Euractiv*, 27 January 2023.

Foxall, A., and O. Kessler. "Yes, There Are Bad Guys in the Ukrainian Government." *Foreign Policy*, 18 March 2014.

Friedman, G. "The Geopolitics of the United States, Part 1: The Inevitable Empire." *Stratfor*, 4 July 2014.

———. "Interesi RF I SSHA v otnoshenii Ukraini nesovmestimi drug's drugom" [The interests of the Russian Federation and the United States in relation to Ukraine are incompatible with each other]. *Kommersant*, 19 December 2014.

Friedman, T. L. "Foreign Affairs: Now a Word From X." *The New York Times*, 2 May 1998.

———. "This Is Putin's War. But America and NATO Aren't Innocent Bystanders." *The New York Times*, 21 February 2022.

Frum, D., and R. Perle. *An End to Evil: How to Win the War on Terror*. New York: Random House Publishing Group, 2003.

Fukuyama, F. "The End of History?' *The National Interest* 16 (1989): 3–18.

Gaddis, J. L. *Strategies of Containment: A Critical Appraisal of Postwar American National Security Policy.* New York: Oxford University Press, 1982.

Gallagher, J., and R. Robinson. "The Imperialism of Free Trade." *The Economic History Review* 6, no. 1 (1953): 1–15.

Ganser, D. *NATO's Secret Armies: Operation Gladio and Terrorism in Western Europe.* New York: Routledge, 2005.

Gates, R. *Duty: Memoirs of a Secretary at War*. New York: Knopf Publishing, 2014.

Gatev, I., and G. Diesen. "Eurasian Encounters: The Eurasian Economic Union and the Shanghai Cooperation Organisation." *European Politics and Society* 17, no. 1 (2016): 133–150.

Gerschman, C. "Former Soviet States Stand up to Russia. Will the U.S.?" *Washington Post*, 26 September 2013.

Gerth, J., and T. Weiner. "Arms Makers See Bonanza In Selling NATO Expansion." *The New York Times*, 29 June 1997.

Gilpin, R. *War and Change in World Politics*. Cambridge: Cambridge University Press, 1981.

Gjevori, E. "Israel: Former Mossad Chief Urges Rapprochement with Iran." *Middle East Eye*, 16 March 2023.

Gheciu, A. "Security Institutions as Agents of Socialization? NATO and the 'New Europe'." *International Organization* 59, no. 4 (2005): 973–1012.

Global Times. "U.S. 'rules-based intl order' is 'law of the jungle' to contain others: Chinese vice FM tells U.S. envoy." *Global Times*, 26 July 2021.

Golinkin, L. "Secretary Blinken Faces a Big Test in Ukraine, Where Nazis and Their Sympathizers Are Glorified." *The Nation*, 6 May 2021.

Goncharenko, R. "Ukraine, U.S. Black Sea Drills Raise Tensions." *Deutsche Welle*, 29 June 2021.

Graham, B. *Hit to Kill: The New Battle Over Shielding America from Missile Attack*. New York: Public Affairs Store, 2003.

Gramsci, A. *Selections from the Prison Notebooks of Antonio Gramsci*. New York: International Publishers, 1971.

Gray, J. *Enlightenment's Wake: Politics and Culture at the Close of the Modern Age*. London: Routledge, 1995.

Greenwald, G. "The Indictment of Hillary Clinton's Lawyer is an Indictment of the Russiagate Wing of the U.S. Media." *Glenn Greenwald* (Substack blog), 19 September 2021.

Greer, S., and M. Shtekel. "Ukraine's Navy: A Tale Of Betrayal, Loyalty, And Revival." *Radio Free Europe/Radio Liberty*, 27 April 2020.

Grim, R., and M. Hussain. "Pakistan Confirms Secret Diplomatic Cable Showing U.S. Pressure to Remove Imran Khan." *The Intercept*, 16 August 2023.

Grytsenko, O. "'I'm not a loser': Zelensky clashes with veterans over Donbas disengagement." *Kyiv Post*, 28 October 2019.

Guardian. "Full Text: Tony Blair's Speech." *The Guardian*, 5 March 2004.

———. "Ukraine has Offered Neutrality in Talks with Russia—What Would that Mean?' *The Guardian*, 30 March 2022.

Gvosdev, N. "Parting With Illusions: Developing a Realistic Approach to Relations with Russia." *CATO Institute*, 29 February 2008.

Hains, T. "NSC's Kirby: Ukraine Should Reject Any Russian-Chinese Ceasefire Plan." *Real Clear Politics*, 20 March 2023.

Hall, S. "The Question of Cultural Identity." In *Modernity: An Introduction to Modern Societies,* edited by S. Hall, D. Held, D. Hubert and K. Thompson, 595–634. Massachusetts: Blackwell Publishing, 1996.

Hamilton, A. *The Federalist: On the New Constitution, Written in 1788.* Hallowell: Masters, Smith & Company, 1857.

Harris, S., and S. Mekhennet. "U.S. Had Intelligence of Detailed Ukrainian Plan to Attack Nord Stream pipeline." *The Washington Post*, 6 June 2023.

Haukkala, H. "The European Union as a Regional Normative Hegemon: The Case of European Neighbourhood Policy." *Europe-Asia Studies* 60, no. 9 (2008): 1601–1622.

Heappey, J. "Ukrainians are Fighting for Their Freedom, and Britain is Doing Everything to Help Them." *The Telegraph*, 26 February 2022.

Heckscher, E. *The Continental System*. Oxford: Clarendon Press, 1922.

Helmer, J. "Whr. Gen. Kujat: Ukraine War is Lost, Germany Now Faces an Angry Russia… Alone." *Veterans Today*, 25 January 2023.

Herbert, B. "In America: War Games." *The New York Times*, 22 February 1998.

Herman, E., and D. Peterson. *The Politics of Genocide.* New York: University Press, 2010.

Hersh, S. "How America Took Out The Nord Stream Pipeline." *Seymour Hersh* (Substack blog), 8 February 2023.

Herszenhorn, D. M. "U.S. Senators Praise Ukrainian Marines, Slam Putin." *Politico*, 2 January 2017.

Herszenhorn, D. M., and G. Leali. "Defiant Putin Mauls Macron in Moscow." *Politico*, 7 February 2022.

Herwig, H. H. *The Demon of Geopolitics: How Karl Haushofer "Educated" Hitler and Hess.* London: Rowman & Littlefield, 2016.

Herz, J. H. "Idealist Internationalism and the Security Dilemma." *World Politics* 2, no. 2 (1950): 157–180.

———. "Political Ideas and Political Reality." *Western Political Quarterly* 3, no. 2 (1950): 161–178.

———. "Power Politics and World Organization." *The American Political Science Review* 36, no. 6 (1942): 1039–1052.

Hildrebrandt, T., and G. di Lorenzo. *"'Hatten Sie gedacht, ich komme mit Pferdeschwanz?'"* ["Did you think I was coming with a ponytail?"]. *Zeit*, 7 December 2022.

Hill, F. "Putin Has the U.S. Right Where He Wants It." *The New York Times*, 24 January 2022.

Hill, F., and A. Stent. "The World Putin Wants How Distortions About the Past Feed Delusions About the Future." *Foreign Affairs*, September/October 2022.

Hirsh, M. "Hints of a Ukraine-Russia Deal?" *Foreign Policy*, 8 March 2022.

Hirschman, A. "Beyond Asymmetry: Critical Notes on Myself as a Young Man and on Some Other Old Friends." *International Organisation*, 32, no. 1 (1978): 45–50.

———. *National Power and the Structure of Foreign Trade*. Berkeley: University of California Press, 1945.

Hobsbawm, E. J. *Globalisation, Democracy and Terrorism*. London: Little Brown, 2007.

———. *Industry and Empire: An Economic History of Britain since 1750*. London: Weidenfeld and Nicolson, 1968.

Hoffmann, S. "Report of the Conference on Conditions of World Order: June 12-19, 1965, Villa Serbelloni, Bellagio, Italy." *Daedalus* 95, No. 2 (1966): 455–478.

Hudson, M. *America's Protectionist Takeoff, 1815-1914: The Neglected American School of Political Economy*. New York: Islet, 2010.

Hudson, J., and A. Horton. "U.S. Intelligence Says Ukraine Will Fail to Meet Offensive's Key Goal." *The Washington Post*, 17 August 2023.

Huggler, J. "Ukraine Crisis: U.S. Officials Compare Peace Efforts to Appeasing Hitler." *The Telegraph*, 8 February 2015.

Huntington, S. P. "Dead Souls: The Denationalization of the American Elite." *The National Interest,* 1 March 2004.

———. "If Not Civilizations, What? Paradigms of the Post-Cold War World." *Foreign Affairs* 72, No. 5 (1993): 186–194.

———. *The Clash of Civilizations and the Remaking of World Order.* New York: Simon and Schuster, 1996.

———. "The Lonely Superpower,." *Foreign Affairs* 87, no. 2 (1999) 35–49.

———. "The West and the Rest." *Prospect Magazine*, 20 February 1997.

Ignatius, D. "Innocence Abroad: The New World of Spyless Coups." *Washington Post*, 22 September 1991.

———. "The West Feels Gloomy About Ukraine. Here's Why it Shouldn't." *The Washington Post*, 18 July 2023.

Ikenberry, G. J., and A. M. Slaughter. "Forging a World of Liberty under Law: U.S. National Security in the 21st Century." *The Princeton Project on National Security*, 2006.

Ingram, P. *Napoleon and Europe*. Cheltenham: Stanley Thornes Publishers Ltd., 1998.

Irwin, D. A. "Political Economy and Peel's Repeal of the Corn Laws." *Economics & Politics* 1, no. 1 (1989): 41–59.

Ivanov, I. "The Sunset of Greater Europe." Speech at the 20th Annual International Conference of the Baltic Forum "The U.S., the EU and Russia—the New Reality." Riga, Latvia, 12 September 2015.

Johnson, B. "For a Quicker End to the Russia War, Step Up Aid to Ukraine." *Wall Street Journal*, 9 December 2022.

Kagan, R. "The Price of Hegemony: Can America Learn to Use Its Power?' *Foreign Affairs,* May/June 2022.

Kamenetsky, I. *Hitler's Occupation of Ukraine (1941–1944)*. Wisconsin: The Marquette University Press, 1956.

Karp, P. "Paul Keating Labels Nato Chief a 'Supreme Fool' and 'an Accident on Its Way to Happen'." *The Guardian*, 9 July 2023.

Kaonga, G. "Video of Joe Biden Warning of Russian Hostility if NATO Expands Resurfaces." *Newsweek*, 8 March 2022.

Katchanovski, I. "The Far Right, the Euromaidan, and the Maidan Massacre in Ukraine." *Journal of Labor and Society* 23, no. 1 (2020): 5–36.

Katzenstein, P. J. *A World of Regions: Asia and Europe in the American Imperium.* London: Cornell University Press, 2005.

Kennan, G. F. *Around the Cragged Hill: A Personal and Political Philosophy*. New York: Norton, 1993.

———. "A Fateful Error." *The New York Times*, 5 February 1997.

———. *The Kennan Diaries*. New York: Norton & Company, 2014.

Kenney, G. "Rolling Thunder: The Rerun." *The Nation*, 14 June 1999.

Kheel, R. "Congress Bans Arms to Ukraine Militia Linked to Neo-Nazis." *The Hill*, 27 March 2018.

Kieninger, S. "Helmut Kohl and NATO Enlargement: The Search for the Post-Cold War Order." *American-German Institute*, 7 July 2020.

KIIS. "Socio-political Moods of the Population of Ukraine." *Kyiv International Institute of Sociology*, 19 October 2021.

Kindleberger, C.P. *The World in Depression, 1929–1939.* Berkeley: University of California Press, 1986.

Kipp, J. W., and W. B. Lincoln. "Autocracy and Reform Bureaucratic Absolutism and Political Modernization in Nineteenth-Century Russia." *Russian History* 6, no. 1 (1979) 1–21.

Kissinger, H. *Diplomacy.* New York: Touchstone, 1994.

———. "How the Ukraine Crisis Ends." *The Washington Post*, 5 March 2014.

———. "Interview with Henry Kissinger." *The Daily Telegraph*, June 28, 1999.

———. *World Order*. New York: Penguin Press, 2014.

Korniienko, A. "Thousands Rally in Kyiv Against Zelensky's Plan to End War with Russia." *Kyiv Post*, 6 October 2019.

Kortunov, A. "False Conflict: Universalism and Identity." *Valdai Discussion Club*, 11 October 2017.

Kozyrev, A. "Russia and the U.S: Partnership is not Premature, it is Overdue." *Current Digest of the Russian Press* 46, no. 6 (1994).

Kramer, M. "Putin Is Only Part Of the Russian Picture." *The Washington Post*, 23 January 2000.

Kramer, A. E. "Armed Nationalists in Ukraine Pose a Threat Not Just to Russia." *The New York Times*, 10 February 2022.

Krauthammer, C. "The Unipolar Moment." *Foreign Affairs* 70, No. 1 (1990/1991): 23–33.

Kristensen, H. M. "Falling Short of Prague: Obama's Nuclear Weapons Employment Policy." *Arms Control Association*, September 2013.

Krugman, P. "Trouble With Trade." *The New York Times*, 28 December 2007.

Kupchan, C. A. "NATO's Final Frontier: Why Russia Should Join the Atlantic Alliance." *Foreign Affairs* 89, no. 3 (2010): 100–112.

Kuzio, T. "Historiography and National Identity Among the Eastern Slavs: Towards a New Framework." *National Identities* 3, no. 2 (2001): 109–132.

Kuzio, T. "Neither East nor West: Ukraine's Security Policy Under Kuchma." *Problems of Post-Communism* 52, no. 5 (2005), 59–68.

Kyiv Post, "Poll: Ukrainian Public Split Over EU, Customs Union Options." *Kyiv Post*, 26 November 2013.

Lane, D. "The Orange Revolution: 'People's Revolution' or Revolutionary Coup?" *The British Journal of Politics and International Relations* 10, no. 4 (2008): 525–49.

Lapidus, G. W. *Ethnonationalism and Political Stability in the USSR.* National Council for Soviet and East European Research, Council Contract No. 627–3 (1984).

Lasch, C. *The Revolt of the Elites and the Betrayal of Democracy*. New York: W.W. Norton & Company, 1996.

Latham, M. E. *The Right Kind of Revolution: Modernization, Development, and U.S. Foreign Policy from the Cold War to the Present*. New York: Cornell University Press, 2011.

Lavrov, S. "Foreign Minister Sergey Lavrov's Remarks at the 29th Assembly of the Council on Foreign and Defence Policy (CFDP)." *The Ministry of Foreign Affairs of the Russian Federation*, 2 October 2021.

———. "Russia and the World in the 21st Century." *Russia in Global Affairs*, July/September 2008.

Lemkin, R. *Soviet Genocide in the Ukraine*. Kingston: The Kashtan Press, 2008.

Lemon, J. "'Let's Take Out Putin': Graham Doubles Down on Ukraine War 'Off-Ramp'." *Newsweek*, 8 May 2022.

Leonard, M., and N. Popescu. "A Power Audit of EU-Russia Relations." *European Council on Foreign Relations* 9 (2009).

Lieber, K. A., and D. G. Press. "The Rise of U.S. Nuclear Primacy." *Foreign Affairs* 85, no. 2 (2006): 42–54.

Lieven, A. "Russia and Ukraine: A Fraternal Rivalry." *United States Institute of Peace Press*, Washington, D.C., 2009.

Lijphart, A. "Consociational Democracy." *World Politics* 21, no. 2 (1969): 207–225.

Lippman, W. *Public Opinion*. San Diego: Harcourt, Brace & Co., 1922.

———. *The Stakes of Diplomacy*. New Brunswick: Transaction Publishers, 1932.

List, F. *The National System of Political Economy*. London: Longmans, Green & Company, 1841.

———. *Outlines of American Political Economy, in a Series of Letters*. Philadelphia: Samuel Parker, 1827.

Lister, T. "The Nexus Between Right-Wing Extremists in the United States and Ukraine." *Combating Terrorism Center at West Point* 13, no. 4 (2020): 30–41.

Lizza, R., R. Bade, T. Palmeri, and E. Daniels. "Politico Playbook: Double trouble for Biden." *Politico*, 21 September 2021.

Lonas, L. "Crenshaw, Greene Clash on Twitter: 'Still Going after that slot on Russia Today'." *The Hill*, 11 May 2022.

LRT. "Putin's plan includes Baltics, says former NATO chief." *Lithuanian National Radio and Television*, 19 July 2022.

Luttwak, E. *Turbo Capitalism*. New York: HarperCollins Publishers, 1999.

Lyne, R. "The UC Interview Series: Sir Roderic Lyne by Nikita Gryazin." *Oxford University Consortium*, 18 December 2020.

Löwenhardt, J. "The OSCE, Moldova and Russian Diplomacy in 2003." *Journal of Communist Studies and Transition Politics* 20, no. 4 (2004): 103–112.

MacAskill, E. "Ukraine Crisis: Bugged Call Reveals Conspiracy Theory about Kiev Snipers." *The Guardian*, 5 March 2014.

Mackinder, H. J. *Democratic Ideals and Reality: A Study in the Politics of Reconstruction*. London: Constable, 1919.

———. "The Geographical Pivot of History." *The Geographical Journal* 170, no. 4 (1904): 421–44.

Macleod, A. "The Utility of the RussiaGate Conspiracy." *FAIR*, 27 July 2018.

Marszal, A. "EU Will Not Accept Russian Veto, Says Barroso." *The Telegraph*, 29 November 2013.

Maté, A. "Ukrainegate Impeachment Saga Worsens U.S.-Russia Cold War." *The Grayzone*, 13 November 2019.

———. "Siding with Ukraine's Far-Right, U.S. Sabotaged Zelensky's Mandate for Peace." *Aaron Maté* (Substack blog), 10 April 2022.

———. "U.S. Fighting Russia 'To The Last Ukrainian': Veteran U.S. Diplomat." *The Grayzone*, 24 March 2022.

———. "U.S., UK Sabotaged Peace Deal Because They 'Don't Care About Ukraine': Fmr. NATO adviser." *The Grayzone*, 27 September 2022.

Matlock, J. F. *Superpower Illusions: How Myths and False Ideologies Led America Astray—and How to Return to Reality*. New Haven: Yale University Press, 2010.

Matlock, J. F. "Why the U.S. Must Press for a Ceasefire in Ukraine." *Responsible Statecraft*, 17 October 2022.

Matthews, O. "Viktor Yushchenko's Star Has Fallen." *Newsweek*, 13 March 2009.

McCarthy, A. "Steele's Shoddy Dossier." *National Review*, 6 June 2019.

McConnell, M. "McConnell on Zelensky Visit: Helping Ukraine Directly Serves Core American Interests." *Mitch McConnell (*official website), 21 December 2022.

McFaul, M. "The U.S. and Ukraine Need to Reboot Their Relationship. Here's How They Can Do It." *The New York Times*, 23 August 2021.

McGovern, R. "Biden Reneged—Now Russian Army Will Talk." *AntiWar*, 30 December 2022.

McMahon, M. "'If we Don't Support Ukraine, Ukraine Will Fall in a Matter of Days," says Josep Borrell." *Euronews*, 5 May 2023.

Mcleary, P. "U.S. Upgrades Ukrainian Ports to Fit American Warships." *Breaking Defense*, 3 July 2019.

Mead, W. R. *God and Gold: Britain, America, and the Making of the Modern World*. New York: Vintage, 2008.

Mearsheimer, J. J. "Why the Ukraine Crisis is the West's Fault: The Liberal Delusions that Provoked Putin." *Foreign Affairs* 93, no. 5 (2014): 77–89.

Mearsheimer, J. J., and S. M. Walt. "The Case for Offshore Balancing: A Superior U.S. Grand Strategy." *Foreign Affairs* 95, no. 4 (2016): 70–83.

Melanovski, J. "Ukrainian President Zelensky Deepens Alliance with Far Right." *World Socialist Web Site,* 30 April 2021.

Menegay, C., and A. Valles. "U.S., NATO, Ukraine Enhance Interoperability with Rapid Trident Exercise." *U.S. Army*, 21 September 2021.

Mendlovitz, S., and T. Weiss. "The Study of Peace and Justice: Toward a Framework for Global Discussion." In *Planning Alternative Future*. Edited by L.R. Beres and H. Targ, 148–174. New York: Praeger, 1975.

Michel, C. "Decolonize Russia." *The Atlantic*, 27 May 2022.

Mill, J. S. *On Liberty and Other Writings.* Cambridge: Cambridge University Press, 1989.

———. *The Spirit of the Age*. Chicago: Chicago University Press, 1942.

Miller, G., and I. Khurshudyan. "Ukrainian spies with deep ties to CIA wage shadow war against Russia." *The Washington Post." 23 October 2023.*

Milne, S. "It's Not Russia That's Pushed Ukraine to the Brink of War." *The Guardian*, 30 April 2014.

Modern Diplomacy. "Kishore Mahbubani: 'A Russian Defeat Would Not be in the Interests of the Global South.'" *Modern Diplomacy*, 23 March 2023.

Moller-Nielsen, T. "U.S. Protectionism Poses 'Existential Challenge' to Europe, say EU leaders." *The Brussels Times*, 30 November 2022.

Morgenthau, H. J. *Politics Among Nations: The Struggle for Power and Peace*. New York: Alfred A. Knopf, 1948.

Morris, E. J., and G. Fonrouge. "Smoking-Gun Email Reveals how Hunter Biden Introduced Ukrainian Businessman to VP Dad." *New York Post*, 14 October 2020.

Morrison, D. "How William Hague Deceived the House of Commons on Ukraine." *Huffington Post*, 10 March 2014.

———. "Obama Lied About a Referendum in Kosovo." *Huffington Post*, 31 March 2014.

MSNBC, "Transcript: The Rachel Maddow Show, 2/28/22 Guests: Hillary Clinton, Alexander Prokhoren." *MSNBC*, 1 March 2022.

Mudde, C. "Europe's Populist Surge: A Long Time in the Making." *Foreign Affairs* 95, no. 6 (2016): 25–30.

National Archives. "Operation Unthinkable: Report by the Joint Planning Staff." Catalogue ref: CAB 120/691, *The National Archives*, 1945.

National Security Archive. "NATO Expansion: What Gorbachev Heard." *George Washington University,* 12 December 2017.

———. "NATO Expansion: What Yeltsin Heard." *George Washington University*, 16 March 2018.

NATO. "Address by Secretary General, Manfred Wörner to the Bremer Tabaks Collegium." North Atlantic Treaty Organization, 17 May 1990.

———. "Bucharest Summit Declaration, Issued by the Heads of State and Government participating in the meeting of the North Atlantic Council in Bucharest." North Atlantic Treaty Organization, 3 April 2008.

———. "Comprehensive Assistance Package for Ukraine." North Atlantic Treaty Organization, July 2016.

———. "'Post-Orange Ukraine': Internal Dynamics and Foreign Policy Priorities." NATO Parliamentary Assembly, October 2011.

Nelson, S. "'That's Called World War III': Biden Defends Decision not to Send Jets to Ukraine." *New York Post*, 11 March 2022

Neumann, I. B. *Uses of the Other: The "East" in European Identity Formation.* Manchester: Manchester University Press, 1999.

New York Times. "In Bush's Words: Iraqi Democracy Will Succeed." *The New York Times*, 6 November 2003.

———. "Quotation of the Day for Wednesday, March 19, 2014." *The New York Times*, 19 March 2014.

Nierop, T., and S. De Vos. "Of Shrinking Empires and Changing Roles: World Trade Patterns in the Postwar Period." *Tijdschrift Voor Economische en Sociale Geografie* 79, no. 5 (1988): 343–64.

Nietzsche, F. *Thus Spoke Zarathustra*. London: Penguin Books, 1968.

Norman, E. H. *Japan's Emergence as a Modern State*. New York: University of British Columbia Press, 1940.

Norman, G. "Top U.S. Military Official Relays 'Worst Thing' Russia did before Invading Ukraine." *Fox News*, 4 May 2022.

North Atlantic Council, "Brussels Summit Communiqué." North Atlantic Treaty Organization, 14 June 2021. https://www.nato.int/cps/en/natohq/news_185000.htm.

Norris, J. *Collision Course: NATO, Russia, and Kosovo.* Foreword by Strobe Talbott. Westport: Praeger, 2005.

NRK. "Fredsprisvinner: Kompromiss med Russland er ikke fred" [Peace-prize winner: Compromise with Russia is not peace].*NRK*, 10 December 2022.

Nye, J. S. "The Decline of America's Soft Power.' In *Paradoxes of Power*, edited by D. Skidmore, 27–32, New York: Routledge, 2015.

———. "What New World Order?' *Foreign Affairs* 71, no. 2 (1992): 83–96.

Obama, B. "President Obama: "The TPP Would Let America, Not China, Lead the Way on Global Trade."" *The Washington Post*, 2 May 2016.

O'Conner, T. "So, if the United States is Concerned about China and Wants to Pivot Towards Asia, then you have to Ensure that Putin Doesn't Win in Ukraine." *Newsweek*, 21 September 2023.

Oreskes, B. "Moscow wary of TTIP talks." *Politico*, 9 May 2016.

Osang, A. "You're Done with Power Politics." *Spiegel*, 1 December 2022.

Packer, G. "Obama's Iraq Problem." *The New Yorker*, 30 June 2008.

Pan, P. P. "International Observers Say the Ukrainian Election was Free and Fair." *OSCE*, 9 February 2010.

Panetta, L. "U.S. Is in a Proxy War With Russia: Panetta." *Bloomberg*, 17 March 2022.

Parfitt, T. "Ukraine Crisis: The Neo-Nazi Brigade Fighting Pro-Russian Separatists." *The Telegraph*, 11 August 2014.

Parker, G. *The Military Revolution: Military Innovation and the Rise of the West, 1500–1800*. Cambridge: Cambridge University Press, 1996.

Parry, R. "CIA's Hidden Hand in 'Democracy Groups'." *Consortium News*, 8 January 2015.

———. "U.S. House Admits Nazi Role in Ukraine." *Consortium News*, 12 June 2015.

Peleschuk, D. "Ukraine's President Finally Flexes His Muscles." *Foreign Policy*, 12 February 2021.

Perry, W. J. "How the U.S. Lost Russia—and How We Can Restore Relations." *Kontinent USA*, 7 September 2022.

Pesenti, M. "Ukraine's Cultural Revival is a Matter of National Security." *Atlantic Council*, 19 January 2021.

Petro, N. "How the E.U. Pushed Ukraine East." *The New York Times*, 3 December 2013.

———. 2023. "The last Ukrainian peacemaker: Sergei Sivokho remembered." *Responsible Statecraft*, 23 October 2023.

———. *The Tragedy of Ukraine*. Boston: De Gruyter, 2023.

Piketty, T. *Capital in the Twenty-First Century*. Cambridge: Harvard University Press, 2014.

Pilger, J. "In Ukraine, the U.S. is Dragging us Towards War with Russia." *The Guardian*, 13 May 2014.

Plato. *The Republic*. Translated by Benjamin Jowett. Ontario: Devoted Publishing, 2016.

Polanyi, K. *The Great Transformation.* Boston: Beacon Press, 1944.

Polityuk, P. "Ukraine Ready for Talks with Russia on Neutral Status—Official." *Reuters*, 25 February 2022.

Posen, B. R. "The Security Dilemma and Ethnic Conflict." *Survival* 35, no. 1 (1993): 27–47.

Prouvost, T. "Hollande: "There Will Only be a Way Out of the Conflict When Russia Fails on the Ground."' *The Kyiv Independent*, 28 December 2022.

Putin, V. "Address by President of the Russian Federation." Speech presented at the Kremlin to State Duma Deputies, *President of Russia*, 18 March 2014.

———. "Meeting of the Valdai International Discussion Club." *Government of the Russian Federation*, 19 September 2013.

———. "Speech and the Following Discussion at the Munich Conference on Security Policy." *President of Russia*, 10 February 2007.

———. "Valdai International Discussion Club meeting." *President of Russia*, 6 October 2023.

———. "Valdai International Discussion Club Meeting." *President of Russia*, 27 October 2022.

Putnam, R. D. "E pluribus unum: Diversity and Community in the Twenty-First Century." *Scandinavian Political Studies* 30, no. 2 (2007): 137–74.

Quigley, C. *The Evolution of Civilisations: A Historical Analysis*. Indianapolis: Liberty Press, 1961.

RAND. "Extending Russia: Competing from Advantageous Ground." *RAND Corporation*, 24 April 2019.

———. "Future Roles of U.S. Nuclear Forces: Implications for U.S. Strategy." *RAND Corporation*, Santa Monica, 2003.

Rapley, J., and P. Heather. *Why Empires Fall: Rome, America, and the Future of the West*. Dublin: Penguin, 2023.

Rapoza, K. "One Year After Russia Annexed Crimea, Locals Prefer Moscow To Kiev." *Forbes*, 20 March 2015.

Raskin, S., and L. Brown. "Ukraine and Russia to Meet for Peace Talks 'Without Preconditions,' Zelensky says." *New York Post*, 27 February 2022.

Ray, J., and N. Esipova. "Ukrainians Likely Support Move Away From NATO." *Gallup*, 2 April 2010.

Reagan, R. "Remarks at a White House Ceremony Inaugurating the National Endowment for Democracy." *The American Presidency Project*, 16 December 1983.

Reinert, E. S., and A. M. Daastøl. "The Other Canon: The History of Renaissance Economics." In *Globalization, Economic Development and Inequality: An Alternative Perspective*. Edited by E. S. Reinert, 21–70. Cheltenham: Edward Elgar Publishing, 2007.

Rettman, A. "EU Chairman Blames Yanukovych for 'Destabilising' Ukraine." *EU Observer*, 27 January 2014.

Reuters. "Idea of U.S. threat to Russia is "Ludicrous"—Rice." *Reuters*, 26 April 2007.

RFE/RL. "Biden Says He'll Make It 'Very Difficult' For Russia To Attack Ukraine." *Radio Free Europe / Radio Liberty*, 4 December 2021.

———. "Pompeo Says U.S. Will 'Do Everything' To Stop Nord Stream 2 Project." *Radio Free Europe / Radio Liberty*, 30 July 2020.

———. "Right-Wing Protesters Clash With Police Outside Ukrainian President's Office." *Radio Free Europe / Radio Liberty*, 14 August 2021.

———. "Russia's Proposal To Redraw European Security 'Unacceptable,' U.S. Says." *Radio Free Europe / Radio Liberty*, 18 December 2021.

Ricardo, D. *On the Principles of Political Economy and Taxation*. London: John Murray, 1821.

Rice, C. "Remarks by Dr Condoleezza Rice, Assistant to the President for National Security Affairs." Speech presented at the International Institute for Strategic Studies, London, United Kingdom, 16 June 2003.

Rocca, F. X., and E. Gershkovich. "Pope Says NATO Might Have Provoked Russian Invasion of Ukraine." *The Wall Street Journal*, 3 May 2022.

Rochester, J. M. *International Institutions and World Order: The International System as a Prismatic Polity*. New York: Sage Publications. 1975.

Rodrik, D. *The Globalization Paradox: Why Global Markets, States, and Democracy Can't Coexist*. Oxford: Oxford University Press, 2012.

Rojansky, M., and J. Shapiro. "Why Everyone Hates Think Tanks." *Foreign Policy*, 28 May 2021.

Roland, A. *Delta of Power: The Military-Industrial Complex*. Baltimore: John Hopkins University Press, 2021.

Romaniuk, R. "Possibility of Talks Between Zelenskyy and Putin Came to a Halt after Johnson's Visit—UP sources." *Ukraniska Pravda*, 5 May 2022.

Rorty, R. *Achieving Our Country: Leftist Thought in Twentieth-Century America*. Cambridge: Harvard University Press, 1998.

Rubenstein, A., and M. Blumenthal. "How Ukraine's Jewish President Zelensky Made Peace With Neo-Nazi Paramilitaries on Front Lines of War with Russia." *The Grayzone*, 4 March 2022.

Rudd, K. "West is Unprepared for China's Rise." *The Australian*, 14 July 2012.

Ruggie, J. G. "International Regimes, Transactions, and Change: Embedded Liberalism in the Postwar Economic Order." *International Organization* 36, no. 2 (1982): 379–415.

Rumsfeld, D. "U.S. Department of Defense Prepared Statement for the Senate Appropriations Defense Subcommittee: 2004 Defense Budget Request." Washington, D.C., 14 May 2003.

Russett, B., and H. Starr. *World Politics: The Menu for Choice*. San Francisco: Freeman, 1981.

Rustow, D. A. "Transitions to Democracy: Toward a Dynamic Model." *Comparative Politics* 2, no. 3 (1970): 337–63.

Rynning, S. "Reluctant Allies? Europe and Missile Defense." In *Missile Defence: International, Regional and National Implications*.Edited by H. Bertel and S. Rynning, 111–32. London: Routledge, 2006.

Sachs, J. "Ending America's War of Choice in the Middle East." *Horizons: Journal of International Relations and Sustainable Development*, no.11 (Spring 2018): 20–33.

Sainato, M. "Rigged Debates: Wikileaks Emails Confirm Media in Clinton's Pocket." *Observer*, 14 October 2016.

Sakwa, R. *Frontline Ukraine: Crisis in the Borderlands*. London: I.B. Tauris, 2014.

Sakwa, R. *The Lost Peace: How the West Failed to Prevent a Second Cold War*. Cornwall: Yale University Press, 2023.

Sarkar, S. "'There Will No Longer Be a Nord Stream 2': Fingers Pointed Towards Biden after Gas Pipeline Blasts." *News18*, 30 September 2022.

Sarotte, M. E. "How to Enlarge NATO: The Debate inside the Clinton Administration, 1993–95." *International Security* 44, no. 1 (2019): 7–41.

———. "In Victory, Magnanimity: U.S. Foreign Policy, 1989–1991, and the Legacy of Prefabricated Multilateralism." *International Politics* 48, no. 4/5 (2011): 482–95.

———. *Not One Inch: America, Russia, and the Making of Post-Cold War Stalemate.* New Haven: Yale University Press, 2021.

Savitsky, P. "The Geographical and Geopolitical Foundations of Eurasianism." *Orient und Occident*, no.17, Moscow, 1933.

Savranskaya, S., and T. Blanton. *Gorbachev and Bush: The Last Superpower Summits*. Budapest: CEU Press, 2020.

Scarborough, R. "Hillary Clinton Behind Plan to Tie Trump to Russia, CIA Warned FBI's Comey, Strzok." *The Washington Times*, 7 October 2020.

Scarlett, J. "Introduction." In *Prisoners of Geography: Ten Maps that Explain Everything about the World.* Edited by T. Marshall, 1-10. London: Elliott & Thompson, 2016.

Schelling, T. C. *The Strategy of Conflict*. London: Harvard University Press, 1980.

Schepp, M., and B. Sandberg. "Gorbachev Interview: 'I Am Truly and Deeply Concerned'." *Spiegel*, 16 January 2015.

Schmidt, E., and R. O. Work. "How to Stop the Next World War." *The Atlantic*, 5 December 2022.

Schmoller, G. *The Mercantile System and its Historical Significance*. London: Macmillan, 1897.

Sciolino, E. "Yeltsin Says NATO Is Trying to Split the Continent Again." *The New York Times*, 6 December 1994.

Scruton, R. "The Future of European Civilization: Lessons for America." *The Heritage Foundation*, 8 December 2015.

Seelye, K. "Arms Contractors spend to promote an expanded NATO." *The New York Times*, 30 March 1998.

Seligman, L., P. McLeary, and A. Ward. "Ukraine uses secretly shipped U.S. missiles to launch surprise strike." *Politico*, 17 October 2023.

Semmel, B. *The Rise of Free Trade Imperialism.* Cambridge: Cambridge University Press, 1970.

Semonsen, R. "Former Israeli PM: West Blocked Russo-Ukraine Peace Deal." *The European Conservative*, 7 February 2023.

Shelest, H. "Defend. Resist. Repeat: Ukraine's lessons for European defence." *ECFR*, 9 November 2022.

Sherr, J. "Ukraine and Europe: Final Decision?" *Russia and Eurasia,* Chatham House Programme Paper 2013/05 (July 2013): 1–12.

Shulman, S. "The Contours of Civic and Ethnic National Identification in Ukraine." *Europe-Asia Studies* 56, no. 1 (2004): 35–56.

Slocombe, W. B. "Stability Effects of Limited Missile Defenses: The Case for the Affirmative." *Pugwash Occasional Papers* 3, no.1 (2002): 73–88.

Smith, A. *An Inquiry into the nature and causes of the Wealth of Nations.* Edinburgh: Adam and Charles Black, 1863.

Smith, G. "The Legacy of Monroe's Doctrine." *The New York Times*, 9 September 1984.

Smith, L. "Adam Schiff Lied About the Trump Investigation—and the Media Let Him." *New York Post*, 8 May 2020.

Snidal, D. "The Limits of Hegemonic Stability Theory." *International Organization* 39, no. 4 (1985): 579–614.

Snider, T. "Putin and Zelensky Finally Agree. Here's why That's a Bad Thing." *Responsible Statecraft*, 5 December 2022.

Snyder, G. *Deterrence and Defense: Toward a Theory of National Security.* Princeton: Princeton University Press, 1961.

Solzhenitsyn, A. "The Exhausted West." *Harvard Magazine*, July-August, 1978.

———. "The Grain Fallen Between Two Millstones" [in Russian: *Ugodilo zernishko, promezh dvuh zhernovov*], Noviy Mir, no.11, 1998.

Sonne, P., and J. Grimaldi. "Biden's Son, Kerry Family Friend Join Ukrainian Gas Producer's Board." *The Wall Street Journal*, 13 May 2014.

Soros, G. "Toward A New World Order: The Future of NATO." *Open Society Foundations*, 1 November 1993.

Soufan, A. H. "Global Terrorism: Threats to the Homeland, Testimony to be presented before the House Committee on Homeland Security." *U.S. Congress*, 10 September 2019.

Spiegel. "Berlin Reverts to Old Timidity on Military Missions." *Spiegel International*, 26 March 2013.

———. "Putin ist ein Drache, der fressen muss" [Putin is a dragon that has to eat]. *Der Spiegel*, 9 February 2023.

———. "We Are Smarter, Stronger and More Determined." *Spiegel*, 13 July 2016.

Spykman, N. J. *America's Strategy in World Politics: the United States and the Balance of Power.* New Brunswick: Transaction Publishers, 1942.

Stanley, J. *How Fascism Works: The Politics of Us and Them*. New York: Penguin Books, 2018.

Steele, J. "Ukraine's postmodern coup d'etat." *The Guardian*, 26 November 2004.

Stevenson, J. *A Drop of Treason*. Chicago: The University of Chicago Press, 2021.

Stoltenberg, J. "Doorstep Statement by NATO Secretary General Jens Stoltenberg Ahead of the Meetings of NATO Defence Ministers in Brussels." *NATO*, 14 February 2023.

———. "Opening remarks." *NATO*, 7 September 2023.

Sussman, G. *Branding Democracy: U.S. Regime Change in Post-Soviet Eastern Europe*. New York: Peter Lang, 2010.

Talbott, S. *The Russia Hand: A Memoir of Presidential Diplomacy*. New York: Random House, 2007.

———. "Why NATO Should Grow." *The New York Review*, 10 August 1995.

Taylor, P. M. *British Propaganda in the Twentieth Century: Selling Democracy.* Edinburgh: Edinburgh University Press, 2019.

Telegraph. "Tony Blair and John McCain Talk about Israel/Palestine and Russia Handling." *The Telegraph*, 27 March 2008.

Teller Report. "In Kiev, They Announced the Development of a Scenario of a War with Russia with NATO." *Teller Report*, 2 April 2021.

Thiessen, M. A. "Why Should Conservatives Support Ukraine? I asked a Populist Leader in Europe." *The Washington Post*, 10 August 2023.

Thompson, W. R. "Dehio, Long Cycles, and the Geohistorical Context of Structural Transition." *World Politics* 45, no. 1 (1992): 127–52.

Todd, E. *After Empire: The Breakdown of the American Order.* New York: Columbia University Press, 2003.

Towle, P. "British Assistance to the Japanese Navy during the Russo-Japanese War of 1904–5." *The Great Circle* 2, no.1 (1980): 44–54.

Toynbee, J. A. *Study of History*. Oxford: Oxford University Press, 1946.

Traynor, I. "U.S. campaign behind the turmoil in Kiev." *The Guardian*, 26 November 2004.

Trenin, D. "Ukraine and the New Divide." *Russia in Global Affairs*, 22 August 2014.

Trotsky, L. "Nationalism and Economic Life." *Foreign Affairs* 12 (1934): 396–402.

Trotsky, L. *Manifesto of the Fourth International on the Imperialist War and the Proletarian World Revolution: Writings of Leon Trotsky 1939–40.* New York: Pathfinder, 1940.

Tönnies, F. *Community and Society*. New York: Dover Publications, 1957.

Tvedt, T. "Development NGOs: Actors in a global civil society or in a new international social system?" *Voluntas: International Journal of Voluntary and Nonprofit Organizations* 13, no. 4 (2002): 363–75.

U.S. Department of State. "Department Press Briefing." 25 February 2022.

———. "Department Press Briefing." 21 March 2022.

———. "Russia's Strategic Failure and Ukraine's Secure Future." 2 June 2023.

U.S. Embassy in Belarus. "Belarus: Budapest Memorandum." *U.S. Embassy in Minsk*, 12 April 2013.

U.S. Embassy in Ukraine. "Anniversary of the So-Called "Annexation" of Crimea by the Russian Federation." *U.S. Embassy in Kyiv*, 19 March 2015.

U.S. Government. "Comer Statement on Devon Archer's Testimony." Committee On Oversight and Accountability, 31 July 2023.

U.S. Senate. "The Debate on NATO Enlargement: Hearings Before the Committee on Foreign Relations (7 October–5 November)." U.S. Government Printing Office, 1998.

———. "Proceedings of the United States Senate in the Impeachment Trial of Donald John Trump: Volume II: Trial Proceedings." U.S. Government Publishing Office, 31 January 2020.

———. "Resolution 435, Calendar No.608." 14 March 2018.

U.S. State Department. "Memorandum by the Under Secretary of State (Acheson) to the Secretary of State." 9 October 1945.

Vahl, M., and M. Emerson. "Moldova and the Transnistrian Conflict." *JEMIE*, no. 1 (2004): 1–29.

Van Brugen, I. "Sergei Lavrov Accuses U.S. of Nord Stream Pipeline Attack." *Newsweek*, 2 February 2023.

Van der Oye, D. S. "Russia, Napoleon, and the Threat to British India.' In *Russia and the Napoleonic Wars*. Edited by J.M. Hartley, P. Keenan, and D. Lieven, 97–105. London: Palgrave Macmillan, 2015.

Vandiver, J. "Ukraine Plans Black Sea Bases as U.S. Steps up Presence in Region." *Stars and Stripes*, 10 February 2021.

Verhofstadt, G. "Speech at the Maidan." YouTube, 20 February 2014. Video, 4:37. https://www.youtube.com/watch?v=rmAU5QRK4i8&t=1s.

Verma, P. "In Wake of Recent India-China Conflict, U.S. Sees Opportunity." *The New York Times*, 3 October 2020.

Volker, K. "What Does a Successful Biden-Putin Summit Look Like? Not What You Think." *CEPA*, 2 June 2021.

Von Laue, T. H. "A Secret Memorandum of Sergei Witte on the Industrialization of Imperial Russia." *The Journal of Modern History* 26, no.1 (1954): 60–74.

Walla, K. "Boris Johnson: Stop Worrying about Putin and 'Focus Entirely on Ukraine'." *Atlantic Council*, 1 February 2023.

Walsh, A. "Angela Merkel Opens up on Ukraine, Putin and Her Legacy." *Deutsche Welle*, 7 June 2022.

Walt, S. "No Contest." *Foreign Policy*, March 2014.

Waltz, K. N. "The New World Order." *Millennium* 22, no. 2 (1993): 187–95.

———. "Structural Realism after the Cold War." *International Security* 25, no. 1 (2000): 5–41.

———. *Theory of International Politics*. New York: McGraw-Hill, 1979.

Wang, Y. "Exploring the Path of Major-Country Diplomacy with Chinese Characteristics." *Foreign Affairs Journal*, no.10 (2013): 5–14.

Watt, N. "Cameron Accuses Corbyn of 'Britain-Hating Ideology' in Conference Speech." *The Guardian*, 7 October 2015.

Weber, M. *Essays in Sociology*. Milton Park: Routledge, 1948.

———. "The National State and Economic Policy" (Freiburg address, Inaugural lecture, Freiburg, May 1895). *Economy and Society* 9, no. 4 (1980): 428–49.

Webber, E. "Boris Johnson Warns Against Seeking 'Bad Peace' in Ukraine." *Politico*, 23 June 2022.

Weigert, H. W. "Haushofer and the Pacific." *Foreign Affairs* 20, no .4 (1942): 732–42.

Whelan, B. "Far-Right Group at Heart of Ukraine Protests Meet U.S. Senator." *Channel4 News*, 16 December 2013.

White House. "National Security Strategy of the United States." *The White House,* April 1988.

———. "Press Briefing by Press Secretary Jen Psaki and National Security Advisor Jake Sullivan." *The White House*, 13 January 2022.

———. "Remarks by President Biden on Russia's Unprovoked and Unjustified Attack on Ukraine." Speech given at the White House, 24 February 2022.

———. "Summit for Democracy Summary of Proceedings." *The White House*, 23 December 2021.

Whitman, A. "Harry S. Truman: Decisive President." *The New York Times*, 27 December 1972.

Wikileaks. "Eur A/S Fried's September 1 Meetings with Senior MFA and Presidency Officials on Improving Relations with Europe." *Wikileaks*, 9 September 2005.

———. "Germany/Russia: Chancellery Views on MAP for Ukraine and Georgia." *Wikileaks*, 6 June 2008.

———. "NATO: February 28th HLTF and NRC (ACE) Meetings." *Wikileaks*, 7 March 2008.

———. "Norway Standing Alone Against Missile Defense." *Wikileaks*, 12 February 2008.

———. "Russia-Ukraine: NATO and Holodomor." *Wikileaks*, 3 April 2008.

———. "A Tour d'horizon with President Voronin." *Wikileaks*, 18 July 2008.

Williams, M. C., and I. B. Neumann. "From Alliance to Security Community: NATO, Russia, and the Power of Identity." *Millennium* 29, no. 2 (2000): 357–87.

Wintour, P. "NATO Members May Send Troops to Ukraine, Warns Former Alliance Chief." *The Guardian*, 7 June 2023.

WION Web Team. "If Russia Invades Ukraine, Nord Stream 2 Pipeline will not Move Forward: U.S." *WION*, 28 January 2022.

Wong, E., and M. Crowley, "With Sanctions, U.S. and Europe Aim to Punish Putin and Fuel Russian Unrest." *The New York Times*, 4 March 2022.

Woolsey, J. "World: James Woolsey, Former CIA Director, Speaks To RFE/RL At Forum 2000." *Radio Free Europe/Radio Liberty*, 10 October 2005.

WSJ. "Vladimir Putin's 20-Year March to War in Ukraine—and How the West Mishandled It." *The Wall Street Journal*, 1 April 2022.

Xi, J. "Join Hands on the Path Towards Modernization." *China Institutes of Contemporary International Relations*, 15 March 2023.

Xu, Q. "Maritime geostrategy and the development of the Chinese navy in the early twenty-first century." *Naval War College Review* 59, no.4 (2006): 46–67.

Yushchenko, V. "Viktor Yushchenko: Ukraine's Future is in the EU—Address by President of Ukraine to the European Parliament." EP05-022EN, *European Parliament*, 23 February 2005.

Zelensky, V. "Address by the President to Ukrainians at the end of the first day of Russia's attacks." *President of Ukraine* [official website], 25 February 2022.

Zuckerberg, M. "Protecting Democracy is an Arms Race. Here's How Facebook Can Help." *The Washington Times*, 4 September 2018.

Index